Alison R. Marshall

The Way of the Bachelor:
Early Chinese Settlement in Manitoba

UBCPress · Vancouver · Toronto

21 20 19 18 17 16 15 14 13 12 11   5 4 3 2 1

Printed in Canada on FSC-certified ancient-forest-free paper (100% post-consumer recycled) that is processed chlorine- and acid-free.

Library and Archives Canada Cataloguing in Publication

Marshall, Alison R.
  The way of the bachelor : early Chinese settlement in Manitoba / Alison R. Marshall.

(Asian religions & society series, ISSN 1705-4761)
Includes bibliographical references and index.
ISBN 978-0-7748-1915-2 (bound); ISBN 978-0-7748-1916-9 (pbk.)

  1. Chinese Canadians – Manitoba – Social conditions – 20th century. 2. Chinese Canadians – Social networks – Manitoba – History – 20th century. 3. Chinese Canadians – Manitoba – Religion – History – 20th century. 4. Chinese Canadians – Manitoba – Politics and government – 20th century. 5. Zhongguo guo min dang. Manitoba branch – History. 6. Laundries – Manitoba – History – 20th century. 7. Chinese restaurants – Manitoba – History – 20th century. 8. Bachelors – Manitoba – History – 20th century. I. Title. II. Series: Asian religions and society series

FC3400.C5M37 2011   305.38'89510712709041   C2010-906512-3

---

e-book ISBNs: 978-0-7748-1917-6 (PDF); 978-0-7748-1918-3 (epub)

Canadä

UBC Press gratefully acknowledges the financial support for our publishing program of the Government of Canada (through the Canada Book Fund), the Canada Council for the Arts, and the British Columbia Arts Council.

This book has been published with the help of a grant from the Canadian Federation for the Humanities and Social Sciences, through the Aid to Scholarly Publications Program, using funds provided by the Social Sciences and Humanities Research Council of Canada.

UBC Press
The University of British Columbia
2029 West Mall
Vancouver, BC V6T 1Z2
www.ubcpress.ca

To the bachelors

Contents

Table and Figures

Preface

The Honourable Inky Mark, former Member of Parliament
for Dauphin-Swan River-Marquette, Manitoba

I am honoured to write this preface for Alison Marshall's book, *The Way of the Bachelor: Early Chinese Settlement in Manitoba*. As a third-generation Chinese immigrant to Canada, I find that this book answers many questions I still have as an adult. Reading it was like reliving my childhood in Gilbert Plains, Manitoba. Why were my parents so devoted to Sun Yat-sen? Why did they read the Chinese newspaper from cover to cover? Why did they practise their Buddhist beliefs in private? Why did they send their children off to church every Sunday? Why did they always visit the Chinese restaurants in other small rural towns in Manitoba? Why did they make sure that their children integrated into Canadian society? Why was the food that the family ate so different from the food that was served to the customer? Reading Alison's book has given me many answers to how I became an assimilated Canadian of Chinese descent. My grandfather came to western Manitoba over one hundred years ago, and I grew up in a Chinese restaurant named the Rex Cafe in Gilbert Plains. This is the environment in which I learned to understand people of all ethnic backgrounds. I believe this served me well in adult life as an elected official – as city councillor, mayor of Dauphin, and Member of Parliament.

The Chinese immigrant has struggled with discrimination since the first day he set foot in Canada in the 1800s. Officially, the government repealed the Chinese Immigration Act of 1923 (which is known to the Chinese community as the Chinese Exclusion Act) in 1947. Despite the way the Chinese were treated, they remain thankful and loyal to Canada.

Alison's book takes the reader through many of the challenges faced by Canada's earliest Chinese immigrants, especially those experienced by lonely men who had to return to China to marry and have children. As she makes clear, *The Way of the Bachelor* is not about racist practices; rather, it is about how these men survived despite the difficulties they faced. I am the direct beneficiary of the suffering that my forefathers experienced. My generation can only be thankful that Alison Marshall has put into words what very few have written. Thank you, Alison, for opening the window so that all Canadians can see what has gone before us and, with greater understanding, Canada will be a more peaceful place in which to live.

Acknowledgments

I moved to the Province of Manitoba in August 2000, and, coming from the multicultural city of Toronto, I naturally wondered about religious practice and diversity in the small Prairie city of Brandon, which I would now call home. Having completed my fieldwork in Taiwan, which focused on mediumship and other aspects of Chinese ecstatic religion, I was used to examining the various manifestations of beliefs and practices found in lived religions. As I published the results of my research and as other projects came to a close, I began to delve into archival records and to have informal conversations about Chinese customs practised on the eastern Prairies. By late 2005, I obtained funding to conduct my first round of interviews, and I started to see that there was a long and rich history of Chinese settlement in the region: Brandon was an important hub in a network of relationships that radiated out from western Manitoba to Winnipeg, the rest of Canada, and the world.

I would like to acknowledge my family first. From the beginning, my partner Brian Mayes has been a generous and patient listener, proofreader, and supporter of this work. I thank my sons Wells and Ben, and my mother-in-law Gerry Mayes, for their help, inspiration, and cheer. And I thank my sister-in-law Alison Mayes for her invaluable proofreading.

I have been overwhelmed by the generosity of everyone who has contacted me to share memories, photographs, and documents. While I have endeavoured to include them all, some have had to be left out. This book could not have been written without the help of many individuals, including Sarah Ramsden, who worked as my senior research assistant for a year and a half. Helen Wong, daughter of the influential Charlie Foo, who was a leader in the Winnipeg Chinese community for almost six decades, provided invaluable assistance, insights, and photographs to help shed light on the long history of the community in this part of the province. Peiyun

Shih, president of the Manitoba Kuomintang, allowed me to visit the Kuomintang office on Pacific Avenue in Winnipeg, which has been there since 1932. May Yoh, a retired associate professor at Brandon University, showed me a collection of photographs and other materials she had amassed for a project during the late 1980s, many of which were later presented in a jointly curated 2009 exhibition entitled "Windows on Chinese Settlers in Western Manitoba." Countless other people within the Manitoba and broader Chinese community also helped me to understand the history, food customs, and religious dimensions of Chinese settler culture in Manitoba.

Conducting ethnographic and historical research on rural religiosity and history is expensive as it requires numerous trips to examine archives and to do fieldwork in remote parts of the province (and elsewhere in Canada). I have, however, been very fortunate to receive funding and assistance from the following organizations: the Social Sciences and Humanities Research Council of Canada; Brandon University; and the Rural Development Institute. I am indebted to many archives that generously provided materials: Library and Archives Canada; Archives of Manitoba, Winnipeg; Stubbs Archives, University of Manitoba; the S.J. McKee Archives, Brandon University; the Carberry Plains Archives, Carberry; and the Daly House Museum, Brandon.

Throughout my multi-year research, my ideas and analysis benefited from the contributions of many people. R. Stephen Warner went out of his way to teach me important lessons about religion and migration. Both during and after the panel discussion of my presentation at the national meeting of the American Academy of Religion in 2007, he provided me with valuable insights into immigrant religiosity as well as with suggestions for a framework within which to make sense of the conflicting data I had gathered from research participants. This book was also improved by the thoughtful comments I received from the two anonymous readers and the entire editorial team at UBC Press, including Emily Andrew, Megan Brand, and Joanne Richardson, who guided and shaped this project.

Daniel Overmyer, Peter Beyer, Cary Takagaki, and Michel Desjardins provided insightful comments when I presented my material at the annual meetings of the Canadian Society for the Study of Religion. Throughout the various stages of writing and presenting the research behind this book, several people enhanced my work in significant ways, including David Lai, Inky Mark, Kwan Yuen, Pauline Greenhill, Esta Ungar, Michael Puett, John Berthrong, Joseph Du, Philip Lee, Tina Chen, Henry Yu, Scott Grills, Satya Sharma, Jan Walls, Kenny Choy, Sergio Lee, Meharoona Ghani, Walker Wong, Daniel Wong, Adele Perry, Roy Loewen, Charles Mathewes, Gerry

Oliver, David Low, Adam Chau, Sheldon Wu, Bill Turner, John Berry, Harley Grouette, James O'Connor, Vivienne Luk, Carol Vint, Glen Peterson, Ray Berthelette, Carol Steele, and Minnie Oliver (who died while I was revising it). Colleagues at Brandon University listened to my findings and, over the years, suggested sources, articles, books, and the names of potential research participants. For this I thank Jim Naylor, Tom Mitchell, Bob Annis, Kevin Wong, Morris Mott, Kurt Noll, Lynn MacKay, and, especially, Leo Liu. I must also acknowledge my research assistants Coco Kao, Lu Chunwei, Codee Lorrain, Sue-On Hillman, and Miles Crossman. I would also like to thank the students in my Gender, Religion, and Food class.

While I have received assistance and support from a number of people and groups, the shortcomings of this book are entirely my own.

Acronyms

BUCSSA	Brandon University Chinese Students and Scholars Association
CBA	Chinese Benevolent Association
CCP	Chinese Communist Party
CPR	Canadian Pacific Railway
KMT	Kuomintang (Chinese Nationalist League)
UFCW	United Food and Commercial Workers

The Way of the Bachelor

Introduction

The first Chinese to settle in western Manitoba felt as alienated from their non-Chinese neighbours as their non-Chinese neighbours did from them.[1] For thirty-three years they had to live as bachelors, without the wives, daughters, and mothers who normally animate Chinese communities. But it wasn't simply living that was the challenge. Over the course of those thirty-three years, they also had to figure out how to make bachelor life meaningful. This they did through a process that I call the *dao*, or way, of the bachelor. It could not be a way based on the usual duality of men and women; rather, it had to be a way structured entirely through relationships with men. Only through other men could these bachelors sustain their connections to their homes and negotiate their relationships with their hosts.

The first Chinese to reach western Manitoba, according to the accounts that survive, arrived in 1884. The sources documenting Chinese life during the first three decades are meagre, which is why I focus primarily on the period between the national revolution in 1911 and the division of China and Taiwan in 1949. Nineteen eleven was not only the year the Qing dynasty fell but also the year that Sun Yat-sen (1866-1925), the revolutionary credited with bringing down the dynasty, spoke at the Chinese Freemasons office in Winnipeg to hundreds of Chinese who flocked there from all across the eastern Prairies. Within a year, Chinese Manitobans were also congregating at the Chinese Nationalist League, or Kuomintang (KMT),[2] offices both in Winnipeg and in Brandon.[3] By 1914, they were attending events at the Winnipeg Chinese Benevolent Association (CBA). These institutions grew around and through each other, creating a social network and a governance structure in which, in Manitoba at least, the KMT took the lead. And they were entirely staffed, supported, and enjoyed by bachelors.

Sun Yat-sen became an important figurehead for the KMT and the Chinese bachelors (even though he would only be provincial president in China until March 1912). He rose to this position not only because he was a revolutionary who had travelled extensively, visiting many of the world's overseas Chinese communities, but also because KMT leaders worked to put him there. He had lived the same life as had the bachelors, coming from a southern village and living far away from China. Like them he had been exposed to Western life and its religions. When he spoke to large groups of bachelors he drew on these shared experiences to motivate them to donate to his party and to help China. But his speeches didn't just communicate political messages: from 1911 until 1925, when he died, they were designed to inspire belief and faith in nationalism and in him as leader. His speeches also communicated religious messages.

These religious messages combined old Chinese ideas, most often from Confucianism (as well as those from the earlier Ruists, or Emerging Scholars), with new Christian ideas, such as the importance of faith and belief in daily life. In this way, Sun Yat-sen's speeches, which bachelors listened to and were encouraged to study, helped to cultivate the model of an ideal immigrant identity. This immigrant identity incorporated modern Chinese ideas (which emerged around 1900),[4] Western Christian ideas, and Confucian and Nationalist ideas.

The earliest bachelors endeavoured to be like Sun Yat-sen, to become modern and Western. And, in so doing, they not only adapted to foreign life in Canada but also flourished. That the bachelors succeeded is quite extraordinary, given that they were living in a very different cultural, geographical, political, religious, and social world from that in which they grew up. But their successes may be explained by two factors: relationships and efficacy (the dominant idea in Chinese religion defined below). In traditional China (prior to 1900, when the modern period began) there were five traditional relationships. Some people believe that these five relationships were modelled after those in the emperor's own family. These relationships are defined in the Confucian text entitled *Doctrine of the Mean,* which has been attributed to Confucius' grandson Zisi/Kong Ji (492-31 BCE). According to this text, these relationships are, in order of importance: (1) ruler to subject, (2) father to son, (3) husband to wife, (4) brother to brother, and (5) friend to friend. In western Manitoba, where there were no Chinese women for thirty-three years,[5] these relationships had to be re-imagined.

The first relationships to form in western Manitoba were friendships. In China, this relationship was voluntary, equal, and the least important.[6] In western Manitoba, it was the opposite: friendships were non-voluntary, unequal, and the most important relationship a person could have. Some friends had higher positions, and others had lower ones; consequently, friends were ranked in terms of their power in Manitoba's Chinese political hierarchies. But it was not just the absence of women that influenced the new meaning given to bachelor friendships. Most Chinese men in Manitoba lived without family relationships.[7] Some men in rural western Manitoba might have come to Canada with relatives, but very few ended up residing near kin. Their fictive kin were made up of men they met or reconnected with along the journey from China to Manitoba. Homosociality, or friendship with other men (both Chinese and non-Chinese), was one of the key dynamics of the way of the bachelor. As connections developed so, too, did a network of fictive kinship (those treated like family but unrelated by blood). This resulted in the creation of social cohesion, authority, and economic capital, thereby providing important avenues to better-paying jobs, places to live, and a chance for remarriage and family life in Canada. Friendships also came to have religious dimensions.

Unlike friendships in China, friendships in Canada provided for human needs and thus embodied "efficacy," the dominant idea in Chinese religion. Chinese religion should not be understood to refer to one China or to one set of unchanging traditions; rather, modern Chinese religiosity occurs in many places and has many forms within the Chinese cultural sphere, whether that be in China, Hong Kong, Taiwan, Macau, Singapore, Malaysia, Australia, the United States, Canada, or elsewhere.[8] Individuals may simultaneously belong to a number of different religious groups, including those that are categorized as Daoist, Buddhist, or Christian; however, Chinese religious behaviour cannot be adequately defined by these traditional categories as its boundaries are much more porous.[9] If we are looking for a unifying concept that connects all the different layers and aspects of Chinese religion and ritual action, then we should look to the notion of efficacy.

Efficacy *(ling)*, which is at the heart of Chinese religion, refers to human efforts to meet practical needs through reverential interaction with deities and ancestors, whose purpose it is to provide for those needs.[10] I do not think that either mode of action, human or divine, is more important than the other. Nor do I think that one can be considered without some reference to the other.[11] Efficacy requires sincerity from the human and reciprocity from the divine. The implication and expectation is that the deity or ancestor will respond appropriately to a sincere person's wishes or needs.

Sometimes efficacy is defined as miraculous power; other times it is defined as spirit/the numinous. Both of these definitions emphasize the dominance of the divine agent. If we examine the character *ling*, we see that it includes the Chinese radical for rain (three mouths) and the character for *wu* (a name for the male and female mediums who were important in early

Chinese religion). In the *Nine Songs (Jiuge)* of the *Anthology of Chu (Chuci)*, the *ling* are male and female mediums who lure the gods down to possess them.[12] But efficacy as defined by this character is misleading because it highlights only the agency of divine roles. Efficacy is about more than magical actions: it is also about everyday concerns and ordinary people. · Adam Chau defines it well:

> At the core ... is the concept of magical efficacy *(ling)*, which is conceived of as a particular deity's miraculous response *(lingying)* to the worshipper's request for divine assistance ... These miraculous responses are socially constructed: it is people and their actions that enable the establishment of human-deity relations and interactions.[13]

Ritual actions performed sincerely and according to established patterns, on the part of both human and divine agents, have efficacious results. When ritual actions involving human and/or divine agents no longer meet human needs, they are adjusted until they once again become efficacious. Efficacy changes according to the needs of daily life. In Manitoba, these new ritual actions were created both from the top-down and at the grassroots level.

As Chinese settlers adapted to life in Manitoba, new efficacies and rituals developed. For the bachelors, it was no longer socially appropriate, or efficacious, to worship traditional Chinese deities such as *Guanyin* or *Mazu* (Buddhist goddesses associated with salvation, family, and childbirth) or *Guangong* (also known as *Guandi*, a god associated with war, loyalty, righteousness, Chinese triads, and Daoism)[14] in the same way that they did in China, since these deities could provide little assistance in their new home. Instead, Sun Yat-sen, the Father of Modern China, was transformed into a god-like figure, and the earliest settlers became ancestors who were to be acknowledged in a special annual funerary celebration known as Decoration Day.[15] This remained the predominant funerary custom until after 1947, when, with the repeal of the Chinese Immigration Act, wives and children were able to immigrate to Canada.[16]

Quotidian rituals changed too. In China, everyday life and the festivals that punctuated it were organized according to male and female roles within the family and, to a much lesser extent, by district magistrates. In Manitoba, Chinese people seldom lived near family, and there were very few women until after 1947. Under these circumstances, homosocial (not to be confused with homosexual) relationships necessarily took on religious dimensions, connecting men to each other, to Sun Yat-sen, to the Canadian landscape, and to China. KMT offices came to function as Chinese religious institutions where men could congregate and could also celebrate the festivals, revere Sun as their new god, remember early settlers, and read the Manitoba-produced KMT weekly newspaper and the library's traditional texts (as well as those written by Sun Yat-sen). The newspapers and texts inculcated Confucian values, which were deemed both nationalistic and appropriate.[17] It makes sense that, as a new alienated minority community developed in western Manitoba, so, too, did new articulations of efficacy – articulations that replaced those that had been appropriate in China.

The first Chinese settlers reinvented relationships and efficacies so that their lives in Manitoba would be less strange and so that those around them would not perceive them as strangers. For thirty-three years they developed connections to local, provincial, national, and global Chinese and non-Chinese communities,[18] and, through them, forged intercultural bridges facilitated by involvement in the KMT and in Christian missions and churches. Once women began to arrive in 1918, and in greater numbers after 1947, new efficacies emerged to address their needs and the needs of families.

There are strong parallels between the experience of western Manitoban Chinese Canadians and the global experiences of those subjected to institutionalized racism. In the mid-1800s, a number of terrible conditions in southern China drove the bachelors to immigrate and to live apart from their families. The Chinese population had swelled dramatically by this point, and there were successive droughts, earthquakes, epidemics, and other natural disasters. People were desperate to survive. This is when the first wave of transcontinental migration to Australia, New Zealand, the United States, and Canada took place. The trend to protect "white" labourers from the competition of Chinese migrants began with New Zealand's Chinese Immigration Act, which passed in 1881. This act was followed by the US Chinese Exclusion Act, which was passed in 1882. Three years later, in 1885, Canada passed its Chinese Immigration Act. Under Section 4, this act, which the Chinese Canadian community often refers to as the Chinese Exclusion Act, imposed a fifty-dollar head tax on all Chinese who entered the country.

The head tax made it too expensive for most wives and children to be able to accompany fathers to Canada. In 1900, the act doubled the amount to one hundred dollars; and, by 1903, the head tax stood at five hundred dollars.[19] Immigration was effectively halted beginning in 1923, when a new version of the Chinese Immigration Act excluded all immigrants except merchants, students, and diplomats and their staff.[20] The act was only repealed in 1947. After 1923, all people in Canada of Chinese descent,

FIGURE 1   Joe Yuen head tax certificate, 1920.
Source: Wade Yuen

whether they were born here or not, were required to register with the federal government within twelve months. Failure to comply resulted in a fine of up to five hundred dollars and/or imprisonment of up to a year.

Studies of large urban settlements and Chinatowns in Victoria and Vancouver have shed light on racism and discrimination in Canada.[21] Other works have attempted to present a broader picture of Canada's Chinese immigrant history.[22] There have also been a few articles and monographs written about smaller Chinese communities in Peterborough and Timmins, Ontario, and Prince Edward Island.[23] As for scholarly writings about eastern Prairie Chinese communities, these, too, have tended to focus on the larger urban centres of Winnipeg, Regina, and Saskatoon.[24] And, while these writings have provided essential context for some of what happened in western Manitoba, they have not been able to fully explain it. Why, for example, was there less bigotry in Manitoba than in other parts of the Prairies, such as in Saskatchewan, especially near Regina and Moose Jaw, where, in the 1920s, the Ku Klux Klan began to form.

The first Chinese to settle in western Manitoba and elsewhere in Canada worked in laundries and restaurants. To open these businesses they relied on chain migration as well as on their own social, political, and economic capital, which flowed to them through global institutions and networks. The Chinese population grew quickly through chain migration,[25] whereby bachelors sponsored other male family and friends to come to Canada and work. Once men reached Manitoba, they raised money to start their own businesses by joining rotating credit associations *(hui)*. These had been used in China since 221 CE and were continued in Canada and other parts of the diaspora to help men obtain private loans from friends.[26] Lai Man Cheung, who was interviewed by Clement Ng in Winnipeg in 1983, explains:

> If twenty people got together, they would have $100 (each contributed $5). If people decided that they needed the money, people would make a bid. If they were willing to pay the highest interest, then they would win. After that, they had to repay the money every week. There must be a sponsor. For example, if I sponsor you, and you failed to repay the other members, I had to pay them on your behalf.[26]

The bachelors asked Chinese friends within their established social networks and institutions to introduce them to groups and individuals who could help raise the capital needed to open laundries and restaurants. In the early period of migration, Chinese men dominated the laundry business.[28] Over time, washing by hand was made obsolete by steam laundries, and, gradually, people turned to restaurant work. Those whose English skills were better moved out of the restaurant profession and into the distribution of tobacco, rice, and meat, and the selling of insurance.

Paul Siu, in his pioneering ethnographic studies of laundrymen in the United States, concluded that Chinese settlers were sojourners who had come to make money and to increase their social status at home.[29] He noted, nevertheless, that they never integrated into the societies in which they lived and that they constantly looked back to China for news of family and friends.[30] There are similarities between Siu's sojourners and Manitoba's bachelors; however, there are also some key differences. Early miners, railway labourers, and some laundrymen may have been sojourners, but many others who were drawn to Manitoba in their wake were not.[31] During my research, it was not uncommon for me to encounter families who had been living in western Manitoba for almost one hundred years. People here made the transition from sojourner to resident more quickly than did people in other places.

In 1977, Frank Quo noted in a government report that people on the Canadian Prairies were less hostile towards Chinese immigrants than were those who lived elsewhere in Canada.[32] I found this to be largely true. At first I attributed the success of eastern Prairie bachelors to a lack of ethnic enclaves and the resultant economic pressure to acculturate to the communities in which they found themselves. Men were welcomed and accepted by small communities that wanted to grow and to have Chinese businesses such as laundries and cafes. All of the communities I examined also had active Presbyterian, Methodist, Anglican (and, after 1925, United) churches, ministers, or missions that would have helped build intercultural bridges between Chinese and non-Chinese groups.

But then I encountered small rural Christian communities in which there were only one or two Chinese settlers, yet in which there was considerable racism, marginalization, and/or separation.[33] These people who lived further away from the KMT centre and had fewer connections were more alone than were others on the Prairies. I noticed that when there were fewer opportunities to create social heat and to be welcomed at Chinese- or Christian-organized events, there was a greater experience of racism. Reflecting on the data, I noted that most of the Prairie communities I was examining in Manitoba and Saskatchewan were white (without large First Nations populations) and that normative behaviour was obviously defined by white society. Conforming to what that society deemed to be socially acceptable enabled one to have power, prestige, and to own property. Racism existed in all of these communities, and the language used to describe Chinese men ("Chinamen," "Chink," "Celestials,"[34] and "Charlie") was usually pejorative at least until after 1947 and, in some cases, much later. In determining the degree of racism shown by a community I could not rely on language as an indicator because it was consistently used in negative and demeaning ways. I came to judge racism by whether a place had a Chinese restaurant or laundry (thus showing that it was receptive to foreign culture), whether that establishment was owned (as opposed to being rented) by the Chinese man (indicating he had quite likely been living there for longer than a summer), and how often he and his business were mentioned in the local newspaper. I came to recognize extreme cases of racism in towns or villages that had one or two Chinese businesses and that only sporadically mentioned them in their newspapers. In these places, there were more frequent references to winter masquerades and school plays in which individuals dressed up as "Chinamen" and in blackface. I also came to notice that the places where there appeared to be less racism were those with large non-British settlements, such as Esterhazy (Hungarian), Dauphin (Ukrainian), and

Baldur (Icelandic). Further, there appeared to be less racism in communities within a four-hundred-kilometre radius of Winnipeg, which was the Western Regional Headquarters of the KMT in Canada. Winnipeg was where most bachelors (even those living in Saskatchewan) went to pick up items from food distributors. Based on my discussions with old-timers in Manitoba and Saskatchewan, I knew that, historically, men in both provinces had travelled by horse trail, train, and sometimes by car each month to Winnipeg or to an outpost of the KMT to attend meetings and to pick up supplies. Winnipeg elders also made regular trips to these outposts to visit members and to solicit donations. I concluded that one likely experienced considerably less racism inside the four-hundred-kilometre radius of Winnipeg than outside it because those living inside it continued to be exposed to Chinese immigrants and their culture through KMT-sponsored intercultural events as well as through Christian and banking institutions and networks.[35] In and through these events, institutions, and networks, non-Chinese residents grew to understand the bachelors and to form relationships with them. Unlike people who lived in more populous cities, where Chinese men were associated with the sometimes "exotic" but mostly "sinful" domain of Chinatown, or were perceived to be a threat to white British labour, those who lived in smaller rural areas regarded Chinese culture more favourably. The tiny Chinese western Manitoba population was mostly rural and dispersed, being historically and physically united not by clan or clan associations but, rather, by the KMT, which facilitated the flow of social, political, and economic capital.[36]

I should add that my research uncovered less racism towards Chinese in Manitoban cities (such as Brandon and Winnipeg) than in some other Canadian cities (such as Victoria and Vancouver). The size of Brandon and Winnipeg's Chinese populations, which were considerably smaller than those in Vancouver or Victoria, helped to produce a better relationship with the dominant non-Chinese society. But here again this relationship could not have happened without the efforts of KMT leaders and, later, other Chinese community leaders. From the beginning, these leaders (who themselves often married British, Ukrainian, or French women) have worked with non-Chinese Christians and politicians to organize and host events. This has been a consistently important aspect of community life. Unlike many Chinese communities elsewhere in Canada, the one in Manitoba has been less inward-looking. Its strength and longevity has depended on the consistent involvement and support of non-Chinese people who have been asked to take active roles as event-organizing committee members, treasurers, and fundraising directors, some for more than three decades. In these ways, since 1912, the Manitoba Chinese community has successfully used traditional and political events to create understanding between Chinese and non-Chinese communities and to reduce (though not to eliminate) racism.

Contained within the way of the bachelor are the religious dimensions of friendship and new forms of efficacy whose architecture may be discerned through four intersecting themes: (1) everyday religious practices, (2) ambiguity, (3) foodways, and (4) social heat. The everyday religious practices I describe are those that emerged as Chinese immigrants settled into Canadian Prairie society, got involved in Chinese political and non-Chinese Christian organizations, and strove to become modern and Western. Meredith McGuire suggests that, in order to recognize the everyday practices that characterize lived religion outside of the realm of traditional religiosity, "a good starting point might be a better appreciation of the many and complex ways ... [in which] religions are the products of considerable human creativity, cultural improvisation, and construction from diverse elements, only some of which [are] inherited from the same tradition."[37] Everyday religion makes room for things that, ordinarily, are classed as social rather than as religious activities, such as banquets and other food events and customs discussed in this book. But the term "religious practices" also includes the "boundary resources" provided by ethnic associations that help define the community as a group, connect it to others, and serve practical and therapeutic needs.[38]

The everyday practices that evolved in Manitoba reflected the influences of emerging social, political, and economic hierarchies and identities. For example, although the men lacked experience and knowledge related to the domestic sphere, they were free to enter it and to cross traditional boundaries that had prevented them from doing "women's work" in China.[39] Laundrymen and restaurant owners became very successful in the inner (private) spheres as opposed to the outer (public) spheres to which they had been traditionally relegated in China. Gender relationships and status in both China and Canada were determined by and intricately connected to labour roles and the various economic aspects of the public and private spheres.[40] In Canada, Chinese women were very few in number and, before 1947, practically invisible. While the dominant society was aware of Chinese "bachelors" (who, in the period before 1912, were usually referred to as "Chinks," "Chinamen," "Charlie," and "Celestials"), white males (and members of Western society in general) tended to view them as feminized and weak. These bachelors apprenticed with other Chinese men, who taught them how to wash, cook, and run their own small households.

Located outside the boundaries and understandings of normative Chinese gender and labour roles, the men in Manitoba eventually became modern Westerners who used relationships here in Canada to ascend hierarchies just being conceived.

Chinese men who worked together in laundries and cafes may not have been brothers by blood, but they were perceived to be family and, therefore, as "brothers" by race. In Chinese Canadian political circles they were also brothers in another sense, being united by Sun Yat-sen's three principles of democracy, livelihood, and nation. Theirs was a religiosity focused on the modern moment and the meeting of everyday needs, but it seldom concerned the "spiritual." The veneration of Chinese deities – with incense, spirit money, mediums, blood oaths, and other ritual actions that, from a modernist perspective, appeared as "superstitious" – was a blight on the image of the modern Western Nationalist gentleman. While it was acceptable for the small numbers of Chinese women (and a few men) who lived in western Manitoba after 1918 to use prayer beads or to practise other Buddhist or Daoist rituals, in general, "superstitious" practices sullied an otherwise modernist self-image. Private rituals and customs belonging to these modalities could only be tolerated in the remotest backwaters of life: if performed indoors, then it must be in a bedroom; if performed outdoors, then it must be in the backyard or garage or before the sun's rays touched the front lawn. People could offer lit incense, meals, whisky, and flowers in public at gravesites during Decoration Day, or Qingming (in the spring) and Chongyang (in the autumn) (the traditional Chinese grave-sweeping festivals), but these non-normative behaviours had to be offset by actions vested with the authority and power of nationalism. The leadership thereby encouraged KMT members to forge relationships within and beyond the Chinese community. It also prodded them to venerate Confucius as a teacher; to study Confucian classical texts that inculcated virtues such as loyalty, humaneness, and righteousness; to read their newspapers; and to become familiar with Sun Yat-sen's will. Sun Yat-sen had written two wills, both of which were legal documents. The first one, which I mention throughout this book, was addressed to his Nationalist colleagues, and the second one was addressed to his family. Sun's first will became a key Nationalist text and attained scriptural status. It explained the social significance of the three principles of livelihood, nationalism, and democracy and encouraged people to continue to work towards the creation of a free and democratic China.

Borne out of efficacy and practical needs, the ritual actions of bachelors enabled them to move back and forth between the public and the private, and between Chinese/traditional and Christian/modern. Erving Goffman's notion of front-stage and back-stage behaviours offers a useful lens through which to view what motivated the "doing" of everyday religion in these settings, which, for Chinese settlers in western Manitoba, ranged from picnics, ice cream socials, and banquets to KMT offices, churches and cemeteries, and political processions. By adapting theatrical terms such as "performance," "roles," and "stage," Goffman attempts to express the motivation for all kinds of social interaction. He argues that how people behave (or the roles they take on) in various settings changed, depending on whether they were doing something at the front of the stage (i.e., in public) or at the back of the stage (i.e., in private). People adjusted their behaviour to be in accord with different situations (e.g., at a funeral, people behave solemnly; at a picnic, people behave jovially). As Goffman reminds us: "When the individual presents himself before others, his performance will tend to incorporate and exemplify the officially accredited values of the society, more so, in fact, than does his behaviour as a whole."[41] Thus, bachelors behaved as Christians on the front stage and in more traditional ways on the back stage.

Because everyday religious practices and identities changed, depending on the public or private context, they were somewhat ambiguous. Ambiguity, the second intersecting theme of this book, characterized all realms of social interaction, including those related to religion and those pertaining to gender, labour, and politics. Identity needed to be flexible in order to straddle these boundaries and to accommodate the differing demands of home and host nations. In Canada, immigrants lived like peasants in order to save enough money to support their wives and growing families in China. These distant families imagined the settlers as gentry because they lived in Gold Mountain, a place that conjured visions of infinite opportunity. These men existed in a world whose spatial and temporal existence, though anchored in China's past, was oriented towards an uncertain present – one that was neither wholly here nor wholly there. As a result, the men adopted new modalities and rituals to cope with a changing and often foreign world. As Seligman et al. point out:

In dealing with ambiguities, ritual engages boundaries: boundaries are crossed, violated, blurred, and then, in an oscillating way, reaffirmed, reestablished and strengthened. Among the paradoxes that attend the performance of ritual is the paradox that ritual plays out a completion, a closure that solves the problem at hand. Yet, at the same time the very nature of the repetitiveness of ritual implicitly shows that the problem is not solved once and for all, that all is not complete and perfect. There is, at bottom, a quality of "either-or, both-and" in the realm of ritual.[42]

In traditional Chinese religious practice ambiguity is a component of efficacy, and Chinese immigrants adapted it to modern Western life in order to survive. On official documents, under "religion," Chinese men put "Anglican," "Presbyterian," "Methodist," or (after 1925) "United Church." While we can't be sure that everyone in the community realized that they were self-identifying on these documents, certainly some people did. This public Christian identity was efficacious as it helped them gain acceptance and trust in small communities.

The men did not fill in these documents dishonestly. Indeed, they appreciated the opportunities to attend missionary and church Bible lessons, where they could learn about Canadian values and practise their English. Most of all, they enjoyed the chance to make friends and to form relationships. In other words, their ambiguity was genuine. While public religious identities and behaviours were often nominally Christian, private ones were traditional. Among fellow Chinese friends and co-workers, most settlers would say that they had no religion, or were not religious, or did not believe in God. During Chinese New Year, the Mid-Autumn Festival, or Confucius' birthday, they would gather with other bachelors and share a meal in the back regions of laundries and restaurants (and, after 1912, in the KMT hall).

In dealing with the third intersecting theme of this book, foodways (or food ideas and food customs), I divide the discussion into (1) the traditional significance of food and (2) the everyday food practices that materialized in western Manitoba. That food is tremendously important in traditional Chinese society and culture should not surprise most readers. As E.N. Anderson notes:

> Chinese use food to mark ethnicity, culture change, calendric and family events, and social transactions. No business deal is complete without a dinner. No family visit is complete without sharing a meal. No major religious event is correctly done without offering up special food proper to the ritual context.[43]

Lettuce means wealth; circular sweet candies and noodles connote togetherness; kumquats are important because they are gold in colour and symbolize wealth and the comfort associated with it; apples are significant because their name sounds like "peace"; and black moss figures in traditional dishes because its name sounds like "prosperity." The thirty-three-year absence of Chinese women from Manitoba not only transformed relationships but also engendered novel food customs. In China, women made the food eaten during the festivals. They were familiar with the recipes, the ingredients, and the other dynamics required to put together the meals in celebration of the numerous yearly events. But there were no women in western Manitoba until 1918, thus, the responsibility for organizing and hosting key festival meals had to shift to men. In Manitoba, before 1910, it was male elders who took on these roles, had the recipes, and set the menus; after that date, Chinese Freemason and KMT leaders did so. Thus, the absence of women resulted in the understandings and boundaries of traditional food rituals being located outside the home and family.

Gender not only influenced the production of food in traditional private settings but also altered food production in public. The customs that developed around food reflected the mixing of cultures and communities as bachelors strove to become modern cafe owners who transformed ordinary and affordable celery and cabbage into the chop suey (*zasui*, or various chopped and cooked foods) of Chinese Canadian cuisine. Like the food itself, the bachelor, through food production, conveyed to the public a persona that was both pleasant and intriguing. Terry Threadgold elaborates on the power of food to express identity and to translate diasporic culture:

> Food became ... a complex intermediary in this network of actors, a way of translating what they could not tell us in English about who they were, what they knew and why it mattered. It had ceased, in other words, to be no more than an empty sign of cosmo-multiculturalism and become an intermediary of cross-cultural translation.[44]

In other words, food communicates the ambiguities of diaspora identity, labour, and community formation.

The fourth and last intersecting theme of *The Way of the Bachelor* is social heat. Adam Chau, in his study of popular religion in rural Northern Shaanbei, China, uses the concept of social heat to highlight the religious dimensions of events and relationships established when people gather in a specific social space: "The concept embodies a native conception of social life that values the convergence and intermingling of a lot of people and the collective production and consumption of loud noises, vibrant colors, fragrant smells, savory tastes, radiant heat, and heightened excitement."[45] Social heat (red and fiery/*honghuo* in Shaanbei, hot and noisy/*renao* in

Mandarin) signifies a dramatic shift away from a calm ordinary situation towards an excited extraordinary one. The shift occurs when many people gather together in isolated areas of rural China. While western Manitoba is appreciably quieter than rural China (and the settlers who lived here were from the southern, not the northern, part of China), and while the food consumed here is more sweet than savoury, I think the term may still be used appropriately. This is because the essential feature of the shift remains the same. It indicates two contrasting registers – one that is quiet and one that is loud.

The majority of events (and social heat) I describe took place between 1911 and 1949, when there were only a few Chinese men living in each eastern Prairie (i.e., Manitoba and Saskatchewan) town, village, and small city. Hosted most often by the KMT (but sometimes by other Chinese political groups and non-Chinese Christian organizations), the events brought together hundreds and sometimes thousands of Chinese men and transformed spaces in remarkable ways. Newspaper accounts describe the lively sounds and heady smells that came out of Winnipeg's Chinatown during New Year's celebrations and other events. During festivals, men accustomed to a calm life in English-speaking, modest, Christian small towns, where they ate a daily diet of plain rice and a few vegetables, would have been overwhelmed by fellowship, food, sounds, and sensations. And, although these lively events may not have had the same feverish pitch, smells, tastes, and colours as those in China, it would nevertheless have been extraordinary for a bachelor living in western Manitoba to gather with other Toisanese-speaking people and eat. These moments, in which Chinese men mingled and shared food, were therefore socially, politically, economically, and culturally transformative, instilling in them shared Nationalist and Christian values and beliefs, and ritualizing relationships. Food events were not just dinners or picnics: they also contained conspicuous religious elements. Missionary- and church-sponsored events prominently featured Christian prayers, singing, and (often) Bible study. If the events were hosted by the KMT, meals were preceded by toasts to Sun Yat-sen (when he was still alive) or the reading of his will (after his death in 1925). As well, everyone in attendance sang the Nationalist anthem, and some people bowed before the framed portrait of Sun Yat-sen, which was always placed on a table with a vase of fresh flowers at the front of the room. National couplets (four Chinese characters written vertically) were often displayed as well. These ritual actions conveyed the religious significance of event hosting and organization in western Manitoba as well as the religious dimensions of the homosocial relationships they so carefully fostered. They also manifested diaspora efficacies *and social heat,* whereby Sun Yat-sen and others were transformed into deities and the KMT evolved into a kind of church lacking in spiritual elements.

Methodology

More than half of the more than two hundred people whom I interviewed for this book knew some of the early Chinese settlers who came to Manitoba.[46] They were their wives, sons and daughters, grandsons and grand-daughters, cousins, employees and employers, and friends. The majority of research participants were born in southern China; the remainder were from the north as well as from Taiwan, Hong Kong, and Canada. I used semi-structured interview techniques and gathered oral histories in English, Mandarin, Cantonese, and Toisanese. I can speak, read, and write Mandarin Chinese. For those few interviews that were conducted in Cantonese and Toisanese, I employed a translator. Sometimes I exchanged notes in Chinese to clarify important points. More than half of these people immigrated to, or were born in, Canada before 1947, roughly one-quarter came after 1947, and the balance arrived in the 1960s and later, when immigration laws no longer favoured Europeans. Interviews, the collecting of oral histories, and informal discussions, ranging from fifteen minutes to four hours in length, took place in settings that involved food – breakfast, coffee breaks, dim sum, lunch, and dinner.[47] Conversations began in a multi-sited "field," and many continued later over the phone and the internet (these were with people who, like me, spent their work days in front of computer screens).[48]

Ethnographic fieldwork helped me to develop the context of lives spent in rural areas of Canada, where racism was not unusual. However, it was not nearly as prevalent in Manitoba as it was in places such as British Columbia, where ethnic enclaves dominated the pattern of settlement. From the beginning, I used an ethnographic approach to gather personal and complicated data about experiences in rural areas beyond Winnipeg and Brandon's Chinatowns. Relationships developed over the years. Once people no longer perceived me to be a stranger,[49] sometimes during the first interview but more often in subsequent encounters, they would recount their life stories. The collecting of oral histories thus enabled me to tell their side of history. As Paul Thompson notes:

> By introducing new evidence from the underside, by shifting the focus and opening new areas of inquiry, by challenging some of the assumptions and accepted judgements of historians, by bringing recognition to substantial groups of people who had been ignored, a cumulative process of

transformation is set in motion ... The use of oral evidence breaks down barriers.[50]

As I interviewed native and non-native Chinese people, many of the accounts I heard – about fathers, grandfathers, uncles, brothers, friends, and employers – had similar ways of expressing the importance of immigrant integration and success.

My team and I completed extensive ethnographic research and also examined reams of archival and historical documents in English and Chinese. This research yielded a significant amount of information about early Chinese life in western Manitoba. Unfortunately, many documents, photographs, and accounts of early Prairie life have been lost. Local histories contain paragraphs and sometimes pages that tell about the lives, accomplishments, and contributions of early British, Irish, Scottish, and sometimes Ukrainian or Jewish settlers. In contrast, if there is a story about an early Chinese bachelor and his business, it is generally told in one line, perhaps in a paragraph, but never in a whole page. Sometimes the reference is to a "Chinaman" who apparently has no last name. At other times, he is given the generic name "Lee," which was common practice in Manitoba as well as in other provinces. For instance, the entry for Reston, Manitoba's Chinese laundry reads: "'Lee' was his name, if memory serves, but the little Chinese laundry man in Reston was better known as 'No Tickee, No Washee.'"[51]

Given the sixty-two years of institutionalized racism in this country, it is equally difficult to find early bachelors in head tax and other government documents. Some men came here as "paper sons," with fake purchased birth certificates and pseudonyms. White clerks wrote their names down phonetically on immigration registers and on other official documents on their arrival at Canadian ports. In this way, Chinese men came to have monikers that slightly or drastically varied from their native ones. Lee Low's Chinese immigration papers for June 1911 listed him as Lau Kong Lee. The General Register of Chinese Immigration varied the spelling so that he became known as Low Kon Lee.[52] Eventually, Lee Low dropped the "Kong" in his name and simply became known to Carberry restaurant patrons as Lee Low. As a result, many men had alternate versions of their names, which must have been very frustrating and demeaning for the Chinese immigrant. The findings presented here are, accordingly, preliminary.

Overview

The Way of the Bachelor examines the history and religion of Chinese immigrants in western Manitoba, in particular, and in Manitoba and Saskatchewan in general. It is about the lived experiences of mostly male settlers who immigrated to Canada, paid a head tax that ranged from fifty (in 1885) to five hundred dollars (in 1903), and lived outside of Chinatowns in predominantly rural areas. It is also about the ways in which, from 1885 to 1947, institutionalized racism shaped migration patterns, prevented families from living together, and influenced the production of global identities, ideas, labour, and institutions. Throughout these pages I tell the stories of men who, through homosocial relationships, survived and found meaning in their new Canadian lives.

Most of the data I present pertain to communities in Brandon, Manitoba. As the second largest city in the province, it is the hub for the region and has the largest Chinese community outside of Winnipeg. Although the material concentrates on Brandon, there is also information about laundries, restaurants, and everyday rituals in some of the smaller rural towns and villages. Because rural and urban lives often intersect, the reader will be able to learn about the history of the Winnipeg-based Manitoba KMT and Christian and missionary groups. I also write about laundries, restaurants, and customs in that city and in the Prairies more generally (especially in Saskatchewan, which shares Manitoba's western border).

Chapter 1 uncovers the history of the KMT in western Manitoba, relating how Sun Yat-sen drew on the authority of Christianity to motivate overseas men to support the revolutionary cause. It also explains how tradition dictated that political leaders were responsible for taking care of the overseas Chinese bachelors. But the influence of Sun Yat-sen, the KMT, and nationalism on beliefs, practices, and identity is only half the story. Christianity, in particular the United Church, is the other half. The United Church (and, before 1925, the Anglican, Presbyterian, and Methodist churches) helped new immigrants learn English and Canadian values that would enable them to become accepted in local communities.[53] It is important to recognize the significance of non-Chinese and Chinese friendships. These relationships were complex and their meaning was not stable. Young boys, brought over to Canada to work and live with men who might or might not have been their fathers, had better lives because of their relationships with Christians. Ministers and churchwomen became their surrogate parents. Christian relationships with Chinese were ambiguous and, at least until after the First World War, were prompted by a desire to convert and to civilize. Generally, after this time, ministers and congregations were very accepting; and, when men married non-Chinese women, ceremonies were held in churches.[54] The bachelors were as ambivalent towards Westerners as the latter were towards them. In the beginning, a desire to learn English and Canadian values prompted them to make Christian friends. As with many budding friendships, there were many things the two sides didn't know, and didn't want to know, about each other.

Chapter 2 introduces the experiences of the men who first arrived in western Manitoba and entered the laundry business. The hours were long, the work was terrible, and the pay was low. The bachelor-turned-laundryman became legendary for his ability to make shirts whiter and clothes cleaner than anyone else. When the popularity of laundries waned in the late 1940s, the men reinvented themselves and turned to the restaurant business, marketing concoctions such as chop suey as traditional fare that could be served to a Western market.

In Chapters 3 and 4, I focus on the Chinese bachelors who provided food to members of the dominant non-Chinese society, thereby engaging in regular and positive interaction with repeat customers. As interactions intensified, intercultural bridges were built and soon became conduits for the sharing of ideas, cultures, and traditions. Chapter 3 tells the story of the rural western Manitoban restaurant, a business whose strategy aimed at future integration. By the 1950s, almost every village, town, and city on the Prairies had such a restaurant. Chinese Canadian restaurants functioned as Prairie nodes, offering places for people to work, to gather, and to erect altars to *Guangong* and *Guanyin* (and other ancestors and gods) behind the kitchen doors. After 1950, they began to bring some of these back-stage customs to the front and so to add to the Orientalist appeal of eating Chinese food. Yet, restaurants also served the needs of rural communities and Prairie ethnic groups such as Ukrainians and Jews. They ate "ordinary" meals at Chinese Canadian restaurants and celebrated holidays and birthdays there, as well. The Chinese Canadian restaurant enabled Jews and Ukrainians to form a minority community of their own. Chapter 4 continues the discussion of food, integration, and identity, reflecting on the agency of ambiguity and the intentional and sustained fashioning of an identity that was pleasing and exotic to both children and adults.

In Chapter 5, I discuss the fundamentals of the everyday religion of Chinese Manitobans, which grew out of early labour patterns as well as out of KMT leaders' views on Christianity, Confucianism, everyday religion, and education (especially for children, who needed to be able to communicate in Chinese when they returned to visit family in China). KMT Confucianism expressed itself through events that leaders organized and hosted at their district branch offices. It also influenced the formation of everyday rituals that were performed by elders, families, and individuals within the various communities after 1949 (when the KMT retreated to Taiwan) and after 1947 (when large numbers of Chinese women and families started to come to Canada). Throughout my discussion of the KMT, laundries, restaurants, and food, I highlight the expediency of homosocial relationships and the importance of efficacy with regard to enabling early settlers to survive, adapt, and create futures for their immediate families and descendants.

1
Christianity and the Manitoba Kuomintang

I begin my examination of the way of the bachelor with a discussion of the earliest Chinese political and religious groups in the province. Homosociality and the religious dimensions of friendship are inextricably linked to involvement in these groups. While, from the beginning of settlement, there were many political groups, the Kuomintang, being the strongest (at least in this province), had an informal partnership with Christian and missionary groups that had started to coalesce decades earlier in China.[1] This partnership started to form in China when Sun Yat-sen and others became involved in the early stages of the revolutionary movement and formed groups that, after 1911, would become the KMT. Sun Yat-sen and others saw in Christianity a doorway to the West. They believed that, by learning about its tenets, they could begin to understand and be understood by Westerners. They were right. I begin by looking at the history of the relationship among churches, missionaries, and bachelors in western Manitoba.

Protestant Christians and the Chinese

Most western Manitoban Chinese bachelors and, later, Chinese Canadians have always looked to ministers, reverends, pastors, and male and female missionaries for fellowship and support. Although a few of them have also formed strong bonds with Roman Catholic priests in small eastern Prairie communities, it has usually been the Protestant Christians (and those in the United Church) who have been the first point of contact for newcomers. In larger urban settlements these relationships have led to Chinese Christian congregations and churches. For more than fifty years now, these kinds of religious communities and institutions have existed in, for example, Saskatoon, Regina, and Winnipeg. In Brandon, there has been one failed attempt in the past to provide Mandarin, Cantonese, and Toisanese Protestant services and Chinese Bible study classes. In 1979, Vietnamese Chinese refugees came to Manitoba, and some settled in Brandon. In the 1980s, the larger Chinese population created a demand for Chinese services and Bible study classes. But most of the Vietnamese Chinese did not settle permanently in the area, and the special Chinese services and classes did not continue beyond a few years.[2] By 2006, hundreds of Chinese had moved to Brandon to work at Maple Leaf Consumer Foods. Initially, Chinese men came to the province without wives and children. By January 2009 wives and children had arrived and another weekly Chinese Bible study class had been organized in Brandon. By October 2009, the class had grown to seventy and was meeting for Chinese services at a local church. It will be interesting to see whether these new Chinese Canadians convert to Christianity or remain nominally Christian, as has been the tendency in the area.

The majority of Chinese Canadians in western Manitoba have tended to be nominal Christians who publicly identify as Christian when asked questions about religious affiliation by customers or by census survey takers. In private situations, these same individuals often say they have no religion or are Buddhist or Confucian. This pattern of public and private self-identification seems to have been a widespread tactic used by early settlers to adapt to the expectations of the dominant Canadian society. As I explain, this tactic was not based on deception; rather, it was the product of ambiguity and ambivalence – both of which are common aspects of Chinese religiosity.[3] As W. Peter Ward notes: "Protestant missionaries had chosen an extremely difficult task and, in consequence, they enjoyed less success than they must originally have anticipated. The greatest of all obstacles was the indifference, if not opposition, of most Orientals to the message of the Gospel."[4]

An attitude of religious ambivalence enabled one to honestly profess an identity to one person and then adjust that identity for another, depending on what was socially acceptable in different settings and to different actors. Thus, religious ambivalence enabled a new settler to be both a Christian and, say, a Buddhist. Sun Yat-sen himself had been baptized, but in other ways he was only a nominal Christian, and he admired the teachings of Confucianism as well as other aspects of traditional Chinese culture. Sun Yat-sen's persona was famous and presented itself as a model of a Chinese man who had influence in both Chinese and Western circles.

In the 1901 Canadian census, 63.3 percent (19/30) of Chinese immigrants in the Brandon District self-identified as Baptist, Methodist, Presbyterian, or just Christian. By 1911, the pattern continued, and 89 percent (87/97) self-identified as Anglican, Baptist, Roman Catholic, or as Methodist and Presbyterian. While it was not uncommon for immigrants to self-identify

Table 1

Brandon District data for those identifying China as birthplace, 1901 and 1911 censuses

	1901	1911
Total	30	97
Anglican	0	9
Baptist	2	8
Church of England	0	3
Confucian	0	1
Methodist	6	16
Meyzu/no religion	0	6
Presbyterian	10	49
Roman Catholic	0	2
Blank or erased	0	3
Buddhist	11	0
Christian	1	0

Note: The table covers the Brandon District only and does not include the Portage la Prairie District, where, in 1911, there were two additional Confucian Chinese men.

in this manner,[5] these data create the impression that the Chinese newcomers were overwhelmingly Christian (see Table 1.1).

I assumed that data from the 1901 and 1911 censuses reflected the religion of research participants; however, as I interviewed family members and friends of the first wave of Chinese immigrants, and as I read newspapers and archival material, these assumptions were proven incorrect. The men may have attended church or said that they were Christian when responding to a census survey, but, for the most part, they were not religious in this way. Their willingness to give these answers had to do with their desire to fit into local communities, their increased involvement with the KMT and other Chinese political and social institutions, religious ambivalence, the ambiguous nature of Chinese religion, and efficacy. I now turn to a discussion of the relationship between early immigrants and missionary and church work both in western Manitoba and overseas.

Towards the end of the nineteenth century, residents in small cities, towns, and villages throughout western Manitoba began to find themselves with Chinese-operated laundries and restaurants. Although people appreciated the services offered by the new businesses, they were less sure about the foreigners who operated them. The men were strange-looking (they had pigtails!), spoke a different language, had strange customs, and often lived alone. At first the missionaries preyed on the strangers and were overtly racist in their attitude towards them. However, as time progressed and more missionaries went to China and returned, racism became less intense.

Large numbers of missionaries began to travel from Canada to China during the First Opium War (1839-42). After the Taiping Rebellion (1851-64), the Second Opium War (1856-60), and the Boxer Rebellion (1900), many more people were recruited to minister in China and, after 1900,[6] to provide food, housing, medical assistance, and clothing.[7] Jessie Lutz contends that "Western Protestant evangelists increased from 1,296 in 1889 to 3,883 in 1906 to 6,636 in 1919 ... Only 106 *hsien* (counties) out of 1,704 in China proper and Manchuria were without some Protestant evangelical activity."[8] As more people went to China, local newspapers wrote about missionary activities as well as uprisings and various disasters. When Canadian missionaries were killed, newspapers reported these stories, too. Chinese men living in western Manitoba were blamed for the deaths, and restaurants and laundries became targets of white hostility: rocks were thrown through windows and laundrymen were assaulted. Missionary reports only served to reinforce the public impression that the "Chinaman" was a barbarous, curious, dirty, idolatrous, and savage heathen.[9] As W. Peter Ward explains: "Repeatedly mission reports and correspondence emphasized that idolatry, superstition, spiritual indifference, moral inadequacy, and imperviousness to the Christian gospel were typical of the Oriental character."[10] In Canada, Methodists, Presbyterians, and others felt threatened by the new settlers and feared that they would not assimilate.[11]

Over time, Christian views about Chinese immigrants softened, partly because missionaries grew to understand their customs and partly because missionaries were being treated better in China. Local ministers and others who had been overseas became known as experts, and they were called on to give public presentations on Chinese traditions and history.[12] As the immigrants got more involved in missionary activities, some of the barriers between white culture and Chinese culture dissolved. For instance, in 1919, the Carberry, Manitoba chapter of the Imperial Order of the Daughters of the Empire held its tea and sale in the local Chinese restaurant.[13] Missionaries began to sympathize with the men who worked long hours for very little pay and who had difficulty communicating because of limited English skills. Missionaries and members of the church were vocal opponents of the successive racist and discriminatory versions of the Chinese Immigration Act, 1885, which was only repealed in 1947.

In China, after 1911, for the most part the new republican government held Christianity in high regard. I say "for the most part" because, between

1922 and 1927, intellectuals, students, and KMT party activists rallied together to protest missionary activities in port cities and especially in Beijing; however, these protests did not take place in the rural areas from which many of the overseas men had emigrated.[14] The anti-Christian campaigns represented the long-held view that foreign missionary bodies had too much power in China. Nevertheless, Rebecca Nedostup notes that the KMT still regarded "Protestant Christianity as the implied or overt benchmark [of religion]."[15] Protestant Christianity was a Western religion and represented many of the ideals that the KMT wanted modern China to possess.

Sun Yat-sen and others within the KMT were Christians, and, once the imperial era ended in 1911, Christianity was perceived to be the standard by which all other religions were to be judged. This meant that missionaries now enjoyed higher status in China. Many of the Chinese bachelors had emigrated from rural southern areas of China and later had become KMT members in Canada. Coming from the southern coast of Guangdong, the men would have been familiar with Western culture and Christianity. When they became KMT members they became even more predisposed to participate in missionary activities. They wanted to appear as Christians and Westerners like Sun Yat-sen and, thus, to be perceived as socially acceptable and modern gentlemen. According to Jiwu Wang: "Attendance at mission activities increased remarkably, and the attitude towards Christianity of the Chinese immigrants improved noticeably. It was reported that more than 1,000 Chinese attended a series of religious services organised by a local Methodist church in Vancouver."[16] In the rest of Canada and in western Manitoba, missionary efforts to convert bachelors to Christianity continued, but the relationship was never one-sided. Prairie churches, missions, and local women offered Sunday school, Chinese Bible classes, summer picnics, ice cream socials, teas, and recreational activities for the local communities in western Manitoba.[17] When new immigrants attended them they not only learned about religiosity but also how to speak English, and they had a chance to mix with whites in the community.[18] One Winnipeg old-timer explained: "Church socials and church Christmas parties opened their doors to the city's lonely immigrants. Many Chinese were converted to Christianity because of these contacts."[19] Through the church, people made friends and formed contacts that led to opportunities to work outside of the laundries and restaurants. As time passed, the bond between Chinese and non-Chinese religious communities strengthened.

In summary, a Chinese Christian would self-identify as such on census surveys and when asked by the white community. He would also have a church ceremony for his wedding, and, when he died, a minister would speak at his funeral. Being known in this way was efficacious, conveying that you had a network of Canadian and Chinese friends and that you had been accepted. Research participants have repeatedly noted that, while many people in western Manitoba frowned on mixed-race marriages between Chinese men and white women, churches were very accepting of them. On 22 September 1910, the *Baldur Gazette* remarked on one mixed marriage that took place in Brandon: "Mah How and a white girl named Miss Louie Morris got married in St. Matthew's [Anglican] rectory in Brandon, Manitoba on September 15, 1910."[20] I note that several of the marriages of influential early KMT elders in the province were of the mixed-race variety.

In one oral history interview, a research participant told a story about someone who was not a formal Christian but who had always wanted to be welcomed and accepted by members of the larger dominant society:

> I remember once talking with a very fine minister of First Church United and we were arranging a funeral and he called [a particular Chinese-Canadian man] a Christian. And I said, "You know, I don't think [he] was baptized Christian." He said, "It doesn't matter. He was a very Christian man and I list him as a Christian."

For both the research participant and the person who had died, being a good Christian was synonymous with being a good Canadian. As it was explained to me, it would have been a great honour to have a white minister speak this way about an early Chinese settler who spoke broken English and didn't have the right to vote until 1947.[21]

After the repeal of the Chinese Immigration act in 1947, many men were able to bring over their children and wives in what came to be another wave of migration. The children got involved in Christian youth groups, church camps, and bands. And, while their fathers, uncles, and grandfathers might have been indifferent to Christianity, the members of this later wave were much more open to conversion. A research participant commented on the importance of the local church in his own adaptation to, and success in, Canada:

> We [the kids] ended up in the United Church and became Christians. The church opened its doors to us. They offered leadership training and moulded me in many aspects. At the same time, my mother and father forced us to go to church. Through the church I became assimilated and Canadian ... At

New Year and at other times Mom would pray and burn incense and put out food. The Chinese United Church played a huge role too. Ministers took me under their wing ... My parents were both buried in funerals where United Church ministers officiated. But they were not real members. It was a place that their children went to.

It was not uncommon for Chinese to burn incense and, behind the scenes, to torch other symbolic offerings seen to be desirable gifts. The list of these desirable gifts is long. Most items are made of paper. There are paper cars, paper television sets, and paper telephones. But the most important and common gift is spirit money, which is also referred to as Hell Bank Money, Ghost Money, and Joss Paper. Spirit money would have been available for purchase in Chinatowns in oversees communities throughout the world. People would have burned it in metal pails in front of altars and gravesites on the birthdays of ancestors and during Qingming, Chongyang, and on Decoration Day.[22]

Involvement with churches, missionaries, and women who hosted Bible classes and other events in Manitoba helped the men and their families become Canadians, but the KMT helped them too. Many early settlers who were involved in Christian organizations or who attended Bible classes belonged to overlapping political organizations and, especially, to the KMT.

The KMT in Manitoba

Aside from self-identifying as Christians, new settlers also self-identified in a more political and private manner. Although after 1912 the eventual dominant form of political affiliation in the province was the KMT, several organizations predated it. Winnipeg's branch of the Chinese Freemasons (*Hongmen* 洪門/ *Zhigongtang* 致公堂) was formed in 1910,[23] and Wong Muk (Mandarin: *Wang Mu* 王木), Lam Syu (Mandarin: *Lin Shu* 林樹), Lee Yik Chap (Mandarin: *Li Yiqi* 李奕緝), and Lee Hungyeui (Mandarin: *Li Hongrui* 李鴻銳)[24] were its early leaders.[25] While the branch was not recognized by the Grand Lodge of Masons in Manitoba, it was connected to the other lodges that opened covertly in Victoria and Toronto that year. The address of the Winnipeg Lodge was 259 King Street, and it had three hundred members. It could be found in the heart of an emerging Chinatown, along with laundries, restaurants, groceries, rooming houses, and apartments that dotted Portage Avenue, Pacific Avenue, King Street, Princess Street, and Main Street.[26] Baureiss and Kwong note that, in 1909, it was the increasing number of Chinese grocery stores that finally created the core area known as "Chinatown" at King Street and Alexander Avenue.[27] Here, you could find traditional foods as well as medicines, porcelain vases, silk, and a growing Chinese community who came to hear about the political and social events taking place in the region.

In 1910, the Chinese Masonic Lodge also housed the Tongmenghui (Chinese United League 同盟會),[28] which, two years later, became the secret Manitoba KMT.[29] Large handwritten signs in Chinese were posted on storefront windows along Winnipeg's King Street to announce news and events to men who were drawn from other urban and rural areas of the Prairies.[30] The Chinese Freemasons and, by extension, the Chinese United League were most fondly remembered for bringing Sun Yat-sen to Winnipeg in April 1911.[31] Sun Yat-sen had come to Canada in July 1897 and again in February 1910, and Chinese United League leaders convinced him to make a stop in Winnipeg after he spoke in Vancouver in January 1911. They met Sun at the CPR station near Chinatown and acted as his bodyguards (along with the ones he brought with him) as he toured the city, held fundraising meetings, and gave political speeches.[32] If his 1911 trip to Winnipeg attracted any public attention at all, there is no trace of it in local Chinese and English newspapers. The visit appears to have been a private community one and was kept out of the media.

Over the next fourteen years, Sun's 1911 tour to Manitoba and other places in Canada and the United States paid off. He knew many of the local leaders by name and could use these connections to rally support in distant communities. Sun was so successful at fundraising in North America because, in addition to his familiarity with North American leaders and their terrain, his speeches and letters conveyed an air of Western sophistication. They drew heavily on a Protestant Christian rhetoric of faith, support, and belief in the revolution in China.[33] Sun embodied the bachelors' idea of a new China. With him as their figurehead, they were able to imagine a nation that was Western, modern, and new.[34] Donating to the Nationalist cause at any bank in Manitoba, or to the KMT party directly, gave the men a way to lessen the suffering of their nation and to become Sun's martyrs.[35] Member donations to KMT fundraising campaigns were advertised in Chinese and, later, in English newspapers. Those who made the largest contributions had the highest status within the community. Six months after Sun Yat-sen's trip to the province and shortly after the Wuchang Uprising, men in Brandon's Chinese community were interviewed by the local paper regarding their financial contributions to Sun:

> Some of the local Chinamen have the $10 bill newly printed by the Revolutionist party in China. According to the local revolutionist sympathizers,

this bill is given in exchange for a Canadian five dollar. If the insurgents win the bill will be worth ten dollars; if they lose it will be worthless. This seems to be a pretty good scheme to finance the revolution, and if the revolution is successful, which seems altogether likely at present, there will be some rich Celestials in the west, as a good many of them have contributed in this manner to the insurgent war chest.[36]

Many of these men lived like peasants on the rural Canadian Prairies, travelling from job to job and place to place. For them, five dollars was an enormous amount of money. They overlooked the costs of these revolutionary bills because they were inspired by the Chinese revolution and by Sun Yat-sen's vision of a new republic.[37] In addition to the 1911 Brandon community contributions, larger branches in the country took out mortgages on their Chinese United League and Chinese Freemason buildings, raising between 63,000 and 100,000 Hong Kong dollars.[38]

While people in western Manitoba had been able to read about Chinese history, politics, and customs in local newspapers before Sun Yat-sen's visit to the province, they knew much more about him, China, and Chinese customs after his visit. Many articles appeared in local newspapers on the queue (the long pigtail worn by Chinese settlers before 1911),[39] opium,[40] and the nation's politics. The *Brandon Weekly Sun* reported on the history of southern Chinese uprisings on Thursday, 18 May 1911;[41] later that same year, it ran stories about the increased rioting and uprisings in China and the danger to missionaries in the region.[42] Local newspapers informed their readers when the Wuchang Uprising took place on 10 October 1911 – an uprising that led to the Xinhai Revolution and the eventual collapse of the Qing dynasty.[43] When Sun Yat-sen became president of China in late December 1911, the *Brandon Weekly Sun* ran the story.[44]

1912 to present

As one research participant noted, belonging to the early KMT in Canada was, for Chinese men, like being a member of one of today's political parties. The only difference was that, if you were Chinese and living in Manitoba in the early part of the twentieth century, you were expected to be a member of the KMT and to support it. Those who chose not to join were branded as "young communists." These men were often associated with the Chinese Dramatic Society.

In Manitoba, the KMT was historically centre-right in its pro-Nationalist views, although at times it forged alliances with left-wing groups in the province to protest against "fascism" and to fundraise.[45] In 1915, the secret

FIGURE 2 Memorial plaque, c. 1929, Huanghuagang,
Seventy-Two Martyrs Mausoleum, Guangzhou, China.
Source: Kenny Choy

KMT, which was established in 1912, issued a press release to the *Manitoba Free Press* announcing its inaugural meeting.[46] For the next several years, the KMT office frequently changed locations, and, by 1916, it opened its doors at 263 King Street. Five years later, it moved to 77 Lily Street, and by 1932 it had moved to the Johnstone Building (209-13 Pacific Avenue), which it rented for one year and then purchased. The Winnipeg branch was the regional Prairie headquarters of the KMT in Canada, and, by 1914, it was one of the most active and powerful of the country's forty-one branches.

Though now forgotten,[47] a rural KMT outpost had opened in Brandon by 1913. The discovery of this KMT office in the middle of the Prairies came about by accident through a search of *Henderson's Directories* for proprietors of laundries and restaurants. Later, these references were corroborated by an international Chinese business directory that mentioned a local office of the KMT.[48] This was one of the first nine sites of the new party to be located east of Vancouver and Victoria.[49] In 1916, Brandon's Chinese bachelors formally announced the KMT branch in the local newspaper:

The Chinese living in Brandon have fallen into line with their compatriots in other cities and have organized a branch of a national association, the initial meeting to take place at the headquarters on Twelfth Street ... the local association will have a membership of between 150 and 200. This national association is to have branches all over Canada and speakers from Winnipeg, Moose Jaw, Regina and Calgary will be here for the opening night, which promises to be an epoch making event among the celestials here ... Lee James is the president of the local association, Wong Higgins, secretary, and Hum Jink, treasurer.[50]

Wong Higgins,[51] secretary of the Brandon KMT, had been one of the founding members of the Winnipeg Chinese Freemasons, who had arranged Sun Yat-sen's visit and may have been part of the committee that had provided his bodyguards during his stay in the province. Wong's involvement with the early rural group had no doubt helped foster the widespread loyalty to Sun Yat-sen during his lifetime and the veneration for him after his death.

Through discussions with old-timers I learned that Brandon's office was the rural headquarters of the provincial KMT. Located in a house at 135-12th Street, it was used as a residence for migrant workers in the laundries and restaurants, and it formed the core of Brandon's tiny Chinatown. Unlike Chinatowns in other small Canadian cities, this one was several blocks away from the CPR station. Like the others, it was defined by Chinese residences and rooming houses, businesses such as laundries and a grocer, and the KMT office.[52] The city's four Chinese Canadian restaurants were a few blocks away, outside of Chinatown.[53]

Brandon's Chinatown was plain. There were no roof tiles in brilliant yellow hues or exotic creatures lining winged roofs of buildings. Chinese in Manitoba didn't construct their own buildings. They rented and purchased pre-existing Western ones, and this is why, unlike Victoria and Vancouver, Brandon and Winnipeg have no original Chinese architecture and/or historic buildings. And there are certainly no underground tunnels connecting basements. However, calligraphy was visible from the street on a sign above the KMT office door, and the posters, written in Chinese, that were periodically hung on its windows advertised rural Chinese and Chinatown events as well as those in Winnipeg. In this office people could find a bit of China and someone to organize traditional events.[54] As with many older buildings in Brandon, this one was demolished decades ago.

During the First World War, many Canadian KMT leaders encouraged members to contribute to the war effort and to support the Allied soldiers.[55] But they also communicated with each other by code, and there was a growing concern that Chinese bachelors were becoming too well organized and well connected during the war. In any case, midway through it, members of the Department of Justice began to monitor the intelligence networks of KMT offices in Canada. Two years later, KMT activities were suspended after an incident in which a Chinese barber in Victoria murdered a Chinese diplomat and then committed suicide. The diplomat had reportedly been passing through Canada on his way back to China. The Canadian government investigated the murder and determined that it was a political crime related to the KMT's revolutionary efforts in China.[56] As a result, on 18 September 1918, the government declared the KMT illegal, along with twelve other ethnically based political organizations. It closed all KMT offices from 28 September 1918 to 2 April 1919, when Order in Council PC 2384 was repealed. During the time that the offices were closed, many Chinese, including L.S. Quong, a student in Vancouver, wrote several letters to the Department of Justice protesting the ban and lamenting the loss of the organization, which had functioned as a moral compass for overseas Chinese. He noted:

> Some of the other aims of this party are: to reform China socially, politically and *morally* both at home and abroad, and to attain these only by peaceful and lawful means. To accomplish these objects the League has established branches throughout the whole world where Chinese are to be found ... Outside of China its work is more of a moral rather than a political character.[57]

Chinese throughout Canada were very interested in reopening the KMT offices that had been closed during the ban, and they began a letter-writing campaign to that end. As mentioned above, in 1919 the order was repealed and, shortly after that, the offices reopened and resumed their activities. While the Canadian government had been aware that the CBA, Chinese Freemasons, and KMT offices were communicating in code, it seems to have been unaware that Sun Yat-sen had built an aviation centre in Saskatoon (and later in other places) and had started to actively train revolutionary pilots there in the early 1920s.

From the 1920s to the 1950s, Sam Wong, a prominent local restaurant owner and KMT leader from Montreal, whom I discuss in Chapter 3, was close friends with a man named Charlie Foo. Like Foo, Wong was an experienced local KMT leader with ties to Winnipeg and Montreal,[58] fundraiser, and one-time KMT building owner. Foo was president and an executive member of the Winnipeg KMT, the CBA, and Chinese Patriotic

League (branches of which had been established across Canada in 1937) for more than four decades. This significant relationship eventually produced a marriage alliance between the Foo and Wong families, and, through this, the KMT secured the allegiance of the Wong Association within Winnipeg and beyond. Historically, however, it should be noted that the relationship between Foo and Wong may have had deeper family roots. Foo's Chinese name was Au Foo (Mandarin: *Ou Fu* 區富), and, like Wong's first wife, he was from the Au 區 clan in China.[59]

Although the KMT maintained a presence in Brandon until the 1950s, its Chinatown office had disappeared by 1934, when Sam Wong was the last recorded owner. The Chinese population sharply declined in the 1930s,[60] in part because of the Depression and in part because of the 1923 version of the Chinese Immigration Act, which massively curtailed immigration to Canada until years after its repeal in 1947.[61] Members could no longer support the operation of two provincial offices and still afford to send donations to China following the 1931 Japanese invasion and the Second Sino-Japanese war in 1937. Membership fees (which were really more like prescribed donations) soared in this period, causing too much of a financial burden for the many who eventually left the area.[62] From 1935 until the late 1950s, the KMT maintained a presence, but not an office, in the city, operating boarding houses on Sixth Street and Twelfth Street.[63]

The year 1947 brought the repeal of the Chinese Immigration Act, and two years after that the Chinese Communist Party (CCP) took control of mainland China. By 1949, when the KMT retreated to Taiwan, it was said to have ten thousand Canadian members.[64] Membership dropped steadily after that, and many annual events were no longer organized. As women and children began to immigrate to Manitoba in large numbers, men returned to the way life was practised in traditional families, with their wives managing their religious and social lives. Chinese communities once dominated by bachelor societies were now filled with families, and, accordingly, KMT governance responded to the needs of this new group, using various events to educate newcomers about citizenship rights in Manitoba.[65] Thus, in the 1950s, Brandon was the site of the Chinese Canadian Citizens' Association of Manitoba, which lasted for a decade.[66] The association was one of many groups operated by the leaders of Winnipeg's KMT, but it was the only one located outside the city. Like the KMT, the Chinese Canadian Citizens Association of Manitoba had an intercultural aim: to encourage Chinese Canadians to become familiar with non-Chinese customs, groups, politics, and, mostly significantly, citizenship.[67]

Today, many of the older members of the community still feel connected to the KMT; however, they also feel a little lost. The local branch and the party leaders with whom they and their parents identified as children disappeared long ago. One of the oldest members explained:

> The Chinese people here in North America still support the KMT and that support came out of their support of Sun Yat-sen. We still support them, but Communist China is not communist anymore and China is being recognized and Taiwan is not. In a way now, we don't know who to support ... I have the twelve-pointed star of the KMT in my heart. There is still a lot of the KMT in me.

National KMT membership had fallen to just three thousand by the end of the 1970s,[68] and today, in Manitoba at least, there are approximately fifty members. And, although the membership of the branch is small, it nevertheless has status and agency among Canadian branches, gauged by its real estate holdings. The Manitoba KMT, along with those in Montreal, Ottawa, and Vancouver, still owns its building. The office has been relocated upstairs and is barely noticeable unless one can read the Chinese characters (written by Sun Yat-sen and sent to Manitoba in 1920) on the building's sign. It and others in Canada used 10 October 2008 (Double Tenth Day, or Nationalist Day) to mark the KMT's return to power in Taiwan. In recognition of this victory, the Manitoba building received a much-needed new coat of blue paint, and the Nationalist flag (which had flown over the building from 1933 to 1979) was redeployed on its roof. Today, I have been told by KMT executive members that the building appears as it did when it was first purchased in 1933. The branch holds two meetings a year and has a library and games room, where elderly men still come to play mahjong and to read the Chinese newspaper. At one time, the basement housed a community kitchen, but today this space is used for storage of the Chinese Dramatic Society trunks, old furniture, and other items no longer in use. The·main hall where Chinese events were once held is now rented by Chingwu Athletic Association, which offers Tai Chi, Kungfu, Chinese wrestling, and Lion Dance[69] instruction and performance. In the fall of 2008, the branch started to offer periodic tours of the building.

Roles of the KMT
While the KMT was first and foremost a political organization, in rural areas it performed other, equally important, roles.[70] If you were new to the area, an elder would pick you up at the train station and take you to the KMT

branch.[71] He would then take you out for a meal and find you a place to live. In the meantime, you would live at the KMT house, where you would have had an opportunity to the meet (or reconnect with) people who could become your sponsors in a rotating credit association, your partners in a business venture, or your companions for fishing, hunting, hockey games, or movies.[72] The house would have had some sort of community kitchen and a small library with Chinese books and issues of the local KMT-produced newspaper.[73] Leaders (who were well connected to others in Canada) visited those who had been arrested, secured lawyers (the Manitoba KMT and CBA had one on retainer who defended the community and wrote press releases on its behalf), and worked hard to fight for justice and to end discrimination. One man, Lai Man Cheung, said that the KMT helped people raise funds for trips and for medical expenses and that it also arranged transportation and found restaurants that would serve free food to those who had no money: "For one to two years, I was looked after by them [KMT], otherwise I would have died of hunger."[74] In spite of the help they received from the KMT, men did die from hunger, some committed suicide, and some were murdered while living on the Prairies. The exact number of the men who died from hunger, suicide, or murder is difficult to determine. But there were periodic accounts in newspapers of men whose lives ended in these ways. Some of the poorer and disconnected men also became ill and ended up in mental hospitals, where they became almost invisible because none of the medical staff could communicate with them. Henry Ying ran the Dominion Cafe in Gilbert Plains, Manitoba, from 1922 until 1940, when he was hospitalized with syphilis and lost his ability to communicate in English. He spent the next forty-four years of his life alone there, without a single visitor. In 1984, a KMT member in the region heard about him by accident, reconnected him with his family in China, and took care of his funeral when he died shortly after their meeting.

Even after Chinese men moved out of the KMT house, it remained at the heart of their social life. Bachelors returned to the house on their days off work to play a game of fan-tan, paigow, or mahjong, and, late at night, tiny Chinatown would be filled with the sounds of tiles turning and men laughing. Today, the men reminisce about these nights and the games that filled them; however, in the early period of settlement, a Chinese man would never have referred to himself as a "mahjong king" in the presence of non-Chinese as the betting game was considered illicit. Evidence of this is presented in a story about events that took place on Sunday, 11 February 1917, when twenty-nine men were charged with frequenting a gambling house. According to the *Brandon Daily Sun:*

A nest of twenty-nine Celestials was ruthlessly disturbed by the police at 135 Twelfth Street, at ten o'clock Sunday evening. From information received, Chief of Police Easlemont, Sergt. Carter and three officers visited the premises at the time stated, with the result that twenty-nine smiling Chinese put in an appearance at the police court this morning charged with frequenting a gambling house. Mr. N.W. Kerr defended, and J.L. Baird appeared for the crown. The hearing was adjourned until this afternoon.[75]

On Friday the same week, these twenty-nine men returned to court to learn their fate. George King, who ran the house and who was presumably also known as "George Chong," who was listed as the owner in *Henderson's Directories*, received the largest fine – fifty dollars – and had to pay the costs. O You, Ding Dong, Lee Gott, and others were given fines ranging from ten dollars to five dollars. The lawyers and the judge then had a discussion about what needed to be done to keep the Brandon Chinese community out of trouble:

they had a little confab as to what should be done to provide social entertainment for the solitary Chinamen in the city. It was pointed out that they were single men and unmarried, and most of them only earning small wages. It was suggested that the churches and institutions like the YMCA might take up the matter. In the meantime the Chinks were advised to find a nice clean room for social intercourse, and that they abandon the national vice of gambling.[76]

King and the other men appear to have stayed out of trouble for the remainder of the year, possibly because the local churches and YMCA, under the direction of the legal authorities, took a more active role in directing what should constitute their "entertainment."[77]

KMT leaders also tried to provide entertainment for the men. Most often this came in the form of political events that were organized to rally support for the Nationalist cause in China. Bush Chan, the editor of a New York Chinese newspaper, and his wife stopped in Brandon on their way through Canada and spoke to KMT members about nationalism and the need to support and have faith in the new republic.[78] Newspaper accounts showed that there was close contact among all of the groups in the country. Brandon, as a rural outpost of the regional Prairie headquarters, drew people from Regina, North Battleford, Medicine Hat, Moose Jaw, Yorkton, Winnipeg, and even from towns in Northern Ontario. As such, the Brandon KMT office was an important node for various intersecting homosocial relationships.

Men may have lived isolated existences from Tuesday to Saturday, but on Sundays and Mondays they crowded the horse trails, branch lines, and (eventually) highways, tracing the boundaries of their local, provincial, Canadian, and Chinese identities and communities in journeys to and from KMT offices. These weekly sojourns connected them to other co-ethnics, to other places on the Prairie landscape, and to Canada. Because they were so familiar with the people and terrain of these community networks, when the laundry, restaurant, or grocery business began to lose money, the men moved easily into another business somewhere else.

To outsiders, the KMT offices were strange places identifiable by signs they couldn't read, where Chinese men might be doing "Chinese" things like washing clothes or gambling. Leaders of the YMCA, police, and business community saw them as political or social clubs, but to the men and their leaders in Canada and China, they were a connection to home (if only imagined)[79] and a means of governance and of executing the sacred task of harmonizing the realms of heaven, earth, and human being, which was so important in Chinese tradition. In doing this, the KMT leadership observed the millennia-old tradition of Chinese statecraft and the need for ritualized relationships. Sincere members had legitimate expectations of the organization and its leaders who, to them, were de facto Nationalist representatives in Canada. Sun Yat-sen and KMT officials followed the Mencian doctrine that political leaders had to ensure the well-being of their subjects or risk disharmony (in this case, threatening the success of the revolution in China) and a loss of the mandate to lead. According to Elizabeth Perry: "Chinese statecraft since the times of Mencius has envisioned a more proactive role for government – which was expected to promote economic welfare and security. Such expectations carried important practical consequences."[80] Unlike inward-looking and isolated Chinatowns elsewhere, the Manitoba KMT offices were actively promoting homosociality, intercultural understanding, and cooperation. The Lee and Wong families were particularly influential in Manitoba. For decades the two families dominated Chinatown businesses and informal trade guilds. The tide of Chinese nationalism merged fragmented clan identities, uniting them in one understanding of a southern and imagined China. Until the 1950s, most Chinese men in Manitoba had come from Toisan (Taishan) China; they spoke Toisanese and recognized Sun Yat-sen as their native leader.

KMT Events
In addition to their fundraising and other political duties, the KMT leadership also took on many of the roles of the women in Chinese society,[81] like

the hosting of traditional events (e.g., the big meal on the evening before the first day of the lunar new year and the banquet that followed Decoration Day cemetery visits). Some of these were formal intercultural events, such as KMT banquets in the best Winnipeg Chinese Canadian restaurants. Charlie Foo explains:

> Occasionally, the churches held a big party for [the Chinese] and they, in turn, invited the church people to a banquet, sometimes for as many as 400 guests. Thus began friendship and social interaction with other Canadian people. Strangeness and misunderstandings were broken down gradually.[82]

Banquets brought together dignitaries from both communities, providing opportunities for bachelors to mix with others outside their group. One of the most memorable events was the Ninth International KMT Dinner, which was hosted in Winnipeg at the New Nanking Chop Suey House a few months before the First Quebec Conference in 1943.[83]

FIGURE 3 Manitoba KMT,
Chinese Nationalist League banquet, 7 June 1943, at the New Nanking.
I have seen at least four copies of this important photograph.
Source: Manitoba KMT

The banquet, held in honour of the Chinese minister to Canada, Dr. Liu Shishun, was hosted by KMT chairman Frank Chan. The guest list included delegates from Canada's forty-five KMT branches. As well, there were several other distinguished guests in attendance, including Manitoba's then lieutenant-governor, provincial court judges, the US consulate-general, elected members of the legislative assembly, high-ranking officers in the Canadian military, prominent lawyers, doctors, dentists, businesspeople, labour council representatives, and many others. It should be noted that the guest list was ethnically diverse and included a mix of people from the United Church, the Roman Catholic Church, the YMCA, and the Jewish community.[84]

Another notable occasion involved the more informal KMT annual picnic, which began in 1918 (*Manitoba Free Press,* 4 July 1918) and continued into

中國國民黨
駐溫地辟分部
歡讌
第九次全加代表大會
代表圜暨
中央特派監誓監選員
劉師舜同志
秩序表

The Winnipeg Branch of the

KUO MIN TANG

(CHINESE NATIONALIST LEAGUE)

BANQUET

IN HONOUR OF

His Excellency the Chinese Minister to Canada
and the Delegates to the

NINTH CONVENTION

of the

CHINESE NATIONALIST LEAGUE OF CANADA

June 7th, 1943

FIGURE 4 Program, Chinese Nationalist League banquet, 7 June 1943.
Photo: Stubbs Archives

FIGURE 5 Chinese national anthem song sheet, Chinese Nationalist League banquet, 7 June 1943.
Source: Stubbs Archives

FIGURE 6 Manitoba KMT picnic, 1938.
The English and Chinese text indicates that this is the 24th anniversary
of the Winnipeg KMT. However, the Winnipeg KMT secretly formed in 1912.
Source: Manitoba KMT

the late 1940s. This was a public food event in which the "doing" of food, and the social heat, thereby produced, created religiosity. Every year it was advertised in the *Winnipeg Free Press* and up to two thousand people (both Chinese and non-Chinese) attended.[85] Local Chinese restaurants and non-Chinese food distributors donated the items for the mostly Western menu of sandwiches and drinks. The actual food, which was quite plain and "white," was on the periphery of this event, in contrast to the entertainment and opportunities to create relationships with the non-Chinese community, which were paramount.

Each year, the picnic began with significant everyday rituals. There was always the singing of the national anthem of the Republic of China and a toast to Sun Yat-sen. There were also sports events: "fat"-man and

"tall"-man races, three-legged races, football games between KMT members and the Chinese YMCA.[86] At this and other events there were short perform-ances put on by the Chinese Dramatic Society, which had been started in Winnipeg by two laundrymen in 1921.[87] Plays and other performances were derived from Chinese historical and dramatic texts and featured "culture heroes" such as Confucius. While Chinese Dramatic Society members were often recruited by KMT and other political leaders to perform at events, they didn't necessarily belong to the KMT or subscribe to Nationalism. It was an uneasy relationship fraught with political tension. Pictures from the annual picnics made clear the paucity of women and children in the com-munity. They also displayed the large numbers of Chinese and non-Chinese dignitaries who were invited, and who attended, year after year. While some people attended out of self-interest and/or for political reasons, others attended because they were fond of the men, who reminded them of the benevolent gentleman from the small-town Chinese restaurants of their youth. Thus, such events and their rituals created and reinforced relation-ships and intercultural bridges. In the picnic's annual photograph, the dignitaries are in the front row, which was divided by a table, on which was placed a framed picture of Sun Yat-sen and some flowers. Visible above the crowd are two flags – the Nationalist twelve-pointed star and the Union Jack. Towards the end of the 1930s and into the 1940s, attendees were increasingly non-Chinese. The picnic was shifting away from being a way to fundraise and for Chinese to reconnect with each other while working towards building intercultural bridges.

When Sun Yat-sen died on 12 March 1925, Chinese communities all over the world – from Canada to Singapore to China – marked his passing with parades and funeral processions. It was a global event. In Manitoba, over four hundred people from the Winnipeg KMT, the Chinese Benevolent Association,[88] and Chinese Christian organizations (and others) joined together to celebrate his life and accomplishments:

> They marched two abreast, all wearing mourning crepes on their sleeves and badges ... Thirty five cars took part, and there were two trucks, bearing Sun's portrait and his books beautifully decorated with flowers ... Five minutes' silence was observed in the theatre, in respect of the first president of the republic, and then began the speeches, which lasted until six o'clock ... Around the walls of the theatre were displayed nearly 200 banners on which were written poems in tribute to the man who was being honored.[89]

In this civic ceremony to honour the first president of the new republic, Sun Yat-sen was elevated to the status of a Confucian sage. Ritual offerings (such as incense) were replaced with flowers, and prayers were replaced by five minutes of silence and then speeches. I imagine that most people would have been moved by the hundreds of Nationalist couplets (which the Western reporter unfamiliar with Chinese customs recognized as poems) written in classical Chinese that festooned the walls of the theatre that day.

Twelve years later, in 1937, there was an even grander occasion when the Second Sino-Japanese War broke out. Publicly, the purpose of the affair was to celebrate the twenty-fifth anniversary of the formation of the Republic of China, and it was held to coincide with the annual picnic. Privately, the purpose of the affair was to raise money for the Chinese Patriotic League (branches of which had been established across Canada that year).[90] These funds were then sent to China to help the orphaned and the wounded. In addition, the league was set up to protect the democratic vision of Sun's new nation, and, accordingly, every sheet of its letterhead was decorated with his will (written in traditional Chinese characters). Toasts at this and other events for the next eight years, until the defeat of Japan, were offered to Sun Yat-sen and to the military general charged with fighting for his legacy – Chiang Kai-shek.

Over three thousand Chinese and non-Chinese people attended the picnic that year and were treated to free lunches. In addition to the regular races and games featured annually, the reporter noted a special tribute to Sun Yat-sen and the singing of the anthem of the Republic of China (during my interviews, rural old-timers spontaneously sang the anthem in a show of national pride):

> The staccato-like tones of the Chinese voices, the solemn, mysterious Oriental faces as the league members repeated in unison before his picture, the beloved Dr. Sun Yat-sen, founder of the republic, and the wail of the Chinese orchestral music, all blended into a quaint whole – a bit of the old world in the new.[91]

There were countless other events and activities put on by the large Winnipeg KMT group until the late 1940s and early 1950s. The KMT organized and hosted Manitoba Chinese celebrations like the one shown opposite to mark Winnipeg's 1949 seventy-fifth birthday with fireworks (Roman candles, giant firecrackers, rockets with coloured flares, and those on long chains hung from poles) set off on King Street between Alexander and Pacific avenues. A Chinese band with cymbals, gongs, drums, and horns would have introduced the lion as it approached.[92]

As evidence that the office continued to be a powerful hub of nationalism, it hosted the KMT's annual Canadian conference in 1943 mentioned earlier.[93] When King George VI and Queen Elizabeth came to Winnipeg in 1939, the KMT organized welcoming floats that were part of the large city parade. Traditional costumes worn on the floats were borrowed from the Chinese Dramatic Society. It recruited old-timers to work as teachers in after-school and Saturday-morning Chinese-language and calligraphy programs for children. Children who lived outside of Winnipeg studied with private tutors. One research participant noted:

> His father hired somebody to teach him Chinese when he was little – he was very small. He didn't go to school until he was 9 but he could read the Chinese newspaper ... All the kids spoke Chinese, they all spoke Chinese in the home but it was the village dialect.

FIGURE 7 Chinatown Lion Dance in celebration of Winnipeg's
75th Anniversary, 1949.
Source: Barry Chan

Ensuring that your children were educated primarily in Toisanese (the
southern Chinese village dialect here referred to), by either a tutor or at
the KMT Winnipeg school, was standard practice among early Chinese in
Manitoba. Both children and adults needed to be able to converse in Toisanese when they visited China and to read the Chinese newspaper (and
its Nationalist messages) published by the KMT.

The Manitoba KMT also organized Double Tenth Day, or National Day,
festivities; dinners and celebrations to mark the Western and Chinese new
years; and the Mid-Autumn Festival. These events, along with the social
heat they generated and the ritual actions they perpetuated, created and
reinforced hierarchies and new efficacies, providing the men with an alternate world – one in which they no longer existed just as Reston's "Chinaman" or Brandon's laundryman. Instead, the way of the bachelor provided

them with status in both Canada and China, with positions in emerging political hierarchies and Christian communities. It also gave them new rituals and gods.

When bachelors died, through Decoration Day customs, they became god-like figures to the men left behind. KMT elders usually arranged for a Methodist or Presbyterian minister to perform a service. Then KMT (and others within the Chinese Freemasons and the CBA) and Christian groups would follow the body to the cemetery, where it would be lowered into the grave. Once this part of the funeral was finished, everyone would share a meal in a Chinatown restaurant or in the KMT hall. Each year, in late spring and around Father's Day, when the snow had melted, Chinese settlers would return to the cemetery and visit all of the graves in which Chinese men had been buried.

This Decoration Day, which some Toisanese today refer to as *hangsaan/ hangshan* (行山), or the procession to the mountain, was different from the spring Qingming and autumn Chongyang (traditional Chinese grave-sweeping festivals) as it was held for individuals who were not related by blood and was observed at a different time of year. People would go to the graves and offer their respect to whomever they knew. The *Winnipeg Free Press* commented on the custom in 1936:

> Despite unfavourable weather conditions, members of the local branch of the Kuomintang (Chinese National Society) turned out in full force Sunday to observe the annual Decoration Day ceremonies. Gathering at the league's headquarters, 211 Pacific Avenue at 2:30 the cars paraded first to Elmwood cemetery and later to Brookside.[94]

In Winnipeg, the custom would begin in Chinatown, with a police escort stopping the traffic to allow the large number of cars to move through the intersection. KMT leaders would be at the front of the procession, followed by lower-ranking members and friends of the Chinese community.[95] It is hard to speculate as to when this custom started, but it was likely around 1914.[96] Everyone in Brandon and many in Winnipeg agree that it was when one of the poor bachelors died alone without family. As he had no money, his bones could neither be shipped back to China for a proper burial nor be buried here. It might have been begun when Wing Lee died on a Friday night at the Brandon General Hospital, three days after Christmas in 1917.[97] Lee was a laundryman who had lived for many years in Dauphin, become a naturalized Canadian, and rented a room at the Brandon Hotel. When he died he likely had little money to pay for his burial and the funeral that was held at Brockie's Undertaking Parlors.[98] Or, possibly, the moment came three years earlier, in 1914, when Sing Lai, who died in Gainsborough, Saskatchewan, near the Manitoba border, was buried in the Brandon cemetery.[99] Presumably the community fundraised to purchase the headstones and lots in which many of the bachelors were buried.[100] The annual late spring event continues in Brandon and Winnipeg. In Brandon, it is loosely organized and hosted by a group of Chinese elders; in Winnipeg, it is organized and hosted by the CBA. One western Manitoba interviewee commented: "We go and collectively remember the early settlers and what they did here. Some people might go and remember individuals." While in Brandon people are buried in the main cemetery, in Winnipeg they are buried at Elmwood and Brookside cemeteries:

> Every year my father took our family to the Chinese community Decoration Day to pay our respects to the Chinese buried at Brookside Cemetery. The custom would be observed in the swampier [and inferior, according to fengshui beliefs] part of the cemetery where most of the Chinese were buried. People would bring incense sticks, flowers and visit the graves.

That Chinese were given plots in the swampier parts of the cemetery may have been dictated by cost, with swampier plots being cheaper than others. It was also no doubt dictated by racism. Both cemetery visits are followed by a community meal at a Chinese Canadian restaurant or the KMT hall, as in the case of Winnipeg. One research participant noted:

> After hangsaan [*hangsaan/hangshan* (行山), or the procession to the mountain] is the best part. The food. We get to eat after. The KMT used to host the banquet. The food would be laid out on tables on the main floor. They would put all the tables together and then put tablecloths and chairs out. There would be all kinds of food, tea, 7-Up and Orange Crush. Chinese really like Orange Crush. And behind the tables on the wall would be a large picture of Sun Yat-sen and a smaller one of Chiang Kai-shek.

I return to this important KMT custom in Chapter 4.

Involvement with the KMT, the Mythology of Sun Yat-sen, and the Route to Social Acceptance

Homosocial relationships and roles in the KMT, along with those in Christian governance structures, provided agency and connections in Manitoba Chinese society. These intercultural connections among Chinese and non-Chinese settlers followed the example set by Sun Yat-sen. As I mentioned earlier, Protestant Christianity influenced the formation of the KMT in Manitoba, providing the powerful vocabulary that Sun Yat-sen used to rally support for the Republic of China among overseas Chinese. Sun had spent three years in an Anglican missionary school in Hawaii and was very familiar with the tenets of Christianity. He was also a skilled diplomat who knew how to use language to convince people to do the things he needed them to do. Ordinary men joined the KMT and continued their traditional beliefs and practices in private. Through the KMT, they became Westernized and repudiated claims, perpetuated by early missionaries (as well as other Canadians and European immigrants) that they were heathens and bootleggers who ran opium dens and brothels.[101] In addition to helping them integrate into white Christian communities, joining the KMT also elevated their status in China, where some resented those who had abandoned the nation for migrant work.[102]

Pictures from KMT events such as parades, banquets, and picnics always feature the prominent display of three emblems: the framed picture of Sun Yat-sen set on a table with a vase of fresh flowers; the flags of Canada (the Red Ensign Union Jack) and China (the twelve-pointed star). A mythology developed about the man and his personal interest in the people who lived in Manitoba.[103] It is entirely possible that Sun was personally drawn to the men in this province and others in the country. Canadian KMT members distinguished themselves by mortgaging their buildings in order to be the leading contributors in the months before the Chinese Revolution in late 1911, and they were second only to San Francisco eleven years later in 1922.[104] The dedication many felt to Sun Yat-sen caused them to go out of their way to help their comrades in China. After he died in 1925, he continued to be remembered and revered through the recitation of his will at meetings and events, and through the elevation of traditional Chinese thought and culture more generally. Even today, the KMT office in Winnipeg has at least four framed pictures of Sun (in addition to framed pieces of his calligraphy and other writings) displayed on its small office walls. I had been (wrongly) told by KMT executive members that Sun had come to Winnipeg again in 1917 and a final time in 1920. In 1917 he had supposedly come to present the branch with a special couplet that he had written. Unlike traditional couplets, this one was not written vertically on red paper; rather, it was produced horizontally in Western style on white paper (although it still needed to be read right to left). Like traditional couplets, it was written in a calligraphic style and signed "Sunwen": "To move forward and not idle (*Jinxing budai* 進行不怠)." When I saw it, this piece of calligraphy was festooned with a silver garland, two silver bells, and artificial red holly berries. I was told that these were remnants from a Christmas party that had taken place over two decades ago. Large pieces of peeling green paint were also hanging down from the ceiling above the calligraphy. To me, these were ominous reminders that the activities of the KMT in Manitoba had not moved forward but, rather, had stopped shortly after the KMT headed to Taiwan in 1949.[105] On his visit to the office in 1920, according to KMT executive members, Sun Yat-sen apparently painted the exterior sign.

Sun Yat-sen's biographies clearly state that he never visited Canada after 1911. Therefore, it is unlikely that he visited the Winnipeg branch of the KMT in 1917 (when he was exiled in Japan) or 1920 (when the KMT was banned under the War Measures Act). It is entirely possible that Sun Yat-sen did write the sign for the Winnipeg KMT branch, but that would not have required an actual visit. The couplet and sign were likely sent to the branch to thank it for donations during fundraising campaigns in 1917 and 1920. To the leaders and members of the Manitoba branch, the collective memory of Sun Yat-sen's apocryphal visits in 1917 and in 1920 conveyed both the importance of the Manitoba office in the early history of the KMT and the charismatic leadership of Sun Yat-sen. Prairie men admired him and wanted to see his Nationalist vision succeed. He was transmogrified into a god in what began as a top-down effort by KMT leaders and ended as a grassroots Prairie myth.

A restaurant owner in western Manitoba whose family had been living in and running restaurants on the rural Prairies since the 1920s displays a picture of Sun Yat-sen. It was bequeathed to him by another KMT member, and underneath it are the words "President 1912 China." This is a reference to Sun Yat-sen's brief status in the KMT as provisional president of the Republic of China from 1 January to 1 April 1912. This Canadian understood his own national identity through a connection to Sun Yat-sen and the KMT:

> Sun Yat-sen is ... most kindly and loving to the people. When he died he had nothing left – no house, just a few books. He lived a pretty clean life. Today in Canada the policy is a copy of his principles: Canada is running on his principle in terms of human rights, nationalities, minority protection. That was what he was calling for and trying to protect – your rights – also your living standards.

Several of the old-timers emphasized that their grandparents, parents, and other relatives revered the man as though he were a god. Some of the older ones still say that the twelve-pointed star of Sun Yat-sen's Nationalist party is inscribed in their hearts. To both newer Mainland immigrants and older Southern immigrants, Sun functions as a positive unifying figure because he brought an end to Imperial China and, with it, the new Republic of China. Sun represented the way of the bachelor, whose Confucian undercurrents shaped and guided behaviour in western Manitoba. Like many of the overseas men, he came from a modest background and, for some of his life, lived outside of China. He was comfortable in a number of different social circles, in each of which he was able to display appropriate interests and influences. As Marie Bergère notes:

> Sun Yat-sen, whose sole strength frequently lay in his powers of persuasion, knew that in order to convince, you need to speak the language of the person you are dealing with. He was as capable of operating in missionary circles as in lodges of secret societies, in merchant guilds as in students' cultural societies and was as active in Tokyo, London, and San Francisco as he was in Hong Kong, Hanoi, and Singapore.[106]

It would be easy to write pages praising Sun Yat-sen. Almost all of the old-timers whom I interviewed mentioned him at some point in their discussions with me. But one person, sensing my growing fascination with and admiration for him, hastened to add that Sun was also known for embellishing the truth. This research participant was concerned that people might not realize that Sun, being human, was fallible. If I included this fact, then people might have a better understanding of him and be able to see both sides of the story. I agreed.

It must be said that with Sun's charisma came a fair share of bluster, for which he earned the nickname "Sun Dapao," or Sun, the Big Gun. Nonetheless, through homosociality and the worship of Sun Yat-sen, Chinese bachelors in western Manitoba created new efficacies for themselves and became united in a common vision and goal. Sam Dong's story, narrated below, reflects the contributions of the KMT and Sun Yat-sen to the Manitoba Chinese community.

Sam Dong

Sam Dong (also known as Dong Sum and Dong On) (1891-1960) was a life-long friend of Charlie Foo and Sam Wong (who are mentioned earlier in this chapter) as well as Harry Chan, a prominent Winnipeg restaurateur. Dong's life and identity represent Chinese and Western ideals and intersections. People remembered Dong as a kind, well-dressed and prosperous man who was often invited to dinner at the houses of prominent white

FIGURE 8   Sam Dong, Weekes Studio portrait, c. 1924.
Photo: Moon Dong.

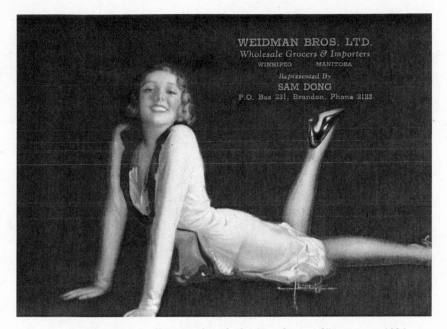

FIGURE 9 Sam Dong calling card with the "modern girl" image, c. 1924.
Source: Moon Dong

businessmen and dignitaries. Having come to Canada when he was quite young, Dong was known for his near-fluent English.

Dong first appeared in *Henderson's Directories* as the proprietor of Brandon's Sam Dong Cafe on Tenth Street, which was in business from 1913 to 1914. Like many other men, Dong had come to Canada long before that and had lived elsewhere on the Prairies before settling in Brandon for a time. The Sam Dong Cafe likely folded in 1914 because Dong returned to southern China to have an arranged marriage and to start a family there.

But, in 1925, Dong was back in the province, and this time he was a travelling salesman, selling candies and tobacco for which there was high demand in the Chinese and non-Chinese restaurants in Manitoba and Saskatchewan. For many years, he did not keep a residence but lived on the road, staying with friends when he was in Brandon or Winnipeg. Eventually, he moved into a house on Brandon's Tenth Street, two blocks away from the city's Chinatown on Twelfth Street. A life-long Chinese friend of Dong's had purchased the house, but, because he lived outside of Brandon, he let Sam use it as his residence. In 1934, the *Brandon Sun* announced that Dong was the first Chinese applicant in Brandon for naturalization papers: "Sam Dong, a commercial traveller, became the first Chinese applicant for naturalization papers here when he appeared before the court today and had his petition given favourable consideration."[107] After the Chinese Immigration Act was passed in 1923, becoming a naturalized Canadian citizen was extraordinarily difficult and very rare. Between 1915 and 1930, only 349 people had attained citizenship in Canada,[108] and eleven years later, in 1941, only eighty of the 1,042 Chinese people living in Manitoba had been naturalized.[109] The fact that Sam petitioned for and became a naturalized Canadian long before most Chinese is remarkable.[110]

In a 1938 photograph, Dong stands proudly smiling in front of the window of the KMT office. His wife and daughter in China saw Dong as part of the gentry because the small contributions he sent home enabled them to enjoy a very comfortable life. But, while here, he and others lived little better than peasants, eating simple meals of rice, with small portions of minced meat and vegetables. In the 1930s and 1940s, monthly contributions sent to relatives in southern China were extremely generous when compared to the few dollars left to pay for food, clothing, rent, and donations to the CBA, the KMT, and the Chinese Relief Fund.[111] When men came to the KMT office for meetings or fellowship, their hardships and ambiguous identity faded. Here, homosociality connected men who were engaged in the same types of work and who were from the same general area in southern China. Visits to the KMT office, therefore, were grand occasions that represented one's status in emerging hierarchies. They warranted being remembered by a photograph taken of the men, dressed in their finest clothing, in front of the building. After these visits, the men enjoyed a fine meal in the 1930s at the New Nanking and in the 1940s at Chan's Cafe. Sometimes they also watched an opera put on by the Chinese Dramatic Society in Winnipeg's Chinatown.

For Sam Dong and many other early Chinese setters in the province, the 1947 repeal of the Chinese Immigration Act came too late. He had had to live most of his life apart from his family. And, although his wife never immigrated, in 1950 his daughter finally arrived in Manitoba. After that, Dong moved to Winnipeg, where he became an art dealer, operating a shop called Oriental Arts on Osborne Street,[112] outside of Winnipeg's Chinatown. Ten years later, on 17 December 1960, at the age of sixty-nine, he died in the Winnipeg General Hospital. By this time, his daughter was no longer in the area, and, for him as for many, the KMT did the things his family might have done. KMT leaders organized his funeral, which was held at the Winnipeg KMT hall in the Johnstone Building at 209-13 Pacific Avenue, and his remains were cremated.[113] One of Dong's last wishes was for his ashes to be returned to China. Harry Chan, who ran Chan's Cafe, and with whom Dong had shared many meals over the years, commented: "Mr. Dong had no relatives in Canada ... He would often talk about the cold. The winters were very hard on him ... If he had to spend his eternity somewhere, he didn't want it to be in the Manitoba winter."[114] In April 1962, Winnipeg lawyer Vaughan Baird, the executor of Sam Dong's estate, delivered the urn containing his ashes to his family and attended his funeral in China.

The story of Sam Dong's life is the story of a man who had been welcomed and accepted by the Chinese and non-Chinese communities in Manitoba. A migrant worker, a Chinese Canadian, a restaurant owner, and a travelling salesman, Dong spent the last decade of his life as a merchant. When he was not working, he spent his free time with an all-male brotherhood and, like others, contributed to Sun Yat-sen's and, later, Chiang Kai-shek's efforts in China.

Unlike other places in Canada, where there were larger Chinese enclaves and, hence, less isolation, the Prairies functioned as an incubator for Nationalist and traditional Confucian views. For a long time after his death, Sun Yat-sen was regarded as a kind of spiritual leader who was charged by heaven *(tian)* to provide for the well-being of all overseas Chinese men – men like Sam Dong.[115]

Beyond the KMT: Other Organizations in the City of Brandon

The KMT's activities tapered off in the 1950s and 1960s, by which time some of the earliest settlers, like Sam Dong, had died. However, during this time, other organizations and newer immigrants had arrived. A representative from the Chinese Embassy in Ottawa persuaded Messrs Liu, Yuen, and Chen to start the Brandon- and Carberry-based Westman Chinese Association in the 1980s. The association offered Chinese who had come from Vietnam, as well as from mainland China, Hong Kong, and Singapore, a place to congregate. Two of its founders had strong ties to the Manitoba KMT, and, in addition to the weekly meetings, they organized many of the same traditional recreational activities associated with the KMT, such as picnics and banquets. When the Vietnamese immigrants moved away in the late 1980s, the association dissolved.

On 9 December 2007, the Westman Chinese Association reformed after approximately twenty years of inactivity. At its first meeting, a local elder, Kenny Choy, and leaders of the newly revived group addressed the crowd in Mandarin, Cantonese, and English, saying that the association was going to help the hundreds of mostly male Maple Leaf Consumer Foods workers and other Chinese newcomers in any way it could. They also used the meeting to announce a new Chinese pavilion, which was to be opened at the lieutenant-governor's multicultural Winterfest in February 2008. More than two hundred people attended this 2007 event, which was held in the large hall at Brandon's Knox United Church. Christian groups from the rest of Manitoba as well as from Vancouver had also been invited. They used the meeting to introduce themselves to new members and to hand out literature. There were traditional and modern performances of dance, songs (including a Mandarin version of "Amazing Grace," which none of the Chinese men seemed to know), martial arts, and calligraphy demonstrations. There were also traditional and Western dainties, along with Chinese tea. Most of the people in attendance were young men, and there were very few families. Since then, most of the wives and children of these men have arrived in Canada.

Another group, called the Brandon University Chinese Students and Scholars Association (BUCSSA), was started in August 2004 by a Mainland Chinese student named Sunny Sun. It was intended to be a group through which students could feel some connection to China and to other students in Canada. Planned as a way to help students contribute to the Brandon community, its operations (as well as the operations of others on university campuses across Canada) have traditionally been funded by the Chinese Embassy and the Brandon University Student Union, with donations from local individuals and businesses. BUCSSA offers discounts to its members at many of the Chinese Canadian restaurants in the city as well as at other Chinese and non-Chinese businesses. The main event organized and hosted by the group is the annual New Year's party, which is attended by around three hundred mostly non-Chinese guests. In addition, BUCSSA hosts and organizes other traditional events that mostly Chinese student attend, such as the Moon Festival, as well as basketball and football games and excursions to Clear Lake, a resort located fifty minutes (by car) north of Brandon.

In 2008, the United Food and Commercial Workers (UFCW) Local 832 (the union representing Maple Leaf Consumer Foods, Brandon) purchased an old bingo hall on Richmond Avenue in Brandon's east end. Here it established a training centre for Maple Leaf workers, including those from China (of which there are approximately 482). The UFCW delivers health and safety as well as shop steward training at the site; however, its primary purpose is to provide the workers with English-as-an-additional-language courses. The funding for these courses comes from the provincial government, Maple Leaf, and the UFCW itself. Like other government agencies in the area and Chinese community groups, the training centre assists with tax preparation as well as with helping members to prepare their immigration documents, photocopying, and translating various items. The union has one part-time fluent Mandarin speaker who writes grievances for the group. In terms of recreational activities, the union organizes and hosts the Westman Picnic for all UFCW members in the area.

The Westman Picnic usually offered hot dogs, chips, and drinks; but, as of 2009, and given the increasing number of migrant workers from China, El Salvador, Mauritius, and Mexico, the organizers were considering offering a more diverse menu. There are many activities, including games and races for adults and children, some prizes, clowns, and face painting.

Other small groups in Brandon meet informally, their members overlapping with those who belong to groups mentioned earlier. A group of southern Chinese male elders meets for coffee Monday to Friday for an hour or two each morning. On Sundays, they gather for what they call "church" at a local fast food restaurant. It should be noted that, while they call the gathering "church," there are no religious elements involved except for the fellowship and the social heat produced when one gets together with old friends. They host Brandon's annual Decoration Day, which has been celebrated for the last one hundred years and which a hundred or more people attend each year. It functions to connect the Chinese community to the earliest settlers and creates connections among first-, second-, third-, and fourth-generation Chinese Canadians, permanent residents, students, new immigrants, and temporary foreign workers. Another group, consisting of Southern Chinese women, also meets for coffee three times a week in the afternoon. Yet another group organized by former KMT members meets late Friday nights at another local fast food restaurant. It provides Chinese newspapers, coffee and donuts, and an opportunity for newly arrived Chinese (most of whom work at Maple Leaf) to socialize. In the next chapter, I tell the story of the earliest group of Chinese immigrants to arrive in Brandon.

2
The Western Manitoba Laundry

Laundry Man

Man of another race and creed,
Wrinkled, yellow and old,
As you pass by upon the street –
What are your thoughts: What are your goals?
Do you dream of cherry blossoms,
Or hear the tinkling temple bells
From that faraway land from whence you came?
Many years you have been here,
Yet an alien still you seem.
Is it that our hearts are cold
As the snow the winter brings?
Do you think our Christian faith
Would be the life to copy?
Or does it make you closer cling
To Confucius and his order?
O man of China, aging fast!
These things I ponder as you pass.

   – Gertrude Carr, 24 January 1940,
    Minnedosa, Manitoba

Before Kuomintang offices opened, the laundrymen and clan associations were the first points of contact for newcomers to the region. While Chinese men resided in places that were geographically, culturally, and socially different from those in their homeland, they were not alone in western Manitoba, contrary to what most people in this area thought. Gertrude Carr's poem "Laundry Man" is a valuable record conveying past (mis)conceptions of the early Chinese settler; however, it also shows a remarkable degree of empathy for him. Carr, who lived in Minnedosa from 1936 to 1943, worked in the family business, Carr's Grocery. She also taught Sunday School at the United Church in Minnedosa. She was familiar with the traditional teachings of Confucianism but unaware that the Chinese immigrants continued to read and reflect on the meaning of these teachings once they arrived in Manitoba. She also wondered what the Chinese man thought of Christianity, the Western notion of faith, and whether he had considered becoming Christian. Carr was similar to most Westerners whose impression of Chinese men was the result of Erving Goffman's notion of front-stage behaviour. She and others could not have been aware that the Minnedosa Chinese laundryman who had been the inspiration for this poem was likely already self-identifying as Christian on assessment rolls and on the census. She could not have known that he had become accustomed to the idea of faith through Sun Yat-sen's speeches and other political writings.

Below, I describe some of western Manitoba's earliest laundries and the complicated lives and customs of the men who operated them. I also discuss institutionalized racism at the municipal and provincial levels, which prohibited Chinese men from employing white women in their laundries. Through these accounts I hope to show the resilience of early Chinese settlers, who appeared to be alone but who were actually part of a homosocial network that connected them to others in Baldur, Dauphin, Minnedosa, and beyond. It was because of their ability to live connected but ambiguous lives, straddling the boundaries between China and the West, that new settlers were able to succeed in remote rural areas of Manitoba.

Western Manitoba Laundries

Early Chinese settlers dominated the laundry business in western Manitoba and, indeed, in Canada.[1] Towards the end of the 1870s, they were relying on clan networks to open wash houses, and, initially, those with the surname Lee (Li) flooded the province, coming from the village of Chen Shan Tsun in Haoshan County. Strong clan ties enabled Lee bachelors to band together to keep other Chinese out of the Winnipeg laundry business. As David Lai writes:

> For many years, they had lookouts posted at the roads and railroads entering Winnipeg and tried to prevent by all means other Chinese from coming to compete with their laundry business in the city. The lookouts were removed only after the Li Society in Vancouver persuaded their clansmen in Winnipeg to change their attitude.[2]

Nevertheless, the Lees continued to vie for control of Manitoba businesses into the 1930s and 1940s. On 4 November 1931, Wong Sam (Sun), a Winnipeg Chinatown tea merchant and KMT member, was shot dead on the corner of Alexander Street and Stanley Street by two Chinese men. The gunmen were presumed to have come from Vancouver.[3] An article in the *Manitoba Free Press* added that Wong Sam had been shot because of a fight between two Chinese clans (one of them the Lee clan) that, throughout the Depression, wanted control of Chinatown gambling dens.[4]

Chinatown warfare subsided during the 1930s. A new alliance was formed between the Lees and the Wongs to control access to Winnipeg's Chinese businesses. By posting family members at railway stations, these clans managed to keep most newcomers who were not Lees or Wongs, and others without the appropriate family name, somewhere outside Winnipeg's boundaries (e.g., Brandon or Carberry). In western Manitoba, names recorded on the census range from the dominant clan name "Lee" to one individual who apparently had the surname "Fuck."[5] In 1901, 100 percent of the Chinese immigrants living in the Brandon District were laundrymen;[6] by 1911, 69 percent of them were still laundrymen.[7]

Laundry work was difficult, but it provided a way for uneducated and non-English-speaking Chinese labourers to make lives for themselves. Most of the men who went into the profession eventually left it for better work in restaurants. Ban Seng Hoe paints a grim picture of the daily routine:

> The work of the Chinese laundrymen and their families was tedious, difficult and physically demanding. A lifetime spent sorting, soaking, boiling, washing, scrubbing, rinsing, starching, drying, ironing, pressing, folding, packaging, collecting and delivering could break the health of even the strongest laundry worker.[8]

A few Chinese men found the lifestyle intolerable. One young Brandon man named Yuen Tuk Foo was driven mad by too many consecutive days working in the hand laundry. A front-page article in the *Brandon Daily Sun* described his disappearance:

> Friends of Missing Chinamen Anxious. Fear he may have jumped into river while temporarily insane. Missing for a week. The local Chinatown is very anxious these days on account of the disappearance of Yuen Tuk Foo, aged twenty-two years, son of a celestial who runs a laundry on Rosser Avenue and who is one of the Chinese longest residents in the city. A week ago last Monday the young man disappeared after leaving a cafe and has not been

seen by any of his compatriots since. On or about that day E. Barnwell, a C.P.R. engineer, reported seeing a Chinaman answering the description of the missing man waving his arms wildly near the track at the iron bridge east of the city and concluded that the man was gone out of his mind. It is feared by Foo's friends that while temporarily insane he committed suicide by drowning. Meanwhile they are searching the country in the hope of finding him or his body.[9]

In 1917, Leong Lee was the proprietor of a Chinese laundry in Blucher, Saskatchewan, who was mocked by his customers for his goatee, which they described as a "little black beard." This derision drove him mad, and he was eventually committed to North Battleford, Saskatchewan's asylum.[10]

Almost all of western Manitoba's early Chinese settlers worked in a hand laundry before moving on to careers in the restaurant business (as cooks, waiters, and/or owners), as salesmen, or as grocers. And long after people had changed their careers, white society continued to refer to them, not according to their ethnicity or their new careers, but according to the profession of laundryman. As they did when forming political organizations such as the KMT and (later) restaurant businesses, early settlers drew on personal connections in Chinese culture *(guanxi)* and rotating credit associations to create opportunities for themselves.[11]

While labouring on the railroad required Chinese to work for whites, working in a hand laundry enabled them to work for themselves. This being the case, they could employ brothers, fathers, grandfathers, uncles, sons, cousins, and friends. They now had spaces that were large and private, so that when the stores were closed they could host and organize traditional events. These events took place behind the screens that divided the front from the back regions of the stores, where they were free to erect altars[12] to honour their ancestors and other gods who would help them to succeed in Gold Mountain (a name given to Canada and other places that offered migrant Chinese workers "golden" opportunities).[13] Here is one account of what was encountered in the back of an early Winnipeg laundry:

Wait here, commanded my uncle in stern tones. We stood where we were, suddenly afraid. As my eyes became accustomed to the gloom, I saw candles and small dishes of rice and chicken in front of a shrine. This was something I understood – offerings to the family gods. Were they in thanks for bringing me safely to Gum San? I bowed to the shrine, as to my ancestors. My heart lifted.[14]

Before Chinese organizations such as the Chinese Freemasons, the Chinese United League, and the KMT opened Prairie offices, it was the rural laundry that connected Chinese to one another. The laundry was a space that facilitated the homosocial networks through which men could develop friends on whom they could rely in difficult financial times and in times of racial intolerance. These same connections were later drawn on when political leaders needed to galvanize support for Sun Yat-sen. It was through these nodes that identities, communities, and the way of the bachelor began to form and give agency to the earliest Chinese Canadian Prairie bachelors.[15] In 1905, Brandon had three Chinese laundries listed in *Henderson's Directories*. By 1911, that number had jumped to thirteen. Three of these 1911 businesses were run by men with the last name of Li (Lee), and they were located in the downtown core between Eighteenth Street and First Street, clustered around Rosser Avenue. By 1921, there were still at least eleven Chinese laundries in the city.

As laundries became more common and competed with white labour, more restrictions were placed on their operations. At a special 1913 city council meeting in Brandon, council members enacted a bylaw that imposed a twenty-five-dollar licence fee on laundries and regulated their use:

Laundries employing chiefly manual labour must pay a licence fee of $25, and this will affect the Chinese laundries principally. The bylaw contains provisions for the regulation of the interior arrangements of the laundries which make it illegal for the workrooms to be used for domestic or sleeping purposes, and also stipulates that no clothing from houses where there has been a case of infectious diseases shall be removed. A discussion took place with regard to restricting laundries to certain districts, but no decision was made.[16]

Laundries were seen to be dirty places lacking proper sewage systems – places where sanitation inspectors could often be found.[17] It was also well known that some Chinese men congregated in the upstairs areas of laundries to gamble and smoke opium. People did not want this kind of activity in their neighbourhoods. Although in 1913 there had been discussions to restrict the areas in which wash houses could operate, it took four more years to enact the bylaw. In 1917, Brandon City Council declared that laundries could only be opened "between the Northern boundary of Pacific Avenue, between the East side of Sixth street and the West side of Twelfth street, and on Tenth street as far as Lorne Avenue."[18] Laundrymen were outraged by this decision, having invested large amounts of borrowed money in their businesses – money that they depended on to survive, send home, and pay off head tax and other immigration debts. One man complained that his wash house had just opened in one of the restricted areas on Thirteenth Street when the bylaw was passed. The *Brandon Daily Sun* reported:

> The only person whom the latest city by-law, that governing and control-ling laundry establishments, seems to have hit, is a Chinaman who says he has just expended $150 to start a laundry just within the limits of the pre-scribed area in the neighborhood of Rosser Avenue and Thirteenth Street.
>
> Mr. Chinaman is haunting the City Hall offices today with the view of persuading the authorities to make the provisions of the by-law a trifle more elastic, so that he may go on with his little job.
>
> The officials are adamant in the case, and the Chinaman is resting his hopes on an appeal to Mayor Cater after His Worship returns from Regina.[19]

Unfortunately, it does not appear that this man was able to "go on with his little job." He became a victim of the view that, as a "Chinaman," he was dirty and uncivilized and, moreover, that he was taking jobs away from white citizens.

The unclean Chinaman (and laundryman) was a common stereotype in Canada,[20] and it was related to other racist images that depicted the Chinese as godless heathens and barbarians. This familiar identity was perpetuated by municipal governments and sanitation officers throughout Canada and western Manitoba.[21] Often there was very little evidence to substantiate fears that the places in which Chinese men lived and worked were filthy or disease-ridden. Here are the details from one report that followed on such a complaint:

> That the Chinese laundries of the city had for the most part been overrun with vermin, but had now become clean, was the most interesting item of the Sanitary Inspector's report at the meeting of the City Council on Monday evening. He also reported that forty-five notices had been served [to] property owners in the centre of the city to have sewer and water con-nections duly installed, and asked for further instructions. The request was not dealt with.
>
> I am pleased to report that considerable improvements have been made in all the Chinese laundries, and that they now look clean and respectable. Some of the laundries were overrun with vermin, bed bugs chiefly, which found ideal quarters behind many layers of old and filthy paper which hung

loose and torn upon the walls and ceilings. An endeavor is also being made to correct a dangerous and filthy habit practised among workers in these laundries, namely expectorating on floors of workrooms and other places.[22]

Members of the dominant society continued to get their clothes cleaned at the Chinese laundry, despite its reputation for being dirty. Chinese men provided quality service at cheap prices. They kept their prices low by working around the clock, unencumbered by family and social obligations. But it was precisely because Chinese men did not live "normal" lives with wives and children but, rather, lived in the company of other lone men that they were the objects of scorn. In larger cities and towns throughout western Manitoba, men lived with six or eight others, sharing sleeping quarters in what were mainly laundries. Health inspectors and police were constantly investigating washing businesses in which too many men ate and slept or gathered to smoke opium.

Nineteen thirteen was also the year in which the Manitoba provincial government followed the precedent set by Saskatchewan in 1912 of prohibiting white women from working in Chinese-operated businesses. The text of the Saskatchewan law enacted in 1912, and revised in 1919, was meant to eliminate the racial and Chinese focus. It was repealed in 1969 and read as follows:

No person shall employ in any capacity any white woman or girl or permit any white woman or girl to reside or lodge in or to work in, or, save as a bona fide customer in a public apartment thereof only, to frequent any restaurant, laundry, or other place of business or amusement, owned, kept, or managed by any Japanese, Chinaman, or other Oriental person.[23]

Meanwhile, in Manitoba, politicians and other officials feared that the employer-employee relationship between young white women and Chinese men would lead either to sexual abuse or marriage. Intermarriage was not uncommon, but sexual abuse charges by white women were. By implication, these laws were continuing manifestations of the racist urge to create more business opportunities for white immigrants. Manitoba's act to restrict the employment of women in Chinese establishments, which was based on Saskatchewan's act, passed in February 1913. However, it appears that it was never proclaimed, possibly, as noted by David Lai, because of the organized protest by members of the CBA throughout Canada. In 1923, the City of Winnipeg added language to its city charter, which enabled it to restrict Chinese from employing women in their restaurants, laundries, and other businesses.[24] Other white labourers found it difficult to compete with the low prices and quick service of the Chinese laundry.

Religious groups also scrutinized the practices of some laundries. The hand-washing business required long hours and labour-intensive work for very little pay. When very young nephews, sons, and other male relatives were recruited to work in them, groups such as the local YMCA started to notice and complain.[25]

Among politicians and religious groups (up until 1920 and after the First World War) it became de rigueur to defame the "Chinaman's" character, denouncing his unclean habits, his unnatural all-male community, and branding him as a sojourner who had little interest in staying and assimilating.[26] The widely circulated myth that the Chinese bachelor was nothing more than a sojourner who was only interested in making money and returning to China was common in Canada in the last decades of the nineteenth century, even though large Chinese communities were beginning to form throughout North America. In 1875, Peter O'Leary, who was travelling through Manitoba and the United States wrote:

> The Chinaman never intends to become a citizen, he in his heart despises the citizens of the United States as Outer Barbarians, and will not bring his wife and children with him to be contaminated by their (to his thoughts) uncivilised and savage ways; he will not even leave his corpse to enrich the American soil; the bodies of Chinamen are therefore carefully shipped back to their celestial land.[27]

Writings of the time still routinely portrayed the "Chinaman" as a mere sojourner who disliked North America so much that he would not be buried here.[28] This characterization was deeply flawed. It is true that Chinese settlers who died in Canada and in the United States preferred to be buried in their homeland. But this was not because they disliked the country in which they had been living. Sam Dong, whose story I told in the previous chapter, requested that his ashes be buried in China because he could not imagine enduring one more Manitoba winter, let alone an eternity of them. But Dong's decision was also shaped by his traditional Chinese religious beliefs. He wanted to be buried with his ancestors, where his living brothers, sisters, wife, and children could visit his grave, make offerings, and remember him. This involved efficacious ritual actions. As racist immigration laws prevented Dong's family from joining him in Canada and performing these rites after his death, Dong and others in his position naturally wanted their bodies returned to their homeland so that the traditions associated with

Confucianism, which had been in place for over two millennia, could be properly conducted. In the early days of settlement in western Manitoba, this was part of the way of the bachelor. Burial in China reconnected him to the people from whom he had been forced to live apart for most of his adult life.

Another misconception about Chinese settlers developed when the appearance of laundries was conflated with the character of their owners and operators. If they were small one-man operations, Chinese wash houses could be found in the most run-down apartments and shacks; medium-sized two-man operations often operated out of part of a house. In these smaller establishments, workers slept on ironing boards, folded beds, or bunks in the back. But the larger shops took up an entire building and were operated by four or more men who slept upstairs after closing. In the largest establishments, men slept anywhere they could find space, in beds affixed to each wall and on the floor underneath them. In some North American cities with substantial populations (but not in western Manitoba), these large establishments worked in shifts.[29]

From the street, one could recognize laundries from the newspaper that covered the windows, the house plants just inside the door and visible from the street, and/or the wooden laundry carts parked at the back. An old-timer interviewed in Winnipeg in the late 1970s recalled the appearance of a typical Chinese laundry on the Prairies:

> A laundry shop usually had a red and white sign-board, and house plants decorating a front window. On opening, a front door jingled a chain of small bells and metal pieces. Inside a laundryman stood behind a counter; beyond this were ironing tables and shelves. Farther in was a washing and drying area; at the deep interior end was the laundrymen's living quarters, consisting of a kitchenette, a bedroom and a toilet.[30]

On entering the shop, one was overwhelmed by a cloud of steam commingled with the smell of soap and sweat. One then encountered the person assigned to the counter. This person could speak passable English and collected and returned items to customers. Larger businesses were advertised in the local newspapers, where it was often noted that the methods used were "Chinese." One man interviewed in Brandon in the late 1980s explained: "The Brandon Chinese laundrymen used to advertise themselves as specializing in hand-laundry and thus taking more care of individual shirts and garments. They laundered a lot of nurses' uniforms."[31] Those who worked in smaller rural shops went door-to-door asking people if they had any dirty clothes; sometimes they wandered the streets, variously shouting and singing that they were collecting items for washing that day. After the laundry was rounded up, it was put in large bags and carried or carted back to the shop on home-made wooden carts.

When you handed over your laundry, you received one-half of a ticket with a red Chinese character, which was a number that corresponded to that on the other half of the ticket kept by the laundryman. The ticket and the character inscribed on it was an oddity to whites in western Manitoba. An 1895 article in the *Minnedosa Tribune* tried (and failed) to explain what was written:

> The Celestials have a system of their own. It is based on the many gods and goddesses of the laundry. Although the system is very complicated, seldom does a Chinese laundryman deliver a package of washing to the wrong person ... The Chinese laundryman at the beginning of each week makes out a batch of checks in duplicate, to be used as wash tickets. He selects the name of some god or goddess or of some object, as the sun, the moon or the stars. To this name he puts a number, as "Moon No. 1," "Moon No. 2," and so on. In the space between the two writings he has his own name, as for instance, "Wah Lee."[32]

The "Moon" reference on the ticket was simply a reference to the days of the week, not to Chinese gods or goddesses (which the writers of the article associated with celestial worship and other more "primitive" forms of religion where people revered the sun, moon, and stars as gods). Why the laundries continued to use the tickets when the owners and workers spoke some English and most customers could not read Chinese is a good question. Perhaps the men felt that the ticket and its foreign inscription gave some kind of exotic appeal to the laundry. In any case, it was an efficient system of cataloguing items sent for washing. One man explained:

> Chinese laundrymen were in the habit of identifying their customers as "lady with big eyes," "man with huge nose," and so on, and in this way, without asking for customers' names, they were able to return the laundered articles to their corresponding owners; and they seldom made mistakes in so doing.[33]

Interviews and historical research indicate that men seldom lost something that had been sent for washing. Customers were confident that, within a few days, their clothes would be washed and ironed, with collars starched and pressed. Linens would be whiter, too. The items would be folded, packed in brown paper, and delivered.

In the very early period, laundries used irons that had been crudely fashioned from pans and other pieces of metal. These would be heated on a stove and would inevitably turn parts of the clothing brown. Sometimes, in an attempt to clean items, the men scrubbed so hard that clothing was returned in a threadbare state. While the methods used to hand wash and iron were hard on clothing, people sought out these services because they were quick and cheap.[34] Chinese were able to offer their services at afford-able prices and to compete with others because they lived where they worked, and they worked for long hours – from seven in the morning until well after midnight.[35] Prices varied. In 1901, in most parts of western Mani-toba, men's dress shirts could be cleaned and made whiter for between five and fifteen cents. Socks could be cleaned for two and a half cents a pair, and work shirts were washed and pressed for five cents each.[36]

Manitoba Laundrymen

The first Chinese businesses in Manitoba were laundries. In 1877, Charley Yam, Fung Quong, and an unnamed woman arrived in Winnipeg by stage-coach from the United States (likely from Chicago). On Monday, 19 November 1877, the story of their arrival was front-page news in the *Manitoba Daily Free Press*:

> This trio of Celestials have been in America for some time – one of them six years and they can speak the English language in a fractured manner, although they discount any Winnipegger in talking Chinese. They come here to enter into the washee clothes business for which there appears to be an excellent opening for "the honourable members for China." Hoop-la![37]

Two months and ten days later, Charley Yam was again front-page news in the *Manitoba Daily Free Press*. He was the boss of a laundry on Winnipeg's Post-Office Street and had been assaulted and robbed by three of his "almond-eyed" employees.[38]

Brandon

In 1884, just two years after Brandon was declared a city, and the year the Chinese Benevolent Society formed in Victoria, British Columbia, Wah Hep was the first Chinese laundryman in the area. The 1884 Brandon assessment roll lists him as a single man who was a Protestant Christian. He rented the space from J. Moodie,[39] and he was likely one of the railway workers and cooks who had been dismissed from the railway between 1883 and 1884, when many of the branch lines had been completed.[40] Possibly Wah arrived in Brandon in the summer of 1884. There are two accounts of how CPR railway workers ended up near Brandon at this time. On 5 June 1884, the *Brandon Weekly Sun* reported that "the CPR discharged forty employees between [Brandon] and Winnipeg."[41] One month and five days later, the paper reported: "Three hundred people some of whome [sic] have been working for the CPR in the Rockies, and others in coal mines, for the past two years, passed through Brandon yesterday en route for the old country."[42] The writings of a twenty-four-year-old Englishman named Robert Miller Christy, who was travelling through Canada in the mid-1880s, offer his impressions of Wah Hep and the laundry located on Eighth Street in downtown Brandon:

> The enterprising Chinaman seems even to have reached Brandon, and is already at his favourite trade. I left some garments to be washed at the laundry of Mr. or Mrs. Wah Hep (I am obliged to confess complete ignorance as to which it was) who gave me a receipt with curious inscriptions thereon, which he (or she) subsequently informed me represented merely the number twenty-five. This surprised me, for I never imagined that even in China, such an amount of learned-looking calligraphy (there were thirteen distinct strokes) was required to express so simple a matter.[43]

Christy's account stands out as one of the few anecdotes about early Chinese Prairie settlers and a Westerner's impression of them. The "Chinaman" was a mystery. He wore a queue, which required the daily shaving of the side of his head, leaving a long pony-tail hanging down the back. Wah's long braided hair hinted that he might be a woman, and his "learned-looking calligraphy" suggested he might be educated. Westerners marvelled at the intricacy of Chinese characters and the beauty of many expressions; however, language and other cultural barriers prevented the development of more than a front-stage understanding. Until 1911, Wah Hep and most western Manitoban Chinese men[44] wore their hair in the traditional queue.[45]

Wah Hep was also known by two other names – Johnson and W.H. Johnson (who, in 1884, was listed as the financial scribe of the Sons of Temperance). It is difficult to determine whether this was the same Wah Hep Johnson as "Johnson" was a very common name.[46] When Wah Hep Johnson voted

FIGURE 10   Lee Low with queue, reverse side of oceanliner ticket, 1911.
Source: Family of Lee Low

in the 1884 election, his name appeared on the Brandon voters list as "Wah Hep." City officials decided that, since his name did not match the name on the voters list, he could not be able to vote.[47]

Many of the early settlers frequently moved from place to place in search of better work. A year later, Wah Hep had moved on and joined others on an odyssey that took them on the branch lines of the railway and the earlier horse trails[48] they would have used to travel among cities, towns, and villages throughout the country.[49] After him, the wash houses in western

Manitoba were operated by men with the surnames Chong, Dong, Fong, Kee, Lee/Li, Lie, Low, Sing, Wah, Wang, Wing, Wong, Yam, and Yee.

It did not take long for Chinese laundries to become popular in Brandon, and, by 1885, Lee Kee was living and operating a business on Brandon's Sixth Street.[50] Like Wah Hep, he also responded to assessment roll questions about his religion with "Protestant Christian." Another man arrived in 1891 and operated a wash house, providing "first class work" with "satisfaction guaranteed,"[51] on Ninth Street at the old CPR ticket offices. Scores of men came to work in Brandon over the next few decades, including On Li Men (also known as L. Men On), Wang Chan, and Sing Hing,[52] Tom Lie,[53] and Li Men Chang.[54] There is no trace of them in the local cemetery or in later newspapers or archival materials, and I assume that they moved on after they finished with their businesses.

In my archival research I found one man who was variously known as Long Gee Lan,[55] Long Yee Kan, Kan Long Lee, George King, and, most commonly, George Chong (1870-1940). This person stood out in the early period of Chinese laundries.[56] Born in the District of Sunning (Toisan/Taishan as it was later called) and immigrating to Victoria via Hong Kong on 25 July 1892, Chong was five-foot-four and three-quarter inches (164.5 centimetres) tall. When he arrived, he listed his occupation as labourer. According to the 1911 census, he was a Methodist. Seventeen years after he immigrated to Canada, *Henderson's Directories* for 1909 listed him as the operator of Li Men On Laundry at 144 Eighth Street. Unlike Wah Hep and others, Chong would live out his life in Brandon and be buried in the cemetery there. In other ways, his life on the Prairies was typical. He spent it apart from his wife, who remained in his homeland, and he was a nominal Christian who socialized with his "brother" Tom and the seventy or more Chinese men living in Brandon at the time.[57] The two men were part of a large network of overseas Chinese men whose isolated lives were made better by Sun Yat-sen's vision of democracy and nationalism.

One of the most important moments for Nationalist supporters like George Chong and his brother Tom came in 1910, when there was a growing movement for Chinese men to cut their hair. This movement had started in China when a memorial written by Wu Tingfang (1842-1922), the Chinese minister assigned to the United States, was made public in August of that year.[58] In the memorial, Wu had asked the Qing court to abolish the queue. Edward J.M. Rhoads summarizes Wu's thoughts:

Wu Tingfang claimed to be speaking on behalf of the seventy thousand Chinese residents in the United States, who found the queue particularly irksome. It made them look outlandish in the eyes of other Americans, and it endangered their lives if it got caught in a piece of operating machinery.[59]

The publication of the memorial had an enormous impact on members of overseas communities, who took it as a sign that they should cut their queues.[60] The hairstyle represented over two centuries of Manchurian cultural dominance and, by implication, cutting it implied the rejection of that culture. Many of the leaders of the revolutionary movement, and most notably Sun Yat-sen himself, already wore the new style, thereby announcing their political views. Thus, the moment when the memorial was made public was rife with symbolism. As Henrietta Harrison notes:

> Short hair for men was one of the first symbols to emerge [in the new republic] since ... the queue had been a Manchu innovation. All three of the men being inaugurated to high office had already cut off their queues before the ceremony. In keeping with his many years as a declared revolutionary Sun Yat-sen had long worn his hair short.[61]

Cutting off one's long braid signalled the dawn of a new republic and a Nationalist spirit that was growing in China and elsewhere. In addition, a short hairstyle indicated that China and Chinese men were becoming more Western and less "strange."

Short hair, in contrast, was modern, Western, and evinced a desire to conform. A poem of unknown authorship in the *Brandon Sun Weekly* depicts the Chinese settler in pejorative language. He was a poor "Chink," a laundry-man and cafe worker. But a haircut would change this bounded identity. He would be able to become a barber too, and possibly even assimilate:

> The End of the Chinaman's Queue.
>
> Have you heard of the order of Wu T'ing Fang
> To trim the poor Chink of his queue
> They're changing the laundry of Lee Wo Chang
> For a barber named Ong Tsi Lu:
> They're trading their irons for clippers and shears
> And starch for bay rum and pomade
> And King Joy Lo will have barber shop chains
> Where chop suey banquets were laid
> The tables of teak and the lantern hung booth

And the bowls of cooling "sam shu"
Will soon be a memory of boys of our youth
When they cut off the Chinaman's queue
We never did relish their food, but the place
With its Orient ways was so rare
Now would it seem real for an almond-eyed face
Not to dangle a pigtail of hair.
It may be that Morgan and Hong Ming [S]et
Are behind such an order as that:
They're forming a human hair trust you can bet.
And will soon raise the price of the "rat." ·
We thought they would quit when they cornered the crop
Of our food and our clothing and shoes
But you never know now where the mergers will stop
When they cut off the Chinaman's queue.[62]

The poem also forecast that the burgeoning demand for haircuts would create many Chinese barbers. It didn't.

When the *Brandon Sun Weekly* ran the story on this emerging trend, it interviewed Tom Chong, the "brother" of George Chong. What Tom said in this interview expressed the desire, shared by both Westerners and Easterners, to assimilate. Chong explained that cutting one's hair was a good idea as it would save time and end the shame people felt when they were ridiculed for wearing a queue: "After Feb. 14, said Tom Chong this morning, the Chinaman will be just as good looking as any other fellow, and he will be right glad to discard the foolish fashion forced upon him by a hated dynasty 250 years ago."[63] What Chong did not say was also significant: that cutting his hair would signal his support for Sun Yat-sen and Sun's vision of a new Nationalist republic. His appearance would now match his nominal Christian and Chinese hybrid identities. Men throughout Manitoba continued to cut their hair, and, in July 1911, the local paper in Birtle reported that "Birtle's Chinese, Lee Tong and son, gave up traditional pigtails."[64] While many of the younger men, such as George and Tom Chong, cut their hair in 1911, before the Wuchang Uprising in October of that year, some of the older men (in their forties and fifties), in a show of loyalty to the Manchurian government, refused to do so.[65]

The simple haircut represented significant global, national, and local changes to the way that the Chinese bachelor was regarded by Western society. He began the transition from being regarded as an effeminate, weak, dirty, and strange "Chinaman" to being a modern Western gentleman. Nineteen eleven was a remarkable year for other reasons, too. [66] George and Tom Chong participated in an international fundraising effort to buy revolutionary ten-dollar bills for five dollars each to support Sun Yat-sen's army. Manitoba and Canada saw the largest growth in their Chinese population between 1910 and 1912, coinciding with the revolution.[67]

George Chong was one of the key KMT members in the region, but when he died on 3 August 1940, his obituary noted that he was first and foremost a laundryman:

> Long Yee Kan, a Chinese laundry proprietor here for more than 20 years, and known to many in this city as George Chong, died here over the weekend, and funeral services were held this afternoon from Macpherson and Bedford's parlors, with interment in Brandon cemetery. Deceased operated the Lee-Men-On laundry on Eighth Street, and some years ago was a member of a Chinese Bible class in St. Paul's church. A widow in China, and a brother here, survive.[68]

The obituary notably emphasized that Chong was a Christian who attended St. Paul's Chinese Bible classes. While it omitted his activities in the KMT and his one-time ownership of the branch office, I assume that the branch helped to pay for his headstone and funeral. His headstone, although unremarkable, resembles those of other early settlers buried near him, noting his surname "Long" and given names "Kan-Lee" as well as his natal county and village in Canton Province. One of the first Chinese men to settle down in the city, George Chong played a large role in the formation of the Brandon KMT; sadly, however, his grave has not been maintained. Perhaps that will change if people recognize the enormous contributions he has made to the area.

People admired George Chong, a laundryman for over thirty years, for his hand-laundering skills and his willingness to work long hours for very little money. In public he was known to be a Christian and must have gained a large measure of respect for his involvement in the church during his many years in Brandon. Through the church he also learned English and Canadian values and made non-Chinese friends and business contacts like other bachelors. Charlie Foo, a prominent KMT elder in the region, was also a meat supplier to Manitoba restaurants. He relied on churches to learn English and Canadian customs: "I attended ... three English classes every week, going from one church to the other for seven years."[69] Many early laundrymen kept a Chinese-English dictionary under the counter and studied it throughout the day. They learned English in order to survive and make a living. As time passed, this new knowledge enabled them to communicate with their clients and others in the community and to be better understood. Although many men became bilingual, they continued to use Chinese characters on their laundry tickets. However, without Westernizing their appearance, many men could never have become accepted. The fact that George Chong spoke English and had cut his queue no doubt contributed to his success as a KMT political leader who straddled the cultural divide of East and West.[70]

In private, laundrymen had become involved in Sun Yat-sen's quest for a new republic, but in public, after 1911, they continued to be objects of curiosity and were sometimes alleged to be involved in criminal activities. This sentiment was fed by a resentment of the "Chinaman" who took away white labour. People admired his hand-laundering techniques but reviled him in other ways. He worked for less money, and he lived cheaply and in squalor.[71] Most Manitoba families only allowed the men to deliver or pick up the laundry, thus protecting mothers, daughters, and wives from unknown but suspected dangers. In the first decade of the twentieth century, this resentment expressed itself in claims that Chinese men were involved in criminal activities, ranging from dealing in opium, to bootlegging, and even prostitution. Of course, for the most part, this was not the case at all; however, there were a few incidents of this sort.

In 1913, Brandon's Le Chung Laundry at 134 Rosser Avenue was raided by Chief Berry and the City of Brandon police on suspicion of opium possession. The police entered the building and followed the billowing blue cloud of smoke up to the attic, where they found four Chinese men, an opium pipe, and a lamp. Chief Berry discovered additional supplies of crude opium hidden under the floor boards in another room. Magistrate Bates sentenced Le Chung to a fine of $150 or three months in jail, Ho Chung to $50 or one month in jail, and Wo Kee to $25 or one month in jail. Bates reminded the "Chinese colony" that it had been warned repeatedly about opium possession and that future offences would merit fines of $500. Further, he cautioned that if this did not deter opium smoking, he would simply jail those who broke the law.[72] One week later, a business operated by Low On (also known as Lu Kong) at 202 Fifteenth Street was raided by Chief Berry and the Brandon police. Berry, allegedly acting on a tip from the Chinese community, discovered crude and other forms of opium in an outhouse as well as large amounts of money. After a failed attempt to bribe him with $25, Low On received the $500 fine and appealed the decision. Two additional men, found sleeping in an upstairs bedroom, were also arrested.[73] Later that year, chief and magistrate worked hard to end another problem: Chinese bootlegging.

> A fine of $125 and costs was imposed Tuesday afternoon on the celestial. Man Hop, was found guilty by Magistrate Bates on a charge of selling intoxicating liquor without a licence. Evidence was given by Chief Berry who raided the place kept by Hop on Sunday night and found a game of fan tan in progress, also a large supply of spirits and bottled beer. The chief asked for half the fine to go to the city, which could be done under section d) of the Liquor Licence Act. This was done, half the fine being turned into the city exchequer.[74]

While these cases obviously indicated involvement in the opium trade and bootlegging, they were rare. A small number of Chinese were engaged in these activities, but there were far more criminals to be found in other ethnic groups, including whites.[75]

By the middle of the First World War in 1916, all of Manitoba, like many of Canada's provinces, was legally dry and would remain so until 1923, when the control of liquor was taken over by the government. Some of their customers asked Chinese laundry and restaurant operators if they could supply them with whisky and other kinds of prohibited alcohol. Seeing a business opportunity, some did so. Chinese men drank occasionally, but most did not have the time to be heavy drinkers. The bachelors engaged in bootlegging for financial reasons, not because they were alcoholics. A book that describes the role of whisky on the Prairies recalls the "Chinaman" as a target of drunken ruffians: "'Cleaning out the Chinks' became a common phrase of the small-town toughs and livery-stable loafers. When they got sufficiently imbued with whisky courage, they would wreck the place, and in the riot that developed it was usually the Chinese who were arrested."[76]

One of the first non-Chinese laundries in Brandon was the Pacific Laundry, which opened in 1883 and was run by W. Webb, a man known for his love of drinking and for beating his wife. After a night of boozing and arguing, Webb murdered his wife and was later executed for the crime.[77] Small non-Chinese laundries had difficulty staying in business and competing with the Chinese-owned-and-operated businesses. An Englishman named Robert Goucher ran a laundry for years with an Icelandic man named John Johnson.[78] After the partnership with Robert Goucher ended, Johnson and his wife went on to run a laundry for thirty years. Other small laundries also opened and closed. Some Irishmen with the surname Crozier and a few

Irish laundrywomen – Isabella Callaghan (1901),[79] Minnie Jackson (1909),[80] and Charlotte Maddus (1911)[81] – ran laundries in Brandon for a brief time. However, most of these people were out of business within a year or two.

Non-Chinese laundries that did succeed were often very large ones, such as the Brandon Steam Laundry. These laundries attempted to distinguish themselves by promoting the Canadianness of their establishments and the superior quality of their work. A 1905 ad stated: "We guarantee to do dyeing and cleaning equal to any in Canada. Come and look at our work. The Brandon Steam Laundry."[82] Five years later, the advertisements explicitly criticized Chinese laundries and evoked stereotypes. For example, the Brandon Steam Laundry promoted itself as a sanitary place that protected "girl" labour:

Are you Interested in Protecting Girl Labor ... There appears to be no limit to the number of hours or days worked each week in Chinese laundries. Our careful workers work nine hours a day, six days a week, which is long enough for white folks. Our wages help a little to build up Canadian industries and our fair city ... WE DO GOOD WORK in a modern, sanitary way, and use thoroughly purified water.[83]

In 1910, when this advertisement ran, there were at least eight Chinese laundries in Brandon.[84] The laundry business was competitive, and the Chinese men could work longer hours than the whites and endure all kinds of difficult situations. As the *Brandon Weekly Sun* explained:

Under good conditions the white man can beat the yellow man in turning out work. But under bad conditions the yellow man can beat the white man, because he can better endure spoiled food, poor clothing, foul air, noise, heat, dirt, discomfort and microbes.[85]

The Brandon Hardware Company, managed by J.B. Curran, was another large business that advertised laundering services, in addition to selling kitchen appliances, pots and pans, paints, oils, and sporting equipment. In a 1911 campaign, the company used the popular "Yellow Kid" to advertise itself.[86] Mickey Dugan, otherwise known as the Yellow Kid, first appeared as a minor New York cartoon character in 1892.[87] The everyman of 1894, he was a hybrid personality created out of the imagination of Richard Felton Outcault (1863-1928) and based on a mostly Irish immigrant who lived in New York City's slums; but he had characteristics that suggested his African, German, and Chinese ancestry.

Using stock advertisements produced by Outcault studio artists for campaigns throughout North America, the Brandon Hardware Company recruited the popular image to suggest the "Chineseness" of its laundry services. Yet, the Yellow Kid was not Chinese, even though the long tunic, bald head, and slanted eyes, as well as the eponymous reference to "yellow," pointed to his Oriental derivation. Outcault himself was aware that the Yellow Kid was often misunderstood in this way. When the Qing dynasty official Li Hongzhang (1823-1901) visited New York in 1896, Outcault drew a special cartoon for the occasion, with the following words written on the Yellow Kid's tunic: "Me and Li has made a big hit with each oter. Say! He tinks I'm a chinaman – don't say a word. I'm goin ter give a yellow tea for him – I know my q."[88] It is hard to know whether those who purchased the advertisements from Outcault's studio knew of the provenance of the Yellow Kid. Nevertheless, the ads successfully used the image of a smiling Yellow Kid holding up a shirt to convince the public of the merits of non-Chinese laundries. Behind the Yellow Kid were three black socks and in front of him was a basket of laundry. The caption read:

> Laundry! We have all the Newest Things. When things are put through the wash you can tell what they are. Our store has stood the test of time. We keep up with the new things in our business. When you need wash-day things, remember we have them. We keep up our stock in all lines of hardware. You can find it at our store.

Two years later, the Brandon Steam Laundry at 1215-19 Rosser Avenue advertised its reopening by offering "modern and hygenic methods of laundering clothes."[89] Now it was manager W.H. Hurley who offered this "modern and hygenic" laundry work (in contrast to the traditional and "dirty" work performed by the Chinese laundryman). Hurley also boasted of the dyeing and cleaning that took place on three floors, all of which were accessible by elevator.[90] Four years later, the laundry had been replaced by Rumford Laundry, managed by G.W. Butler.[91]

So far I have only discussed laundries in the City of Brandon. Beyond this urban domain, laundries could be found throughout small villages and towns in western Manitoba. However, without local homosocial networks and a larger community of KMT members, life was harder and more solitary than it was in Brandon or Winnipeg. One or two men had to collect, wash, iron, fold, package, and deliver clothes several days a week. As a result, they worked longer hours, endured more harassment, and travelled much greater distances to attend monthly KMT meetings and other events than did their compatriots in Brandon and Winnipeg.

Nevertheless, some rural Chinese businesses and their owners thrived without the competition they would have had in larger centres. By all accounts, most small towns and villages had some kind of wash house. And for many men who were not from either of the Lee or Wong clans, small towns and villages were often the only places where they could open a business. By 1911, rural western Manitoba had laundries run by men with the surnames Fong, Gee, Dong, Wee, Woo, Wing, and others. Unfortunately, there is very little evidence of these wash houses today. In what follows, I present the history of two rural laundries that, based on what I have been told by my research participants, typified the Chinese experience on the Prairies.

Baldur

One year before its official founding in 1890, the Icelandic community of Baldur, Manitoba, had a Chinese laundry.[92] From 1899 to 1901, Baldur, located approximately seventy kilometres southeast of Brandon and just over seventy-three kilometres north of the American border, was an important entry point and node for Chinese immigrants. During this decade, scores of men came to Baldur to apprentice before settling elsewhere. In 1900, a writer for the *Baldur Gazette* noted: "Wee Chee, late of Roland, has opened a Laundry in the building next to Davidson, the Jeweller. He commenced regular business Monday with a goodly pile of linen on hand. Wee Chee is a welcome adjunct to our cosmopolitan population."[93] By 1902, Wee Chee had left and another laundry was opening: "A Chinese Laundry will open here on the first of March. It is to be hoped that he will receive courteous treatment from all."[94] Between May and September 1900, Wee Chee bought weekly advertisements for his laundry, advising that he laundered shirts, collars, cuffs, linens, and household washing.

The editors of the community's newspaper were fascinated by the constantly changing population of laundrymen in their community. Most Baldur laundries were in business a short time and served as outposts where bachelors could apprentice before moving on. In 1908, the *Baldur Gazette* noted: "There has been a regular merry-go-round of Chinamen in the laundry here lately. One day last week we had three new ones here, but two have gone and we now have one that looks as if he might stay a while."[95] Often when the men left Baldur the editors explained that it was because the winters were too harsh or because they had gone to live in another city. After only a month in business in November 1900, Lee Man Yuen went to Winnipeg to spend the winter because "it was too cold to washee in countree in winter."[96]

Compared to other rural papers of the time, the *Baldur Gazette* was disproportionately fascinated with its small and ever-changing Chinese community and, indeed, with Chinese culture and customs in general. For example, it displayed an understanding of Confucianism and the complex reasons why Chinese persecuted missionaries during the Boxer Rebellion.[97] Some issues dispelled the myth that most Chinese use opium: "It is generally understood that a large percentage of the Chinese are addicted to the use of opium. This is a misconception. The belief that the Chinese of rank and culture use the drug is due to the prominence given to the cultivation of the plant and the manufacture of opium in the Celestial empire. As a matter of fact, a native who uses opium is looked upon by his superiors as we discuss and classify our drunkards."[98] Others reported on the brutal murder of Chinese men in Winnipeg.[99] Was this favourable reportage due to the fact that the *Baldur Gazette*'s owners, editors, and reporters were fond of the Chinese residents whose advertisements were a steady source of income for the paper? Or was it fuelled by reader demand? Beginning in 1899, issues of the *Baldur Gazette* were filled with accounts of the town's latest laundry.

The *Baldur Gazette* was also quite diligent in reporting the many visitors who came to see the men. Over the years, several came to Baldur from Wawanesa, Belmont, and Miami to visit their friends. In 1902, the paper noted: "Our Chinaman enjoyed a visit Monday from two of his confreres from Belmont. The visitors were apparently keen sports spending the afternoon shooting along the river."[100] But the newspaper also included stories about remarkable men in other places. For instance, in 1905, the *Baldur Gazette* noted: "A Chinaman who ran a laundry at Glenboro has been appointed by the Chinese government to go to England and study the art of shipbuilding."[101] After examining rural newspapers in many towns and villages throughout western Manitoba, it became very clear to me that the *Baldur Gazette* held Chinese culture and immigrants in high regard: there appeared to be less racism here. An article in this paper in 1912 describes the positive characteristics of a Chinese person:

> The Chinese are orderly, law-abiding and well-behaved: they have a strong sense of right and justice – are fair-minded; they are reliable in commercial dealings – pay their debts and keep their agreements, whether verbal or written; they are dutiful to parents, fond of children and mindful of etiquette

and punctilious about returning courtesies or favours: they are respectful to elders and superiors.[102]

Although for a decade several men came to and left Baldur, eventually some (and later their families) settled in the town. The first one to settle was Woo Tom. Woo Tom arrived in Baldur between 1908 and October 1909, when, the *Baldur Gazette* noted, using common and negative language: "Tom Wootom, our celestial Washee Washee, chin chin, had a visit from his brother on Saturday."[103] On the 1911 census, Woo Tom listed himself as a thirty-two-year-old male widower who immigrated to Canada in 1896 and had no religion.[104] Woo had a brother in Wawanesa, a son who eventually joined him to work in the shop, and friends in Winnipeg.[105]

A town celebrity, Woo Tom's activities were often displayed for all to see on page eight in the "local and general" section of the *Baldur Gazette*. In 1909, shortly after Woo Tom arrived, the paper divulged that A.W. Playfair had built a new laundry for him.[106] Two years later, in April 1911, probably when the snow had melted and the trails were passable from the branch line to Baldur, Woo Tom received a visit from the Winnipeg-based Woo Wing.[107] This visit happened around the same time that Sun Yat-sen visited Winnipeg. Later the same year, the paper noted that Woo Tom "got an extension put on his home."[108] By May 1912, Woo made local news yet again. This time it was because he had "purchased a gramophone and nearly fifty Chinese records, mak[ing] night hideous to the passer-by."[109] Woo Tom earned fifty dollars a month from his hand-washing business when he first started out in 1909.[110] Apparently, this income enabled him to put an extension on his home, purchase records and a gramophone, and sponsor his son, Woo Sing, to come to Canada.[111]

Were Baldur's dirty clothes sufficient to enable Woo Tom to accumulate enough money to purchase all these items? Perhaps he immigrated to Canada as a rich man and settled in Baldur. He was not a Lee or a Wong and the village might have seemed like a good place to raise his son, who, by the fall of 1912, was attending the local school: "Tom Wootom's son is attending school here, he will be talking broken English soon, and the Canadian children will probably be talking broken China – hope they don't cut their mouths."[112] The *Gazette* also reported when Woo Tom went to Winnipeg, presumably to gather with others at its KMT office and bring in the Chinese New Year with his son, brother, and friends.[113] In 1916, after having gone to school for a few years and learned some English, Woo Tom's son joined him in the business and then, shortly after that, the two left in the early spring: "Woo Sing has decided to give up the laundry, he says washee no good. He now workee on farm heap muchee. He is succeeded by Mr. Woo Bing, who is prepared to do all kinds of laundry work at the old stand."[114] But Woo Tom's son, Woo Sing, was still there in October when the large advertisement in the *Baldur Gazette* announced his prices, saying that dissatisfied customers could "bring the laundry back and [he would] do it over again for nothing."[115] The advertisement also noted that Woo Sing now spent four or five days a week in Belmont. By August 1917, the Baldur Laundry run by Woo Sing, his father Woo Tom, and others had closed.[116]

In our search of early Prairie newspapers for references to Chinese settlers, the *Baldur Gazette* had the most to offer. As I mentioned earlier, I do not think we can rely solely on racist and demeaning language to measure the degree of racism that Woo Tom experienced in Baldur; rather, the evidence seems to suggest that he lived there for seven years because doing so was fairly lucrative and generally positive. Clearly, he at least interacted with *Baldur Gazette* reporters, all of whom must have had a very limited understanding of Confucianism and other aspects of Woo Tom's back-stage life, including the social heat he experienced with other Chinese men in Winnipeg.

Waskada

From 1926 to 1947 Woo Bong ran a laundry in Waskada, Manitoba, where he lived in the back of the building. Usually, these residences were fairly spartan, being furnished with a bed, a chair, and rudimentary appliances used to prepare simple meals. Woo Bong did not attend the local church, and most of the time he kept to himself. Occasionally, he socialized with Jim Yuen, who ran the town restaurant. None of the wives or children of the town were allowed to go into the laundry alone because it was believed that Woo was involved in bootlegging. On days when he didn't have any laundry, his voice would ring out through the streets, singing: "Laundry, Laundry, here comes the laundryman. I've got the whisky today, no laundry."[117] While Tom Woo Tom had been a favoured citizen of Baldur, Woo Bong's experience was different. Many of the town's young boys would taunt him, shouting: "Chinky Chinky Chinaman wash my pants, put them in the water and make them dance." One time the boys sent an electric shock through the clothesline so that, when he went to hang wet laundry on it, both his hands and the laundry were singed. Woo would have had to explain to his customers the reason for the burn marks on the clothing and reimburse them for the damage. It is likely that he would not have admitted to the singed clothing's being the result of an act of overt racism. In fact, throughout our many interviews, Chinese men seldom complained about the harassment they endured. It was only through the retelling of the story by non-Chinese informants that we learned of this and other cruel racist acts. Woo Bong was rumoured to have become so enraged by the systematic racism that he chased the boys with a knife.[118]

All of the laundries discussed in this chapter were operated by single men who, for the most part, were nominal Christians. By 1940 the number of Chinese-run laundries in western Manitoba was beginning to be eclipsed by the number of Chinese-run restaurants.

3
The Western Manitoba Restaurant

Neither the bachelors nor the earliest non-Chinese settlers on the Canadian Prairies could have anticipated the enormous impact that Chinese restaurants would have on white culture. These eating establishments enabled all kinds of previously unfamiliar foods to flow into the eastern Prairies, from rice to noodles to Cadbury chocolate bars, Orange Crush, and pineapples. And, as these "modern" commodities were consumed in rural and urban parts of Manitoba, people became receptive to the individuals, markets, cultures, and ideas that brought them into their small communities.

Before there were Chinese-operated cafes or restaurants, people had to rely on hotels and rooming houses run by single or widowed women who were European settlers. The women served light lunches and offered "weekly meal tickets" to boarders. However, if a person wanted something to eat other than lunch or supper, the hotels and rooming houses were closed. Chinese men, seeing an opportunity, traded in their soap and irons to become the cooks, chefs, waiters, managers, and owners of a new kind of eating establishment. And, by 1904, they had begun the cultural transformation of Manitoba's prairie landscape. As Chinese-owned-and-operated restaurants began to open in small rural towns and cities throughout the Prairies, they challenged the dominance of white women, who had always made and served food for the predominantly male population. Although most Chinese men had no experience as chefs, they learned to make traditional dishes for themselves and Western ones for their customers. As populations grew and wars ended, the mostly bachelor customer base was replaced by families and by those who wanted to go out for fine meals and experience something of modern global culture.

Like the laundrymen, restaurant owners relied on rotating credit associations to raise money to start businesses. This new enterprise offered another location where Chinese men could work freely, employ those of their own ethnicity, and import novel and modern commodities. Restaurants also served as nodes where, after hours, men would gather during the festivals to establish connections with the Kuomintang office and other institutions in Winnipeg. For the most part, the western Manitoba cafe industry was dominated by the Choy (Choi, Toy, Toye, Tsai, Cai), Lee (Li), Wong (Wang), Yuen (Yuan), Mark (Mauk, Mak, Ma), and Dong (Young) clans. Through hard work, men achieved merchant status, became social capitalists,[1] and used the restaurants to sponsor brothers, uncles, nephews, fathers, sons/ paper sons (see below), and cousins. Later on, their restaurant businesses enabled them to finance bringing their wives and other children to Canada.[2]

In larger urban areas prior to the 1950s, Chinese-owned-and-operated restaurants resembled other popular types of cafeterias and diners and were decorated with wood panelling and linoleum flooring. Most places had a long counter dedicated to workers coming in from the countryside who would sit there by themselves and eat a quick meal. As well, there were big oak booths, each with its own jukebox, table with fresh flowers, and bowl of nuts. Sometimes, in larger centres such as Brandon, the words "Chop Suey" were written in a mock Chinese font on signs placed at the side of the building to add a cosmopolitan touch. Unlike the laundry, whose windows might be covered over with newspaper and which evoked negative stereotypes, restaurant windows fostered a good impression, with their display of fresh fruits and flowers for sale inside. By the 1950s, restaurant owners learned the appeal of "Chinoiserie" (a blend of Chinese and European design) and its power to satisfy the public appetite for more information about both traditional Chinese customs and more modern ones. Harvey Levenstein elaborates on the power of restaurant decor: "The titillation came, not from trying new and different foods but from new and exotic locales. It was a commonplace in the restaurant industry that the nature and the quality of the food in a restaurant took a back seat to its décor."[3] By the late 1940s, when the Second World War was over, people were going out for dinner in larger numbers, and the labourers who had at one time been the most common customers were replaced by families and businesspeople. This was the heyday of the Chinese restaurant and how most people remember it.

In contrast to that of the urban Chinese restaurant, the interior of the rural one varied greatly. Some very run-down-looking restaurants with drab exteriors were, surprisingly, Chinese on the inside, filled with all sorts of scrolls, calligraphy, and various images on the walls. Others appeared to be prosperous from the outside but contained almost nothing traditional inside. In small towns and villages, the restaurant was often the second-generation Chinese business in the area – the one that opened when the laundry closed down (or after it had become established). And, often, as is still the case today, it was the only eatery in town. Cafes performed the role of contemporary convenience stores and, sometimes, Oriental emporiums, where Chinese trinkets could be purchased from the case beneath the cash register.

The local Chinese restaurateur was a respected businessmen who, on one level, was extolled for his kindness and success, yet, on another level, was kept at a distance. Repeatedly, research participants recounted stories of the generous men who gave free meals to needy people throughout the Depression and war years, and who supported local teams and community fundraising efforts. We found newspaper articles that heaped praise on the local cafe owner who sponsored the curling bonspiel and gave the speech at the opening night banquet. And we found photographs of Chinese men seated in the middle of the teams that they had sponsored, smiling proudly.

If a man's wife or someone else in the family had a birthday, the restaurant owner would make a special meal, wrap it up, and have it delivered for the occasion. People were delighted by these thoughtful gestures. Chinese men also gave boxes of chocolates to customers at Christmas, even during wartime, when chocolate and other special items were rationed. Some restaurants offered promotions, whereby each visit counted towards a box of chocolates.[4] Other Chinese men gave Christmas turkeys and small gifts to customers who had become friends. Happy Dong was a Chinese man who owned and operated Chinese restaurants in Brandon and parts of rural Saskatchewan for almost four decades. He had many non-Chinese friends with whom he corresponded. In a letter sent to Happy on 20 December 1952 a friend thanked him for a Christmas turkey:

1039 Louise Avenue,
Brandon Manitoba,
December 18, 1952

Dear Happy,
I wish you would write and tell us about yourself and [your nephew] Bill ... You are such a beautiful writer that it should be no trouble. I am scolding you instead of saying I wish you and Bill a very happy Xmas and New Year. Today there came a big parcel containing such a huge turkey. How am I going to thank you for it? Dr. will be writing you when he sees such a wonderful gift. We had a beautiful card from Dr. Chu and Molly. It is

so good of him to send it. I should have sent our card air mail some time ago ...

Our love to Bill. How we'd love to see him. How does he get on at school. Our friendliest greetings again Happy, and a thousand thanks. This has been a busy time and I am not as frisky as I used to be. Old Age!

Greetings, Best wishes, and thanks

from Wilfred and Grace Bigelow.

Wilfred Bigelow (1878-1967) was a "horse-and-buggy" doctor who operated the Bigelow Clinic, which opened in 1913 to serve Brandon and rural areas of Manitoba and Saskatchewan. His wife, Grace Bigelow (1876-1959), was a midwife and nurse. Chinese settlers like Happy Dong came to be accepted and embraced by their small communities. They developed strong bonds with customers, who helped them to fill out government forms (e.g., to sponsor family members to come to Canada) and to complete their annual tax returns. They shared Christmas meals and sometimes, as in the case of Happy Dong, shared special family news. Happy Dong was very happy when his nephew Bill immigrated to Canada in 1948. Chinese men also had excellent reputations as employers.

FIGURE 11 Rex Cafe servers, Carberry, Manitoba, c. 1940.
Source: Minnie Oliver

The Chinese bachelors were never happy to see loyal employees (most often servers) quit, and they often tried to tempt them to stay on with gifts such as beautiful Chinese brocade robes (which they saved for just such occasions). But the women who worked in cafes were often young Ukrainians, and, though most adored their bosses, they were eager to find jobs with shorter hours or to get married and start families. A few of the bachelors kept in touch with the women after moving on to live in larger cities such as Winnipeg, Calgary, Victoria, or Vancouver. By then, the women had become part of the bachelor's extended family, and the men wrote them annual Christmas letters, sent photographs, and periodically visited. In some instances, the bond between Chinese employer and white employee continued from generation to generation. Families of former servers became kin to second- and third-generation Chinese Canadians who made trips back to the places where their fathers or grandfathers had first worked in Canada.

Still, Chinese men continued to endure all kinds of racism and harassment. To many, the cafe owner and his brother, nephews, or sons were intimidating because of their ambiguous social, religious, and sexual identities.[5] The men worked long hours, and most of the time they lived with male co-ethnics. They did not have the structure and routine of family life, with wives who made their meals, cleaned their homes, did the laundry, and got the family off to church on Sunday. To a lesser extent, cafes shared with laundries the reputation of being filthy places where an all-male population lived, ate, slept, gambled, drank, sometimes smoked opium, and might even have engaged in sexual relations. While the men may have been very polite to the customer, some people suspected that, behind the kitchen doors, they behaved like savages. Rumours circulated that they were chasing each other around brandishing cleavers. There was also talk that some places were so infested with cockroaches that food had to be repeatedly chopped and worked with a cleaver to keep the bugs away. Those more acquainted with traditional cooking methods recognized that the chopping and moving around of the meat and vegetables was a traditional Chinese cooking technique, not a sign of bug infestation. And, most common of all, people sometimes wondered if the meat served in the restaurant might be from a dog or a cat. These misunderstandings about the Chinese restaurant, its owner, and the homosocial relationships that had enabled him to succeed, inspired many acts of violence on the part of ignorant individuals. Consequently, immigrants in small towns and villages learned to stay inside on Halloween nights, when racist acts were at their most violent and excessive.[6]

But it was not only the different lifestyles, unknown customs, and misunderstood relationships that concerned local residents. Like the wash houses, cafes were competitive, staying open longer than the accommodations owned by lone white women who offered weekly meal tickets to boarders,[7] served light lunches, and sold tobacco, cigars, candies, and ice cream.[8] As a result, Chinese businesses succeeded in small established markets, taking business away from white residents. In 1919, the *Carberry News Express* reported on the reopening of a Chinese restaurant in Carberry. The report emphasized that a bylaw should be enacted to exclude these establishments:

> The Chinese restaurant was reopened in Carberry this week. Carberry has no by-law governing restaurants and it is necessary that every public eating house take out a license to do business as pointed out by Mr. May, provincial director of hotel accommodation at a recent meeting of the town council. It strikes us that the two hotels in Carberry can supply all the meals necessary and they should be protected to the extent of the exclusion of Chinese restaurants.[9]

Chinese cafes were perceived by other businesses as unfair competition, but local children adored them. Chinese bachelors offered them a chance to see and taste every kind of sweet confection: a visit to see the Chinese cafe and its bachelor owner was an adventure. Manitobans in their seventies, eighties, and nineties loved to reminisce about the rural restaurants of their youth. But it was not the chop suey or chow mein (*chaomian*, or fried noodles) they wanted to tell me about; rather, what they cherished were the candies and desserts. They remembered the man who ran the cafe and first introduced them to chocolate or taffy. Older kids flocked to the cafe after school dances and the movies to order ice cream floats, sundaes, and pies, and they lingered there until they had to go home. One person explained: "I never had anything to eat there except ice cream cones now and then but we used to go in there as high school students and get a booth and have a drink of 7-Up or Orange Crush and talk away to our friends." Children on an outing with their parents or grandparents got a small piece of candy at the cafe, selected from the collection stored beneath the front counter and for sale along with Chinese teapots and dolls.

A cache of the best chocolate bars was kept in a storage room for favoured customers and their children. Thus, if you were young and living in a small town or village in western Manitoba, this was the "cool" place to go. In many towns, adults were seldom seen in the restaurant, except when they

FIGURE 12   Daniel Lim, Brandon, 1950.
Source: Daniel Lim.

had to retrieve their children. Parents could not have been happy about their children spending long hours chatting with their friends in the restaurant. One research participant commented:

A Chinese man named "Charlie" ran a cafe there. This restaurant was a hang-out for teenagers. The only time I recall seeing an adult in this restaurant would be to find one of their teenagers. I also do not recall anyone ever actually ordering or eating any food – we teenagers could only afford a seven-cent Coke and twenty-five cents for the jukebox. Charlie was very patient with all the noise, but every once in a while he would appear from his kitchen and kick us all out. As I think back I don't recall ever seeing Charlie in the post office or in a grocery store or, for that matter, anywhere outside the cafe. His English was only adequate and I don't recall ever seeing him in a car or talking to an adult in the town. I don't remember ever seeing a wife or any children. He must have been a very lonely man.

Some communities were not pleased that their children were buying candy and other treats with the money they had been given to put into the Sunday School collection.[10] The bachelors and their cafes were competing not only with the local businesses but also with the churches and parents for the patronage of children. But it would be misleading to imply that restaurant owners were not accepted by the communities in which they lived. These people became respected businessmen within their own communities and were generally highly regarded by church groups and missionaries. Still, people harboured suspicions about these men who lived in "unnatural" all-male communities.

As I indicate throughout this book, Christianity, the KMT, laundries, and restaurants all helped Chinese immigrants fit into, and become accepted members of, Canadian society. And one of the most noteworthy ways the bachelor made himself both familiar and understandable to the public was through Chinese Canadian food. Men who owned and operated cafes ate rice every day, stir fries made with ingredients they could get on the Prairies, and dishes with authentic items like tofu and Chinese spices. Chinese food items like chop suey and chow mein only became available in Manitoban restaurants in the 1950s and only became popular in the 1960s; however, in the United States, they were popular decades before this. To western Manitobans, these foods, like the laundry ticket with characters written across it, offered a little bit of a foreign culture – just enough to entice them but not enough to scare them away.

People reminisced about the local restaurant's special foods. The owner remembered whether you liked ginger beef or sweet and sour chicken balls. He made liver and onions, halibut steaks that "hung off the plate," hamburger and chips, and, of course, the legendary banana cream pie. One of my most memorable interviews was with an elderly woman who had made this pie. As with scores of the people to whom I spoke, she had rejoined her husband in Canada years after the repeal of the Chinese Immigration Act in 1947. Given that she worked for decades in a rural restaurant, I am sure she could make any number of delicious Chinese dishes, but on this particular day she served me banana cream pie. After her telling me anecdotes about Prairie life and customs for over an hour, we took a break. She announced that she had baked something very special for the occasion and proudly served me a slice of this pie. And it was fantastic.

It was atypical for a woman to make a restaurant's pies on the eastern Prairies as men usually did the baking and cooking for Western customers. Periodically, the bachelor might emerge from the kitchen where he had been preparing the meals. He would visit with the customers, offering cherished ones a free slice of banana cream or raisin pie, or, on special occasions, a box of chocolates. The young women and, later, his wife would be in the front, serving the food and collecting the cheques. At closing time, the proprietor would emerge from the kitchen and sit at the front, quickly moving the beads of his abacus back and forth, calculating the day's earnings, joining the thousands of men throughout Canada's Chinatowns who were doing the same thing. Other Chinese men might arrive around this time to have a drink of rice wine or whisky, or to have a friendly game of mahjong or fan-tan.

Although these Chinese and non-Chinese relationships made life meaningful in small foreign communities, there were significant economic challenges that had to be overcome. Some cafe owners were especially lucky, diligent, and connected because of the social heat they enjoyed at all kinds of events. They remained in business for twenty or thirty years. Most owners were less stable, even though they found life easier to endure on the Prairies than elsewhere in Canada. They tended to move every ten years.[11] They followed the pattern of other ethnic restaurant owners, who relied on inexpensive family labour and chain migration to survive.[12] The pattern was as follows: a single man would come to western Manitoba to run the restaurant and then bring his family over after a few years of hard work and saving money. After his family arrived, he would then sponsor another male to come and work. Over time, this man would save enough money to buy his own restaurant fifty kilometres or so down the highway, and then he would sponsor his own family to come over.

Since the 1960s and 1970s, immigration to Canada has been based on a point system, and getting here is easier than it used to be. Some families migrate to rural areas and operate small rural restaurants, remaining for five or ten years, saving money, learning English, adjusting to the country, and raising children. When their children go to university, some move to a larger urban city. Since 2006, others have been arriving in the province as temporary foreign workers who can earn more than ten dollars an hour working, say, at Maple Leaf Consumer Foods in Brandon. A few of these newcomers express the hope that they will be able to move into the restaurant business once they are able to speak enough English and their two-year contract with Maple Leaf runs out. But, since the 1950s, the number of western Manitoban Chinese Canadian restaurants has been in decline. Repeatedly, we encountered situations in which the owner had died and the restaurant had closed down. Or we heard about situations in which the owner's mother had died and his father had moved to western Manitoba and not liked the area. The owner, being bound by his filial obligations, would close the restaurant and move his family to a larger urban centre, such as Calgary or Winnipeg, where his father would have access to a larger Chinese community and feel more comfortable. His children would study at universities in these cities and, on graduating, would enter various professions and would not return to run the family restaurants.[13] When parents retire, they either close the restaurants or sell them: they do not want this life for their children.

Brandon

Brandon's first Chinese-operated restaurants began to appear in 1904 and had names like Brandon Restaurant, the BC Restaurant, and the Ideal Restaurant.[14] The Ideal Restaurant was operated by Charles Sing, who self-identified (not surprisingly) as Protestant Christian and lived with others on the premises who, presumably, were co-ethnic co-workers.[15] Most of these businesses existed for a year or two and then disappeared. Three years later, there were six of them in the city, demonstrating the cafe's rapid rise in popularity. Chinese restaurants quickly became the dominant eating establishments in Brandon.

In the oral histories, interviews, and archival research, hundreds of names of men who ran Chinese restaurants were brought to my attention. Curiously, almost everyone I interviewed had known one particular man. This man's name was Yuen Bak Yee (Yu), but he was more commonly known to Westerners as Buddy Leeds and to the Chinese community as Buddy Lee. "Buddy Leeds" was a clever name. The first part, "Buddy," conveys that the man had assimilated with (and was a friend to) non-Chinese people. When he encountered a Chinese person and introduced himself as "Leeds," the person heard the name "Lee" and connected him to the powerful Lee clan. Throughout his life, Buddy maintained an identity between the extremes of East and West.[16]

Yuen Bak Yee was born in 1909 in Sunning District (Toisan), China. He emigrated from Hong Kong to Canada on 7 July 1921 at the age of twelve, along with two other boys from the same place and with the same surname. All three sailed to Victoria, British Columbia, and, while the other two went to Indian Head (Saskatchewan) and Treherne (Manitoba), Buddy Leeds headed to Portage la Prairie, Manitoba. The General Register of Chinese Immigration describes him as follows: "Four Foot Five and one half. Mole on the left side of the neck. Pits on forehead. Pits on upper lip."[17] Shortly after he arrived in Portage la Prairie, Leeds's uncle brought him to Dauphin, Manitoba, where he attended primary school. He never completed

FIGURE 13 Buddy Leeds in Hong Kong, 1960.
Source: Doug Sebastian

secondary school, and, like many immigrants at the time, he went to work at his uncle's restaurant at a young age. One research participant recalled hearing about him as a small boy: "Buddy came when he was young. When he was a child he would be in front of the restaurant and playing outside and the white people thought it was kind of cute and gave him five cents if he could do a cartwheel. Then he did one." Having spent much of his young life in the business, he became very proficient in English. Knowing English made Leeds different from most other Chinese immigrants and helped him to become one of the most famous elders in Brandon. Like Sam Dong, Bak Yuen Yee was always well dressed. Even on hunting and fishing trips he would be wearing a pressed white shirt and often a tie with a vest over top. Until the 1940s, he was also one of the few Chinese men in the region (along with Sam Dong and Sam Wong) to own a car.

By 1941, Bak Yuen Yee had changed his name to Buddy Leeds and had moved to Brandon, where many of his "cousins," or those with the family name Yuen, lived. For much of his life there, he resided on Tenth Street near Sam Dong and, later, on Rosser Avenue. He enjoyed a meal out in Winnipeg at some of the better Chinese restaurants, like the Nanking or Chan's Cafe. Given Leeds's extensive provincial connections, he often visited the KMT office for meetings or to get together with friends to play a game of mahjong.

FIGURE 14 Buddy Leeds (far left) after a fishing trip with friends, 1969.
Source: Doug Sebastian

When in Brandon and other parts of western Manitoba he would go hunting and fishing with non-Chinese men as well as with other bachelors and cousins. One research participant recalled being invited to come along on several occasions:

> Buddy gave me his old shotgun when I was little. And every fall I would come along with Buddy and my dad to hunt for ducks. After we would go shooting we would return to Buddy's car for a snack and he would open the trunk, where there would be all kinds of chips and chocolate bars ... When my dad was working, I'd go hunting with Buddy on my own. If my dad caught a big carp we'd go to Buddy's restaurant to give it to the cooks to eat. Buddy was pretty busy but he always had time for hunting and fishing.

In China, Leeds had a wife through an arranged marriage and a daughter named Kim. He was also rumoured to have many non-Chinese girlfriends in Brandon.

People describe Buddy Leeds as a gregarious and charismatic entrepreneur who, throughout the more than thirty years he lived in Brandon, was engaged in many different business ventures. At first he ran a cafe on Tenth Street called the Ritz. Eventually, the cafe became a grocery store called the Ritz Groceteria, which was in operation from 1949 to 1952. When business declined he went on to own (with partners) the Olympia Cafe in 1953. Unfortunately, the Olympia Cafe burned down that same year due to an electrical fire that started in the basement. This resulted in Leeds's opening a further business. This time he rented space from Brandon's influential Bass family and opened the United Grill and Cafe at 33 Tenth Street, which he managed from 1954 until 1959. The United Grill and Cafe claimed to be the largest and finest restaurant in Brandon, offering Chinese and Canadian food.

The early 1960s must have been a very painful time in Buddy Leeds's life. As a leader in the Chinese community, he attracted the attention of the RCMP and the federal Department of Justice for his role in bringing many Chinese immigrants, or "paper sons," to Canada. According to one research participant, this was how the process worked:

The idiots in Ottawa made this immigration law to limit the number of inferior Orientals. The only way that you could come to Canada was if you had a father or mother or spouse here. So many [boys] came here illegally as a "paper son" ... Back in the old days young Chinese worked hard in a restaurant and then would go home [to China] and get married and leave their bride there and visit once every five or three years, and stay three months and then come back, and then the wife would have a son from the visit. In a lot of cases that was true. When the son grew up you could apply to bring him over. But with a "paper son," people would go home and visit and then come back and then [falsely] report that the wife had a son. That opened the space for that person to sell a spot [in Canada] to someone else for $3,000.

Buddy Leeds was one of the community leaders who helped people bring their "paper sons" to Canada. He brokered deals in which, for instance, a grandfather, uncle, or friend paid someone for the right to use their spot in order to bring over a boy as young as seven or eight years old to work in the restaurant. Another research participant added that, "if someone from the Chinese community died, Buddy would erase their name on the papers and take the papers to China. Buddy got caught doing this ... But he was only trying to help people come to Canada." Although Leeds was not the only Chinese person in the region who was being investigated, his case became famous. On 29 July 1960, he was arrested for three counts of forging immigration documents to smuggle people into Canada. The *Winnipeg Free Press* reported as follows:

> RCMP Friday made their first arrest in Manitoba in connection with a nation-wide alien smuggling ring. Arrested was Chinese-born Brandon restaurant proprietor Yuen Bak Yee, better known to the English speaking community as Buddy Leeds ... Mr. Leeds's arrest was the third made by the RCMP in Canada within the past two days. On Thursday two Chinese operators of travel agencies were picked up by police and charged on 13 counts of perjury, forgery and uttering in connection with the smuggling of Chinese immigrants into Canada.[18]

A year later, after twenty-nine court appearances, the charges were dropped.[19] Buddy Leeds's bad luck continued, and less than a year after that, his first Canadian wife, Marie Evelyn Leeds, was killed one Saturday morning while she was driving fourteen and half kilometres east of Portage la Prairie with her brother Nicholas Skillnick. But soon life returned to normal for Leeds. By 1964, he had married his second Canadian wife and had a child on the way. Buddy Junior (also known as Porky), his first son, was born in 1965. Between 1964 and 1966, Leeds owned the Leichee Garden and Coffee Bar at 1015 Princess Avenue and then opened the Bellair Restaurant at 935 Rosser Avenue, which he managed for almost a decade, from 1966 to 1975. In 1973, Buddy's mother, Lou Tong Yuen, came from Hong Kong to spend Christmas with him, his second Canadian wife, and their seven-year-old son.[20] In 1974 and 1975 he was proprietor of Kam Lung Restaurant, which offered "Brandon's Newest and Finest Chinese Foods." This would be his longest and final business venture. People recount how, a short time later, Leeds was surprised by a visit from his first Chinese wife and his daughter. Sometime after that, he and his Chinese family moved to Vancouver, where he later died. I attempted to find out what happened to Mrs. Leeds and her son but was unsuccessful.

Often the mention of Buddy Leeds provoked laughter from informants – not for his many rumoured dalliances but, rather, for his courage and bluster. Admired for his English-language skills and his ease with the white community, he helped many Chinese become accepted in non-Chinese circles, creating opportunities for the two groups to come together and form business and other relationships. For instance, every year, a white friend gave Leeds twenty-five ducks for a KMT regional supper, which was held in Brandon and Winnipeg in alternating years. Ducks were a special part of these meals because they were symbolic. As one research participant explained, "they represented boats and water – water was one of the categories of ritual food and the other two were air and land."

Buddy Leeds's experience in the restaurant business epitomized that of the typical Prairie Chinese man. Most proprietors changed businesses frequently. Their wives came to Canada late in their lives and often brought with them grown children whom they had never known. But in other ways Leeds's experience was atypical. Relatively early – because of his personality and English fluency – he became a powerful elder in the community and was well connected to KMT leaders, prominent non-Chinese lawyers and businesspeople, and, most important, to the western Manitoba Chinese community.

In 1957, the Chinese Canadian Citizens' Association of Manitoba and Pat Low, as president, organized a float to be included in a parade for the City of Brandon's seventy-fifth anniversary celebration. Buddy Leeds was part of the organizing committee and was well connected to men in Winnipeg's Chinatown and beyond. He borrowed a non-Chinese friend's car for the event, and, when the parade ended, he gave the float to a white family, who put it in their backyard, where, for many years, it functioned as their son's playhouse.

Leeds was admired and loved by both Chinese and non-Chinese in western Manitoba. He was embraced by Canadian society more than were most of the other men of his generation, and he accomplished this through the relationships and festive occasions that occurred in both the back-stage and front-stage regions of his social, political, and business lives.

Turning to other restaurant stories, one finds Chinese eateries with the name "Rex Cafe" all over Manitoba – in Dauphin, Gladstone, Neepawa, Carberry, and Carman. The Brandon Rex Cafe was one of the earliest in the city, in existence from 1913 to 1927 at 119 Tenth Street, with only two proprietors – Frank D. Lung for the first two years and Fong Song (Charles Fong Song) for the remainder. Unfortunately, both men disappeared once they finished working there. Brandon also had a Royal Cafe (1925-31), another familiar name for a rural restaurant, located at 118 Eighth Street. But the restaurant with the longest history and best-known owner was the Carlton Cafe run by Sam Wong (Mandarin: *Huang Xianxi* 黃賢熹), whom I discussed briefly in Chapter 1. Wong and his family ran the cafe located at

FIGURE 15 Chinese community float
becomes a playhouse for Doug Sebastian, 1958.
Source: Doug Sebastian

121 Tenth Street for almost fifty years, from 1923 to 1972. It survived the Depression, two wars, and numerous changes in the city.

Born in 1881, Sam Wong first attempted to leave China in 1906, applying to join his uncle as a migrant worker in San Francisco, California. He was denied entry into the United States because San Francisco had just experienced an earthquake and fires. His second attempt to leave was successful,

FIGURE 16 Sam Wong, immigration photograph, 1912.
Source: Helen Wong.

and, in 1912, he immigrated to Canada and worked in a laundry in Montreal. By 1916, he was the chief executive officer of the Montreal KMT. Late in 1916, he moved to Brandon and entered the restaurant business, working in the Hollywood Cafe, then the Rex Cafe. Finally, he raised enough money to open the Carlton Cafe.

Unmarried, Sam Wong eventually went to China, had an arranged marriage, and brought back his wife, Wong Au (Mandarin: *Huang Ou* 黃區). The first Chinese woman in western Manitoba, she arrived in Brandon in late 1918, when she was twenty-seven years old. Shortly afterwards she

FIGURE 17 Gravestone of Wong Au (W.A. See),
with Decoration Day offerings at Brandon cemetery.
Source: Alison Marshall

became pregnant.[21] Au was a relatively older woman, and, being the only Chinese female in the city, she was very isolated and did not get many opportunities to socialize or exercise. By all accounts, there were complications during her labour and, with neither a Western doctor nor a traditional Chinese midwife present (most of the larger Canadian Chinatowns had significant female populations and therefore a Chinese midwife),[22] she and her infant son died on 19 February 1920. Wong Au's gravestone refers, incorrectly, to her English name as W.A. See. "See" was not her surname but, rather, the Cantonese spelling of the word "Mrs." She was married to a

Wong and came from the Au family. Presumably, the cross erected beside her gravestone marks the place where her son's body is buried.[23]

Sam Wong was devastated by the loss of his wife and newborn son. A Chinese friend in Brandon learned of the tragedy and said that he had a daughter in China who was the right age and that Wong could "take her as his wife." Wong had a chance for a second arranged marriage and, being a relatively affluent Chinese merchant at the time, agreed. Lim Koon Ying (Ying Lim Quang) (1903-93), who was from Toisan, China, paid the $500 head tax that was then imposed on all people who emigrated from China to Canada. Lim boarded the *Empress of Russia* on 8 August 1921 and sailed from Hong Kong to Victoria, arriving less than a month later on 5 September. Wong was there to greet her when her ship docked, and the two were married in a traditional Chinese ceremony in Victoria. Then the newlyweds took the train to Brandon on 15 September 1921. Lim Koon Ying was the second Chinese woman in the area, and she and her husband went on to have five children.[24]

Sam Wong was once again a husband and father. In business, he was a kind, hard-working, and generous man. Wong's strong connections to the KMT, and the social heat he experienced through KMT and Christian events, brought him comfort. He spoke Toisanese at home with his wife and children, and limited English to his customers. In many ways, he appeared to be a modern Western gentleman. In private, his beliefs and values most closely resembled those of Confucianism, while in public he was a Protestant Christian. A nominal Christian when he died, his family arranged for a United Church minister to speak at his funeral. Sam Wong continued his native customs, but he also tried to fit in and contribute to Brandon society. He was almost always dressed in a suit and sometimes wore a fedora. Even family photographs of him on picnics, fishing, visiting local Chinese families, or relaxing with his wife portray him in a pressed Western shirt, tidy pants, and polished shoes.

Sam Wong, like many other men at the time, was active in the local KMT. In fact, it was probably because of a KMT meeting he attended in Victoria in 1916 (as Montreal chief of the KMT executive) that he had a chance meeting with Li Kimkim, then president of the Winnipeg KMT. This meeting presumably led him to relocate from Montreal to Brandon. The photograph on the cover of this book was taken in Brandon in the front of the Rex Cafe in the summer of 1917. It shows Wong in the driver's seat, Li in the passenger seat, Winnipeg KMT secretary Wong Oursheng (Mandarin: *Huang Rongsheng* 黃容生), and an unidentified man (probably Sam Dong) in the back seat. As president and secretary of the Manitoba KMT, Li and

FIGURE 18 Sam Wong, Montreal KMT
delegate to Victoria, BC, meetings, 1916.
Source: Alison Marshall

Oursheng had come to Brandon to solicit donations for a 1917 central party KMT fundraising campaign.

Wong continued to be active in the KMT after he arrived in Brandon and, from 1931 to 1933[25] owned the house in which the KMT office was located. He attended meetings both there and in Winnipeg, where he travelled with others to hear various speakers. His son was eventually married to the daughter of Winnipeg's powerful KMT and CBA leader, Charlie Foo.

During the Depression Sam Wong offered free meals to those in need; during the Second World War he offered them to soldiers. For this act of kindness, the Canadian Legion paid tribute to him in a framed citation: "We commend you especially for the unstinted generosity you bestowed upon members of His Majesty's armed forces during World War II."[26] Not only was Wong a generous supporter of his Brandon community but, throughout his life, he sent money back to China to his hometown association to build homes and contribute to the community's new school and bridge. He also acted as Brandon's Chinese Patriotic League representative during the war relief effort from 1937 to 1945. He was responsible for advertising the league's fundraising campaign, making the necessary arrangements with banking institutions (which would open an account for the funds), and remitting the donations to the Manitoba office of the KMT. A picture dating from August 1943, with the Nationalist twelve-pointed star behind him, shows Sam Wong receiving a cheque from Brandon mayor Fred Young. Wong worked in the restaurant well into his seventies and died at the age of seventy-eight in Winnipeg. After his death in 1959, his sons continued to run the Carlton Cafe until it closed in 1972.

Another famous regional restaurant was run by the Choys. The Choys originally settled in Newdale, Manitoba, led there by Choy Him, who came to Canada in 1911 and eight years later bought a restaurant and hotel near the CPR station. In 1928, he sold that business and bought the Paris Cafe, which he operated until 1939.[27] Choy Him was followed to Canada, and into the business, by his son Choy Soo (1909-83), who immigrated in 1923 (the same year as the Chinese Immigration Act) at the age of fifteen. Seven years later, Choy Soo, finding no Chinese women in western Manitoba of marriageable age, and observing the custom of overseas men, went to China and married Chan Yook Hai (1909-2010).

But Chan Yook Hai (Jade) did not come back with Choy Soo to this country. She remained in her home village, and Choy visited every year and a half. Over the years they had four children – two sons and two daughters. After 1937, and during the Second Sino-Japanese War, many bachelors who were near retirement age and who, for decades, had been forced to live apart from their Chinese wives and children returned home. Some men financed the trip back to China on their own, while others accepted financial assistance from the KMT, which was encouraging those interested to return during the Second Sino-Japanese War. When Choy Soo's father returned to China to retire in 1939,[28] he took over as owner of the Paris Cafe.[29]

Like many rural settlers and his bachelor father before him, Choy Soo had an ambiguous identity and existence. In Newdale, the public knew him to be a hardworking, lonely, and strange peasant. Hidden from their gaze, however, was another life spent with bachelors and relatives in neighbouring Prairie towns and villages during festivals and when the restaurant was closed. In China, due to his generous remittances, people imagined him to be part of a gentry class of overseas men who were thriving on "Gold Mountain." After 1949, when China was under the control of the Chinese Communist Party, the gentry status of her husband made Jade Choy an object of scorn. She and her children lived in fear of retribution, eventually being forced from their home, which had been purchased with migrant dollars. For almost two years they lived an itinerant life, eating cheap salted vegetables and fish until 1951, when they made it to Hong Kong where they could stay with relatives. After the Chinese Immigration Act was repealed in 1947, the Canadian government began to allow people to emigrate from China to Canada, but it would take several years for Jade and other bachelor wives and families to be reunited with their husbands. Canadian and Chinese clerks were overwhelmed by the number of requests that had to be processed in a short time. More than ten years after the repeal of the act, Choy was able to sponsor his wife and youngest daughter, Sue-On, to come to Canada. Kenny, his younger son, came a year later in 1959, and both children completed their education in Newdale.[30] In 1965, Kenny went into partnership with James Lee of Brandon and Philip Yuen of Hamiota, and together the three opened the Chop Suey House in Brandon, which boasted "a special range for turning out Chinese specialties."[31]

In 1970, the Choy family moved to Brandon and took over the operation of the Chop Suey House at 220 Tenth Street. The restaurant, now known as Soo's Chop Suey House, was one block away from, and in direct competition with, Sam Wong's long-running Carlton Cafe. Choy ran the restaurant until his retirement in 1975. During his life here, Choy was involved in many intercultural activities as a member of the Brandon Masonic Lodge and Shriners Club. Choy Soo died on 24 October 1983 at the age of seventy-five. After his death, his son Kenny took over the restaurant, and, when he retired in 1992, his sister Sue-On and her husband Bill Hillman ran it until it closed ten years later.

The Soo restaurant at 220 Tenth Street was a very successful business, and, over its thirty-two years in operation (from 1970 to 2002), it offered customers a craft shop, a banquet hall, an Orient Room, and, for a time in the 1990s, a satellite location at the Shopper's Mall. By all accounts, the Choys' restaurant was the first in the area to market its modern Western Chinese identity, thus demonstrating the way of the bachelor, which blurred the division between East and West. They accomplished this through blending traditional and Chinese Canadian foods and offering a decor that included traditional architectural details, such as circular doorways symbolizing *tian* (heaven) in banquet rooms. Daoist landscape paintings of cypress trees and cranes covered the walls, and Chinese screens divided rooms. Like many other Chinese Canadian restaurants in the region, it had fans, lanterns, red carpeting, and a fish tank, along with an exterior sign in a faux Chinese font.

But, in addition to presenting the hybrid, ambiguous face of Chinese Canadian identity, the Choys used their businesses and spaces to draw people together to celebrate traditional events. Unlike the Lee and Wong clans in the region, fewer of the Choys were active in the provincial KMT.

The Choys have, however, used social heat (the shift from the ordinary to the extraordinary that takes place during festivals and other such events) in the same way as did the KMT – to create a more distinct family community. The Choys have been leaders in the community for several decades and have worked hard to continue Chinese customs and traditions by creating the Westman Chinese Association and organizing a pavilion at the lieutenant-governor's Winterfest. Like many other Chinese immigrants I discuss in this book, the Choys were not sojourners. They followed the way of the bachelor and became modern and Canadian. At the same time, they maintained ties to their clan and hometown associations in China and to the traditions of their homeland. Most of the Canadian Choy clan are nominal Christians who are married in the United Church and are buried by its ministers. Religious efficacy (as discussed in the Introduction) is crucial to this family. They make food offerings to ancestors and deities during traditional festivals throughout the year and participate in the annual Decoration Day. The KMT and other Chinese political involvements are not a dominant theme for this extended family.

Restaurants run by the Choy family and others made Chinese food popular in Brandon. Today, Wah Lee's and Double Happiness Chinese restaurant are two of the other well-known restaurants with proprietors who have been in business for a generation or more (or whose families have been). But the most well-known and successful restaurateur in the city is Sergio Lee, who arrived in Brandon at the age of eighteen in February 1969 and now owns and operates Kam Lung *(Jinlong)*. Some people refer to Lee as Brandon's most powerful current elder. Like all of the other Chinese families in the region, Lee is well connected to previous generations of the Chinese community in Brandon as well as to leaders of the Manitoba CBA.[32]

Rural Western Manitoban Restaurants

For over a century there have been small Chinese settlements throughout rural western Manitoba, including Baldur in Argyle Municipality, Binscarth, Birtle, Boissevain, Carberry, Dauphin, Deloraine, Killarney, Melita, Minnedosa, Neepawa, Russell, Shoal Lake, Souris, Virden, and Waskada. Chinese settlements have historically clustered around the restaurant(s) and, before them, the laundry. Given today's reality of rural out-migration, several of these small towns and villages have neither a cafe nor a Chinese population.

At one time, dispersed bachelor communities were connected by the memory of Sun Yat-sen's visit to, and subsequent interest in, the province. After that, they were united by events that were hosted and organized by KMT leaders in both Winnipeg and rural areas. From 1925 (when Sun Yat-sen died) to 1949 (when the KMT fled to Taiwan), Nationalist supporters were inspired by the efforts of Chiang Kai-shek to unite and defend China. While some of these settlements have diminished and disappeared in recent years, others have continued, even though the KMT, the memory of Sun Yat-sen, and the tradition of hosting Chinese events has faded considerably.[33]

Baldur

The popular Chinese laundryman Woo Tom, whom I discussed in the previous chapter, paved the way for later immigrants to Baldur, which is just north of the border between Canada and the United States. These bachelors, like Woo Tom before them, would not have stayed if they had not been welcomed and accepted by Baldur's small Icelandic community. In 1916, Lee Wee Foon moved to Baldur and bought Charlie King's restaurant and confectionery, renaming it the Baldur Cafe.[34] Over the years, the cafe was a popular place to buy home-made bread, cherries, peaches, apricots, blueberries, chocolates, boxed candy, preserved fruit, barrels and boxes of apples, and fresh oysters (when in season).[35] On one level, Lee Wee Foon was accepted by the community because of his personality (and, after 1919, the personalities of his wife and son) and his food. However, this would not have been enough to keep him in business. He also needed to be part of a network of friends (who could help out when he was in China), banks, and Winnipeg's Chinatown food distributors (from whom he obtained produce). The rules for survival in rural Manitoba were the same whether you lived in Brandon or Melita (with a population, according to the 2006 census, of 1,051). Bachelors needed to have strong relationships with both Chinese and non-Chinese men if they wanted their businesses to survive beyond Chinatown, and the archival records show that Lee had these. They also suggest that he was a devout KMT member. Five years after he opened the Baldur Cafe, Lee and his family travelled to Regina to visit with friends while another friend (named "Henry") ran the shop.[36] In June 1922, Lee went to Vancouver to visit with friends and Henry again came to run the store.[37] Two years later, in March 1924, he went back to Winnipeg and Regina on business.[38] In 1921, the Union Bank in Baldur announced that it was taking donations for the Chinese famine. As Lee was the most well-known Chinese settler in Baldur at the time, I assume he was the KMT's and CBA's representative in the area – the person who collected contributions and forwarded them to provincial leaders.[39]

In 1924, after eight years in his old building, Lee Foon set to work building a cafe and a new grocery store.[40] The building would go through many changes throughout the many decades that Lee Foon, then his son Tommy, and now his elderly son Oscar ran the business. Years later, the restaurant adjoining the grocery store became an ice cream parlour. The Lees sold groceries and sandwiches as well as all kinds of treats that attracted the neighbourhood children, who waited around to pick up freshly baked bread or dropped by after a movie to have a banana split or a slice of raisin pie. The younger children were excited by a visit to the store and the chance to select a candy from the excellent assortment of confectioneries.

Lee Foon was a well-dressed man who had cut off his queue and wore his hair short and neat. Sometimes he would be seen wearing a shirt and sweater or a jacket. But he always wore Chinese pants – the kind that, according to Western taste, were a little too short. This ambiguous appearance enabled him to live as a modern Chinese gentleman in an alien rural community. In 1919, Lee brought his wife, See Yee ("Yee" = maiden name, "See" = "Mrs."), and son over from China.

The couple would have eight more children in Baldur. Unlike Foon Lee's, See Yee's appearance and behaviour were not very ambiguous. Throughout her life, she learned very little English and wore traditional Chinese clothing. I was told that she had bound feet and hobbled around the restaurant. She wore a plain Chinese dress with a mandarin collar and braided detail and trim at the cuffs. Her hair was pulled neatly back from her face and worn in a bun. And she always wore earrings and rings. Other than these superficial details, people knew little about her or her family's private customs. As I have said, an ambiguous identity was key to a bachelor's success; however, it was not a necessary attribute for a Chinese wife, who was considered fortunate to live in Canada with her husband, to remain in the traditional inner quarters, and to do the "women's work" of raising children. See Yee was welcomed and accepted by the Baldur community because of her role as a traditional Chinese wife who took care of her husband and children. She was not a nominal Christian and did not attend church services. She was a very generous and friendly person who was always willing to help customers and the local children who worked in the store.

When the Lee family first arrived, people in the community recalled thinking that they were a bit strange. This perception quickly changed as Lee Foon followed the way of the bachelor, forming relationships, becoming a nominal Christian, and winning the respect of the townspeople. The family lived upstairs from the grocery/restaurant, in which all of their children worked. The children were well disciplined, went to church regularly, and attended Sunday school. People, despite initial fears about the Lees' strangeness, noted that they mixed well in the community. Every morning they could be seen leaving the grocery and walking to school together, the youngest one, Fawnie, wearing a fur bonnet. Eventually, the children became quite popular and socialized with non-Chinese children, making jokes and bringing gifts to those who were ill. Later, their parents employed local children at the grocery. Some of the younger Lees were married by local United Church ministers, and women in the community opened their houses to host the reception teas for the newly married couples.[41]

Waskada

A bachelor named Jim Yuen (also known as Yen Kwong Fong, Yen Quon Fong, "Old Jim," and the "Chinaman"), who was born around 1880, originally worked as a cook at Winnipeg's Seymour Hotel. Eventually, in his late teens or early twenties, he made his way to Waskada to run the restaurant there. Like many of his contemporaries, Yuen was known to have a wife and son in China. He sent money home each month, but no one recalls him ever returning to China for visits. The restaurant required nearly all his time, and people remember that he would stay up until three or four in the morning baking apple and raisin pies. After that, he would sleep until he had to let the servers in to open the restaurant. It must have been very strange for Jim when he first came to Waskada – a lone Chinese settler who worked almost all the time and supported a family in China. But it had to have been just as strange when his son Charlie, who, for all Jim knew of him, could have been a paper son, arrived in 1947. Eventually, Charlie, who had been sponsored by his father to help in the Waskada restaurant, was sent to Estevan, Saskatchewan, where he opened his own restaurant.

Jim Yuen was a well-loved, generous, and seemingly happy person, but the work prevented him from mixing much in the community. The restaurant was especially busy on the weekends (after the beer parlours closed), movie nights in town, and when there were curling bonspiels. During Waskada's annual field day, Yuen would change from being a man who worked alone with no community to suddenly being one who could draw on the support of a network of friends. Around this time each year, when business would swell, another Chinese cafe owner from Deloraine would appear in town to help Yuen for a day.

Although Jim Yuen ate traditional foods himself – rice and stir-fried vegetables with meat – he didn't serve these dishes to his clientele. When customers arrived for a meal he would visit their table and sing out the menu: "Steak, pork chops, ham and eggs, bacon and eggs and sausage. What you like?" In addition to meals, Yuen provided commodities that were in high demand on the rural Prairies, such as candies, cigarettes, and cigars. He would order many kinds of chocolate bars, such as Jersey Nut and Dutch Treat. The best bars would be put in the back and saved for special customers and friends. If he knew that some of his friends were working on a hot day, he would come out to the field and give them a cold drink at no charge. Yuen's customers were his friends and he treated them well.

Jim Yuen was in Waskada for thirty years,[42] and, during this time, he tried hard to fit in and learn English, keeping a dictionary nearby to look up the meaning of unknown words. Although he never joined the rest of the townspeople at church on Sundays, it was not because they did not accept him; rather, it was because the work in the restaurant kept him too busy and, with the exception of his going to the barber's to get a haircut or shave, people do not recall that he ever left the restaurant. In 1948, one year after the repeal of the Chinese Immigration Act and the arrival of his son Charlie, Jim Yuen left Waskada. He told his customers and friends that he was returning home. By 1948, the Second Sino-Japanese War had ended and Japan had been defeated. Now China was crippled by a civil war between the KMT and the CCP. Within months the KMT would lose and retreat to Taiwan. Was Yuen returning because his wife, who had been separated from him for most of their married life, could not or was not willing to come to Canada? Or was it because he longed to return to his homeland? Before Yuen left he gave several self-addressed envelopes to a favoured employee, a boy who had worked for him for four years. The envelopes showed that he had returned to Zhonglou in Toisan County. Years later, people learned that Jim had died in China. The boy kept the envelopes for more than sixty years to remember this fine man and everything he had taught him. I was deeply moved when this now-elderly research participant showed up one day at my office and presented these envelopes to me for safekeeping.

Binscarth

Binscarth celebrated its 110th birthday in 2006. Mark Woo (also known as Mark Wo) ran Mark's Cafe, which opened in 1922. Woo was a kind man and was well respected by the community; he was "never one to cause trouble."[43] He lived a solitary life filled with endless hours of work interspersed with brief periods of respite in his upstairs apartment. He had few friends and survived on what many research participants described as a simple diet of little more than boiled rice so that he could save enough money to be able to return to China to be with his wife and children. Twenty-four years after he opened the restaurant, Woo moved to Saskatchewan. Unfortunately, he never realized his dream of returning to China and was buried in the cemetery in Roblin, Manitoba (seventy kilometres north of

Binscarth). He, too, was a nominal Christian, and when he died a United Church minister officiated at his funeral.

Mark's Cafe was replaced by other Chinese restaurants such as Toy Gene's Cafe, which was in operation from 1946 to 1948. Later, there was the Dominion Cafe, or DY's (1954-76), run by the well-loved Billy Dare (also known as Ming Dare or DY). Billy Dare, like Mark Woo, loved children, and the counter beneath the cash register was always stocked with a great assortment of candies. Like many men who lived in western Manitoba, Dare had been forced to leave a wife and children in China. Dare lived with a boy whom people knew to be his grandson Stanley. Stanley went to school in Binscarth and helped out at the restaurant. When he got older he moved to Winnipeg and opened his own restaurant. In 1976, Dare moved to Winnipeg due to ill health. When he was eighty, his wife and family finally immigrated to Canada. When he celebrated his ninetieth birthday, both his Chinese family and his many non-Chinese friends from Binscarth were invited to the event.

After many years without a Chinese restaurant, Binscarth now has one called Choy Restaurant and Service. The exterior of the building is similar to that of many others on the Prairies. It has plain white aluminum siding, and a simple sign advertising the restaurant hangs below the sign for the Esso station. The interior is equally generic. The carpet is new, the ruffled curtains and the wallpaper are pleasant-looking, and the tables are clean and orderly. Aside from the lucky cat and a few other Chinese decorations and wall hangings, the restaurant resembles most rural diners. It offers the kind of food one would expect at many rural eating establishments. There are chicken balls, egg rolls, fried rice, and chop suey.

The restaurant is operated by David Choy, who is the son of Allen Choy, a restaurant proprietor and businessman who lives in Shoal Lake, Manitoba, and is a relative of Choy Him and Choy Soo, who operated a restaurant in Newdale and then in Brandon. Choy is well known and liked by the Binscarth community. He is a good example of a man who has retained his Chinese traditions but is modern in other ways. He has a Chinese wife and lives with his in-laws in a traditional family arrangement. He is a second-generation Chinese Canadian who speaks impeccable English, and his family has integrated into the community.

Neepawa

Neepawa has the second largest population of the towns discussed in this chapter, and, because of its size, it has always been able to support at least two Chinese restaurants. Although Neepawa is nearly ten times the size of

Binscarth, its history of settlement is very similar. The 1901 census shows that three individuals named Lee resided in Neepawa: George Lee, Wong Lee, and Lee Sing. They typified early Chinese immigrants in western Manitoba: all were male, older than thirty, worked in the laundry business, and self-identified as Christians. Ten years later these men had moved on. The 1911 census showed that James Yuen, Lee Soon (also known as Hong Hong), Chin Mook (also known as Shin Shui), Chin Hee, C. Hone Joe, and C. Hone Sing now lived in Neepawa. At twenty years old, Chin Hee was the youngest Chinese man in the community. They were a mix of hired men, laundry workers, and a restaurateur. All listed themselves as Christians. Lee Soon and Chin Mook, both twenty-five years old, operated the Mountain Avenue S.K. Laundry. They had come to Neepawa in 1907.[44]

For many years, Neepawa laundries and restaurants were owned and operated by men from the powerful Lee clan and by those who were active in Winnipeg Christian groups. Ten years after he arrived in Neepawa, Lee Soon's brother Ling Lee (also known as Lee Hi) (1895-?) began his journey to Canada in the spring of 1916. Like other Chinese immigrants, he first travelled to Hong Kong, where he waited for immigration officials to approve his application. He then travelled to Vancouver and on to Montreal before, in 1917, finally arriving in Neepawa.[45] During his life in Neepawa, Lee visited his wife and two children in China three times.[46]

In 1917, Ling Lee entered into partnership with Sam Toy (1886-1959), another local Chinese bachelor. Together the two operated the two Chinese Canadian restaurants in Neepawa – the Royal Cafe and the Paris Cafe. Eleven years later, Ling Lee bought out Sam Toy's interests in the businesses. Between 1928 and 1940, Lee managed the Royal Cafe and his brother Lee Soon managed the Paris Cafe (with Soon's son, Frankie Lee).[47]

Decades of life in Neepawa made Ling Lee a beloved figure in the Chinese and non-Chinese communities, a position he earned through his generosity during the Depression and two world wars. By 1940, however, he was exhausted by the rigours of restaurant life and was hospitalized. For years after that he slowed down, then transferred his interests in the two restaurants to his nephew Frankie Lee and Bill Toy. Finally, in 1959, Lee made his fourth and last trip home to Hong Kong. His departure from Neepawa was a sad moment for the community. In a ceremony that, on Friday, 16 January 1959, was front-page news, he was honoured by the city that, for four decades, he had inhabited as a bachelor, a laundryman, and a restaurateur:

Friends and fellow businessmen gathered to honour Mr. Lee before his departure. The mayor paid high tribute to him both as a citizen and as a businessman, and spoke highly of his honesty and willingness to help those who needed help.

The mayor then presented him with a boutonniere on behalf of the telephone operators, a lighter on behalf of E.P. Boyle and the Neepawa Creamery, and a gold wrist watch on behalf of many of his friends in the community.

It was estimated that seventy or more people attended the function.[48] Ling Lee never returned to Neepawa and died in Hong Kong. In Mayor William Whitmore's tribute to him, memorialized in the *Neepawa Free Press*, we can see that this man had become a part of the Neepawa community. He paved the way for later generations of Chinese immigrants, most notably, his nephew Frankie Lee.

Frankie Lee emigrated from Hong Kong to Canada in 1922. When he arrived in Neepawa, his father enrolled him in high school. George Rey recounts Frankie's first day in school:

There was great excitement in Grade 11 class the day Mrs. Cochran announced that a Chinese boy was to join us. Frankie Lee soon taught us some of his ways, including writing and arithmetic, at which he was much better than his classmates. Frankie was in his early teens at the time. Nevertheless he had duties and chores to perform after school hours and at times he found the weather bitterly cold.[49]

When he was not in school, Lee worked in the CNR Cafe. He was diligent and friendly, like his uncle Ling, and eventually saved enough money to buy the cafe. Later, he sold it to Sammy Wo. Similar to many other Chinese immigrants in western Manitoba and Canada, Frankie Lee was involved in the United Church. As he got older, he also became active in the Neepawa Lions Club and participated in events at the Neepawa Legion.

By 1927, because of the new restrictions in the final version of the Chinese Immigration Act (enacted four years earlier), there were still very few Chinese women in western Manitoba.[50] So Frankie Lee, like so many before him, returned to China to find a wife. After the wedding, he spent some time with her and their family and then returned to Neepawa. As with so many of these men, for twenty years life was lived transnationally, and Frankie drew on the support of friends within his Chinese and non-Chinese Manitoba community. He periodically returned home to see his wife and growing family, who finally joined him in 1949, two years after the repeal of the Chinese Immigration Act.

Together with Bill Toy, Frankie Lee bought the Royal Cafe and the Paris Cafe, both of which had been operated by his uncle Ling Lee. In 1950, the Paris Cafe changed its name to the Bamboo Restaurant. Several years later, Frankie Lee went into partnership with Dick Lee and Ming Dare to expand it. Meanwhile, Billy Toy ran the Royal Cafe until his retirement. He died in Vancouver in 1974. In 1975, Frankie and his wife retired to Vancouver to be with their children. In 1982, Albert and Sheila Cabildo took over the building that was the Royal Cafe and renamed it Lee's Village Restaurant.

Ming Dare came to Canada in 1950 and moved to Neepawa from Minnedosa in 1964 with his wife Susie and two daughters. In 1965, Dare went into business with Dick Lee and Frank Lee of Neepawa to expand and reopen the Bamboo Restaurant, which still exists today as the Bamboo Garden Restaurant (albeit with different owners). Along with the other owners, Dare was a cook at the Bamboo Restaurant and his wife was a server. Ming Dare and Dick Lee sold the restaurant to Albert Louie and May Louie (nee Toy) in 2002. In 2006, Ming Dare moved to Calgary.

Albert and May Louie now run the Bamboo Garden Restaurant. May is the daughter of Don Toy, who ran the Paris Cafe in Gladstone, Manitoba, and who is distantly related to Sam Toy, who is buried in Neepawa and owned and operated the Paris Cafe between 1917 and 1928, in partnership with the affable Ling Lee. She is also related to Allen and David Choy (who own and operate restaurants in Shoal Lake and Binscarth) and the Newdale and Brandon Choys.

As has been mentioned, unlike Binscarth and many other Prairie towns and villages throughout western Manitoba, Neepawa had not one but two Chinese restaurants. It is a remarkable example of a place in which one extended family controlled the restaurant industry for decades. The legacy of the Lee family is unmistakably positive in this region, where people still remember with admiration the suffering, struggles, and contributions of the area's early Chinese bachelors. Although most of these men have now died and been buried elsewhere, Sam Toy and Fun Lee are buried in the Neepawa cemetery, and, from time to time, incense, candles, and flowers will appear before their graves, having been placed there in private, unseen rituals honouring them as ancestors.

Today, Lee's Village Restaurant is owned and operated by Raymond and Wendy Kwok, who immigrated to Canada in 1990, first living in Montreal, then in Toronto, and finally in Neepawa. Taking over the restaurant in 2006, they were attracted to Neepawa because they believed that its slow pace would enable them to spend more time with their family.

Carberry

Carberry may be the most remarkable area of Chinese settlement in Manitoba. Carberry's bachelors were some of the earliest to self-identify as Confucians and have also been strong KMT supporters and Sun Yat-sen loyalists.

As in Neepawa, several bachelors have resided in Carberry over the last century, but only a few have remained for decades. The first laundry in Carberry was opened in 1891, and, for years after, men came and did not stay long.[51] The 1901 census indicates that Gott Kee (also known as Gott Sing)[52] and his brother Toy Kee resided in Carberry. Compared to other bachelors who were living in the province at the time, these men were young, aged eighteen and twenty-two. However, in other ways they were typical new settlers, being laundrymen and nominal Christians. In February 1910, the two advertised Lee Moon's laundry as offering "first class work guaranteed."[53] Together, the brothers ran the laundry on Third Avenue, having taken over that business from Gott Lee.[54] By 1911, Chinese people in the region, as in other places, were all male and worked not only in the hand-washing business but also as cooks in restaurants and hotels. Brothers Lee Wey and Lee Heng were forty and sixteen years old, respectively, and were the laundrymen in Carberry. On the 1911 census, brothers Bing Tim (also known as Bing Sam) and S. Wow listed their ages as twenty-nine and twenty-six, respectively. They also indicated that they were restaurant operators and Presbyterians.

The 1911 census shows that Carberry's Chinese no longer consisted of all nominal Christians. Cooks Wong Charley and Pip Charley, aged twenty-nine and thirty-five, respectively, stood out because they self-identified as Confucians (something that must have surprised the census taker as the entry shows evidence of having been rewritten at least once). In summary, in 1911 the Carberry Chinese population was six, with four self-identifying as Presbyterian and two self-identifying as Confucian. This important piece of information, which indicates a new category of religious identity, foretold the political and religious history of Manitoba's Chinese population in trending towards a more traditional and hybrid public identity. By 1921, the census showed there were 691 Confucians living in Manitoba and thousands more in every province with a total of over 27,000 throughout Canada.[55]

Over the years, Carberry has had many Chinese-owned-and-operated restaurants. The earliest, called the Royal Restaurant, had been in existence since at least 1907. It was run by Meh How and advertised itself as being "open day and night" and serving "hot meals."[56] Continuing the "royal" theme, Kings Restaurant opened in 1913 and was run by Charles Work and Charlie Kong.[57] In 1913, there was also the Carberry Cafe, which was run by Charles Wong.[58] Ben Town Restaurant emerged two years later and was run by Frank Lee and Charles Yer,[59] while the Brookdale Cafe was run by Wong Lee.[60]

Since the 1920s, Carberry has had a few main Chinese-owned-and-operated restaurants, including the Rex, the Liberty, and today's C.V.M. Cafe. The Rex Cafe was operated by Wing Low (also known as Lowe), Lee Low (also known as Low Kon Lee, Lau Kong Lee, and Lee Lowe) (1896-58), and others. Wing Low came to Carberry in late March 1920 to run the restaurant. The opening was announced in the local news section of the 1 April 1920 edition of the local paper: "A Chinese restaurant was opened in town last week."[61] A welcoming community, such as those that helped Woo Tom and Lee Ling integrate into Baldur and Neepawa, respectively, in the previous decade, was not available to Wing Low. The earlier restaurant had attracted the ire of Carberry newspapers and the community, and Wing Low would have to overcome this if he were to stay and become accepted. The opening of the restaurant caused the editors of the *Carberry News Express* to reflect on what had happened the last time the town had a Chinese restaurant. They were presumably referring to the Ben Town Restaurant that had been around in 1915. Young boys had been seen loitering at the restaurant, which some referred to as a "joint," and spending their "Sunday School" money there. One man in Carberry repeatedly tried to get the police to intervene and close the restaurant. However, the police did nothing, and "the public got wise to the conditions and the Celestial was forced to close for lack of business."[62] The article went on to caution Wing Low, noting that a similar set of circumstances to that found at the Ben Town had been observed at the Rex in the previous week, when it had opened:

> The same thing will occur with the new restaurant if conditions we saw on Sunday last are allowed to continue. At one time during the afternoon no fewer than eleven boys were sitting around, boys from good homes who should either have been at home or out enjoying the bright sunshine. If we must have a Chinese restaurant it is up to the authorities to see that it is conducted according to law.[63]

The article contains the unmistakable inference that a "Celestial" restaurateur was no different from a Chinese laundryman, who was a "dirty heathen." Sundays were to be spent at church, at home, or in the "bright sunshine": they were not to be wasted indulging in the moral turpitude of foreign environments. "Boys from good homes" were at risk. While the opening of Wing Low's restaurant was met with fear and uncertainty, the issue was not revisited in future editions of the newspaper. In the 1920s (and following the First World War), one begins to see such attitudes change as newcomers who adopted the way of the bachelor were gradually accepted in Manitoba.

Wing Low tried hard to fit in and gain the respect and business of the community. By this time, Carberry had had Chinese men living in it on and off for almost three decades. Most small communities welcomed the addition of a Chinese restaurant, and it is difficult to imagine that the majority of Carberry's residents felt differently. Like other Chinese men, Wing Low became a nominal Christian and contributed to fundraising efforts organized by the dominant society. He bought weekly advertising space for his Rex Cafe in the *Carberry News Express.* Week after week the ads read: "Rex Cafe. The New Stand Now Open. We solicit all the farming trade. Hot Meals Served At All Hours. Ice Cream and Soft Drinks, Confectionery and Fresh Fruits. A Full Line At All Times."[64] The advertisements noted that, like other restaurants in western Manitoba, in the winter months the Rex Cafe served cosmopolitan foods such as "fresh oysters in season." On 6 May 1920, Wing Low joined with other local businesspeople and agreed to close his restaurant on Thursday afternoons throughout the summer.[65] But he was getting to be an old man, and shortly after he arrived in Carberry he contacted his younger cousin Lee Low. Lee Low was born in China in 1896 and immigrated to Canada in 1911, when he was fifteen. Like George Chong and Buddy Leeds, Lee Low was also born in the District of Sun Ning (or Toisan).[66]

Lee Low worked in Victoria until 1920, when his cousin Wing Low wrote and told him that he should move to Carberry and run the restaurant. He thought that was a "good deal," and so he came that year.[67] After apprenticing with Wing Low for two years, Lee became the new proprietor of the Rex Cafe in February 1922.[68] Unlike the others who worked in Carberry over the years, and who were Methodist, Presbyterian, and/or Confucian, Lee Low was publicly nominally Christian and privately Buddhist.[69] Over the years he made many changes to the cafe. In 1928, he installed booths, and a year later he expanded the property to include a corner store.[70] Although there was no announcement in the paper about its new proprietor, the advertisements did change and now read: "Rex Cafe. High-Class. We solicit all the farmer's trade. Hot meals served at all hours. Ice Cream and Soft Drinks, Confectionery and Fresh Fruits. Full line at all times. Tobacco and Cigars."[71] People recalled Lee Low with fondness. He was a bright,

FIGURE 19　Christmas Card with Lee Low and Family, 1949.
Family.　L to R:　Tong, York, Lee and Walter.
Source: Family of Lee Low

warm, kind, and thoughtful man with a broad smile, who, not surprisingly, had many friends. They remember much less about his brother George (also known as Tong), who worked at the Rex but kept a low profile.

Lee Low's restaurant was the hub of the community for almost thirty years, from 1922 until 1950. Towards the end of his time in Carberry in 1949, his two sons, Walter and York, joined him.

Work was the dominant activity in their lives, but there were outings too, including one to the Brandon Fair the year the boys arrived. Buddy Leeds, the affable elder mentioned at the beginning of this chapter, arrived one afternoon with his car to pick up the boys, their father, and their uncle. He then drove the group to the Brandon Fair and back. Although Low's friendship with Leeds is proof that he was well connected, and possibly even a KMT member during the decades he lived in the province, neither homosocial relationships nor the KMT community was enough for the family once Lee was reunited with his boys. For Lee Low, the lure of Chinatown was too great. He knew that a larger Chinese community could offer the language and cultural education that the small town of Carberry could not, and so they left, moving to Vernon, British Columbia. Lee Low was finally able to sponsor his wife to come to Canada in 1957. However, the decades of hard work in the Carberry restaurant took a toll on his health. One year later, he died.

In the spring of 2006, Walter Low, accompanied by his wife and son, returned to Carberry to visit with Minnie Oliver, who had spent ten happy years working for his father. For a week, the Low family reminisced with Minnie and her children about the decades that Lee Low had spent in Carberry. Minnie, who had worked for Lee Low in her youth, had become part of his once divided family. She was older than Walter, but, after the visit, the two became like siblings. Walter called Minnie every month; when she got sick, he called more often. Minnie died on 6 May 2009. The last three years of her life were made considerably brighter by the discovery of her "brother" and his family.

The C.V.M. Cafe opened during the mid-1940s and was initially operated by two non-Chinese men named M.P.H. Menlove and W.H. Vopni.[72] The current owner, Kwan Yuen, has been the operator of the cafe for over four decades, and, like others here, he emigrated from Hong Kong. He serves a range of Chinese Canadian food and more traditional dishes. When I interview restaurant owners, I always request "mapo doufu," which is a spicy tofu dish said to have been Deng Xiaoping's favourite. It is not a southern Chinese dish, but it is very commonly served on the Prairies. It is a good sign if a restaurant owner has some traditional ingredients – like tofu, fresh garlic, and fresh ginger – in his kitchen that he uses for his own meals. Often, and here, it is served to me with gailan, or Chinese broccoli. A scan of the wood panelling on the walls of Yuen's restaurant reveals few decorations, except for one intriguing picture. This decoration shows that Yuen's loyalties are not to Deng Xiaoping and the CCP but, rather, to the KMT and the party that lost to the CCP almost sixty years ago. On one of the walls hangs

FIGURE 20 Sun Yat-sen on western Manitoba restaurant wall.
Source: Alison Marshall

a portrait of Sun Yat-sen, with the words "President of China, January to April 1912" (although he was only provisional leader for a few months in 1912).[73] The picture was bequeathed to Yuen in the will of a KMT old-timer who died decades ago. Included just below the picture are the characters of Sun Yat-sen's will. The will became a key Nationalist document with religious status that encouraged men to keep striving to implement the three principles of livelihood, nationalism, and democracy. The will was read at picnics and KMT meetings, and it decorated Manitoba's Chinese Patriotic League letterhead from 1937 until the end of the Second Sino-Japanese War. This powerful sign of patriotism was given religious significance by the addition of a bell and decorative embroidery and a piece of red string – a good-luck ritual object displayed to the right of the picture.

Chinese-owned-and-operated restaurants in Brandon and in rural communities throughout western Manitoba have been around for more than one hundred years, providing hubs where men and (later) their families could gather during the New Year and on other occasions. Beyond enabling these private manifestations of lived religious behaviours, restaurants facilitated Chinese immigration to the Prairies, initially through chain migration and "paper sons." After 1947, the arrival of wives and children brought richness and depth to customs and traditions that had been started decades earlier by the KMT and other clan associations. But this changed Chinese demographic also meant the end to what was once a relatively stable phenomenon on the Prairies. Although the single men had been anchored by the memory and vision of Sun Yat-sen and the KMT, the social heat that these political and other Christian gatherings provided was not enough for their families. Some wives and children yearned for more than small communities could offer, and the pull towards larger communities, with Chinatowns and other ethnic services, was too great. While rural Manitoba still has many Chinese restaurants, there are far fewer than there used to be.

To those on the periphery of restaurant life, the fact that, for decades, it had served as an ethnic hub for Chinese men went almost entirely unnoticed. The white children (now elderly adults) and their parents were, in part, blinded by the exoticism of the place and the magical confections and modern foods it offered. But, in any case, they never had more than a front-stage view of the "Chinaman," who made certain that he controlled their impressions of him. In public, he lived ambiguously as a Christian; in private, he lived more traditionally as Chinese. This was necessitated due to the significant obstacles created by institutionalized racism. These men wanted nothing more than to be socially accepted, to form relationships, and to have their wives and children join them in Canada. In order to do this, it was clear that they had to be very deft in managing what was appropriate for the front stage and what had to be relegated to the back stage. Their hard work provided the foundation for, and the pattern of, the assimilation that later generations built on and followed in order to prosper. All of their efforts were for the later generations, for their children and grandchildren. As one research participant noted:

Despite the hardships and rampant discrimination the Chinese still appreciated the opportunity to be here. They stayed because of their children. They worked hard and believed in the future of their children. Through their children they worked. They were not any different than other ethnic groups. They were very tolerant and passive. The nature of their culture was more accepting and hopeful.

Through the ambiguous and global identity of their appearance, culture, and cuisine, bachelors sought to break down barriers and to become accepted by the dominant society. In this chapter, I have indicated how the men, their foods, and their restaurants became part of a treasured past; in the next chapter, I examine the relationship between Chinese food, integration, and identity.

4
Chinese Food and Identity

Throughout the twentieth century, whether you lived in Carberry, Neepawa, or Brandon, you could go out for Chinese Canadian food. Rural cafe owners, although they were initially opposed by church groups, white businessmen, and parents were widely appreciated during the First World War for providing spaces where Chinese and non-Chinese could gather. Cafes would be open from first thing in the morning until the hockey game or local dance ended late at night. Out of the cafe and people's interactions with it evolved important everyday food practices and a cosmopolitan culture.

In the Introduction, I remark on the significance of the "doing" of food in creating events, community, and religiosity. In my research, I initially focused on questions about religious beliefs and customs, but this was a failure as it merely produced the answers that people thought I wanted to hear. It also elicited strange looks and puzzled faces as research participants struggled to figure out why I was interested in traditional religions like Buddhism and Daoism in a place where there were obviously no native temples and never had been. Over time, I learned the shortcomings of focusing on "isms" in a place where identities were characterized by ambiguity, porous boundaries, and overlapping relationships. For this group of people, living in isolation from larger centres (which contained traditional Chinese religious institutions and Chinatowns), everyday religiosity was ambiguous (as opposed to being defined by one religious identity). When I restructured my data collection methods to focus on what people ate and where, I discovered the heritage of everyday lived religion on the Prairies as well as the centrality of restaurants. People opened up when I asked about food.

Early rural immigrants were resilient men who lived difficult lives and endured years of racism. Life was especially hard during those years when they operated laundries, which offered excellent quality service at very cheap prices. But the dominant community considered laundries to be dirty places where many men worked, ate, slept, and sometimes smoked opium in the back. With laundries, customers were generally able to see into the back; with restaurants, they were not. With restaurants, men lived upstairs, and dining rooms were clean and inviting spaces, where customers interacted with English-speaking European (often Ukrainian) servers while the Chinese owner and cook worked behind the scenes. The food that came out of the kitchen seemed to come from another world, located neither entirely in the customer's own European culture nor in the bachelor's domain. Food was hybrid. Canadianized Chinese dishes like sweet and sour chicken balls and deep-fried shrimp were ordinary foods that had been prepared in Chinese styles and had sweet southern Chinese-inspired flavours. These new Canadianized Chinese dishes and Western staples like steaks and eggs enabled bachelors to overcome the obstacles of race and culture. Food ideas and customs linked Chinese men to Canada and to China. This strand in the way of the bachelor was influenced by ambiguity and the geo-political developments of the day.

The Wuchang Uprising of 10 October 1911 (now known as Nationalist Day, or Double Tenth Day) led to the Xinhai Revolution and the collapse of the Qing dynasty. It also led to the emergence of KMT offices and political and banking networks to facilitate the flow of donations from Canada to China the following year. While KMT offices provided places for men to congregate, functioning as extensions of their nation, they also helped to root the bachelors in communities and to create hybrid customs. Also influencing integration were the First and Second world wars, which inspired everyone, including new settlers, to contribute, thereby demonstrating a commitment to Canadian citizenship. And Chinese Canadian restaurants offered food that, throughout western Manitoba and the rest of Canada, made them popular places in which to dine. This was the welcoming public identity of the restaurant.

Lily Cho writes about the remarkable agency of the Chinese cafe, which serves food that has become standard fare in Canada's rural areas.[1] Over and over again, it has been noted that, across the Prairies, Chinese Canadian restaurants offer reliable meals. I hear this sentiment echoed by research participants who relish their childhood memories of the signature foods and the men who prepared them. Although customers moved away, when they returned for a visit, bachelors recalled whether they liked ginger beef or chow mein. The bachelor remembered his customers' tastes and identified those who patronized his restaurant through the foods they enjoyed eating. Food created positive and sustaining relationships and memories that stayed with people as they moved away from the places where they had first eaten it.

Chinese Canadian foods represented aggregate modern identities and cultures. Steve Penfold, in his discussion of the effect of Tim Hortons on Canadian culture, makes a similar observation about that franchise, which offers "a kind of folklore of mass culture where commodities are used to express important, if ironic, interpretations of national and local identity."[2] Both Tim Hortons donuts and the food items discussed in this chapter are comforting nostalgic commodities linking generations to mass Canadian culture. Chinese Canadian food reminds people of the place and time of their childhood, much as Jell-O brings back the popular culture of 1960s North America.[3] The fusion of Canadian and Chinese food happened long ago and reflects a long history of transnationalism and adaptation.[4] The many actions associated with the consumption and preparation of food have created overlapping Chinese and non-Chinese identities and histories throughout Manitoba. For both the bachelors and non-Chinese settlers, food made them Canadian and helped them to maintain connections to homeland traditions and customs.

The Chinese cafe is a complex space representing the intersection and flow of multiple cultures, commodities, and identities. While it and its owner are often regarded individually as isolated, disconnected entities, they are imbricated in a network of Chinese and non-Chinese global relationships. As Sylvia Ferraro comments:

> When we go to a Chinese restaurant in Chinatown ... we enjoy the flavor and taste of Chinese food but do not think of the intricate social connections that are behind Chinese restaurants in any Chinatown around the world. For instance, we do not think that the renown of Chinese food in transnational contexts can be reason enough for Chinese of diverse origins ... to try to settle down with a Chinese restaurant business overseas.[5]

If connections were important in Chinatowns where hundreds of Chinese bachelors lived in close proximity to one another, they were even more important in rural areas like western Manitoba, where bachelors (and everyone else) lived far apart and needed to find social heat. Cafes were a business the bachelors could operate and a place where people could get together. Through the food they offered, the restaurants provided a way for people to transcend the boundaries of gender, race, class, religion, and nation. These cafes provided for the everyday needs of ordinary working people. Tastes may have differed, but early settlers had to eat, regardless of whether they were Chinese or non-Chinese. When a bachelor served food to members of the dominant society he was nourishing customers, influencing their palates, and joining together various groups of people who liked the sweet and soothing tastes of his food. He was also providing a means for rural people to become familiar with modern commodities and to associate him with the cafe's food and novel culture (as opposed to the handwashing and filth associated with the laundry business). Food was creating boundaries and identities, but it was also dissolving them in ways that were beneficial to the rural bachelor. He was not just supplying food to his customers: he was taking care of them. Over time, serving food to repeat customers became a strategy to create and maintain relationships and to gain the respect of mainstream society. At the core of these practices was the idea that consumption and related acts constructed identity. Like his food, the bachelor's identity was hybrid and global. Even Sun Yat-sen had noticed the ubiquity of Chinese food in North America:

> The popularity of Chinese food has spread rapidly in recent years to foreign countries where Chinese traders have set foot. In New York City alone there are several hundred Chinese restaurants. Almost every city in the United States can boast of at least one Chinese restaurant. The whole American nation has a craze for Chinese dishes.[6]

By the 1950s, almost every village, town, and city on the Prairies had a Chinese cafe, and the appeal was widespread throughout North America.

Even though settlers likely had no experience as chefs, necessity and networks of friends who were doing the same thing gave them expertise. After a town council meeting in Minnedosa in January 1908, the mayor took the councillors out for an "oyster supper" at the local restaurant.[7] On 23 December 1916, the Rex Cafe (and presumably Sam Wong, who was then working there) produced what must have been (even by today's standards) a very expensive Christmas meal. The starter included soup (either cream of oyster à la reine or consommé printanière royale). There were appetizers such as stuffed olives, salted almonds, and celery en branche. For the entrée there was a choice of fish (BC salmon or Manitoba white fish), boiled meats such as leg of lamb with caper sauce or ham, and roasted fare such as beef and sweetbreads, roast prime rib, turkey, goose, and duck. There were two salads from which to choose: Waldorf salad or hearts of lettuce with tomatoes française. And, finally, there were desserts, ranging from plum pudding with traditional hard sauce, to fruit Ireland pudding, to apple, pumpkin, or hot mince pie and assorted cakes, fruits, and cheeses. The meal could be finished off with coffee or tea (black or Chinese green tea).[8] As one might expect, this grand feast was rare, but I want to show the extent to which bachelors tried to learn the cuisine of their new nation and predominantly white European patrons. Ordinary occasions, of course, warranted simpler fare, such as steak and potatoes, hamburgers, eggs, salads, sandwiches, fish and chips, or just a cup of hot coffee.

Today, restaurants continue to offer their patrons favourite dishes that are often deep-fried (shrimp) and sweet and salty. Most Manitoban Chinese restaurants offer spicy mapo doufu as well; but in smaller rural areas it is not listed on the menu (because regular patrons don't order it), and you have to ask the server about it. Adhering to the expected "tastes" of customers means that those customers will come back week after week. Offer something too spicy, "oniony," or with hints of a strange seasoning and they might not return. None of the restaurant owners I interviewed said that they served their customers the food that they themselves ate every day and during festivals. When I asked why, the general response was that they knew that their customers would not like it. Like the bachelors before them, these cafe owners knew their customers through their tastes. A typical special throughout the Prairies includes a mixture of fried dishes liberally flavoured with sugar and soya sauce: chicken rice, sweet and sour chicken balls, spring rolls, and consommé, with a set price that ranges from as low as $4.99 to as much as ten dollars.

Since the Chinese restaurant's early days in 1904, owners and operators have aimed to please their customers and to be accepted by the dominant society. Many used newspapers to advertise their desire to keep their "permanent patrons," who like to "dine away from home," happy by offering them intimate and pleasant environments, expected foods, and proper service at affordable prices. As mentioned, several Chinese restaurants in Manitoba organized free evenings for soldiers during the First and Second world wars. On 2 January 1917, Fong Song, manager of the early Rex Cafe, advertised a celebratory dinner for all returning soldiers: "The Rex Cafe is entertaining all the returned soldiers in this city and district at a dinner at 7:30 on Friday Evening."[9] This generosity was also shown by others in the region, including Neepawa's Ling Lee and Brandon's Sam Wong (see Chapter 3).

Chinese Canadian restaurants became increasingly popular in the 1950s and 1960s. As one research participant commented:

Workmen came in from the country [and] would sit at the counter by themselves and eat lunch. It wasn't a place where people, if they were used to going there for lunch, would eat dinner. High school kids and so on would come in. But it wasn't a place where you would say, "Let's go out to dinner." Once they started to serve some Chinese food, that brought people in.

At this time, customers went out more and restaurants reciprocated with "new" items to draw them back, such as chop suey, chow mein, egg foo young, fried rice in a variety of styles (with chicken, mushroom, pork, beef, or shrimp), with plum and soya sauce as condiments, and fortune cookies at the end of the meal (to add something even more exotic). Restaurants serving Chinese Canadian food in contrived Chinese settings became common throughout North America in the 1950s and 1960s, thereby providing a way for immigrants to overcome negative stereotypes.[10] Some of the pioneers of this trend of offering hybrid food and decor included Brandon's Buddy Leeds, Newdale's Choy family, and Neepawa's Frankie Lee. These and other restaurateurs updated earlier methods employed by Chinese settlers to overcome the social and economic obstacles of racism and to "conquer the world." By the 1960s, the Chinese Immigration Act had been repealed and many bachelors now lived with their wives and (sometimes) daughters, sons, and mothers. Their restaurants were no longer all-male domains, being animated by family and friends.

During the 1960s, bachelors followed some of the earliest patterns of integration as well as new ones, which accentuated the Chinese identity of their business. Laundrymen had been able to communicate with their customers in broken English, but they still used the Chinese laundry ticket to keep track of customer orders because it added a foreign and exotic dimension to the business. Most Chinese cafes served Canadian items like steak, fries, burgers, toast, and coffee. On some level, though, proprietors realized that customers wanted to see more of the Chinese character of the restaurant. They didn't necessarily want to go into the kitchen to see what the cooks were doing, but they did want to see what they imagined would be part of the back-stage life of the restaurant. To present more of this private identity to their customers, Chinese owners decorated their restaurants with Chinese characters, dragons, and other fragments of imagined culture in order to create a more authentic experience. Tulasi Srinivas refers to this experience as "adventure tourism":

The adventure tourism image is expected to be echoed in mood, lighting, decor and ambience of the restaurant to create the feeling of adventure. Restaurants are critiqued favourably if they expend time and attention on creating a "complete" atmosphere of the adventure to a strange and distant land."[11]

Now bachelors were encouraging customers to consume edible commodities and to buy Chinese items from the glass cabinets beneath the cash register. They were commodifying Chinese thought, culture, and identity, and they were also making restaurant experiences more exciting and exotic. As Simon Bronner writes:

[Folk art] is a thinly veiled commodity – a commodity not necessarily, although often, to make money, but one to offer or suggest excitement, reality, and taste for a distinct social world. It is a cultural statement by its owners rather than its makers.[12]

The affable Buddy Leeds was one of the region's earliest promoters of the new foods and a 1960s Chinese identity. When his restaurant, the Leichee Garden and Coffee Bar, opened on Thursday, 23 July 1964, it announced its Oriental(ist) design and food:

Manager of the restaurant Buddy Leeds explained that this will be the first café in the area to specialize in Chinese cuisine. Other spots have, of course, served Oriental dishes, but Leichee Gardens will feature them ... Customers will also be attracted to the smart interior design of the Garden, centred around an Oriental motif, with wood panelling and Chinese lanterns. The restaurant, Mr. Leeds says, is following the popular trend of more interest in Oriental food and customs.[13]

Demonstrating economic, social, and cultural connections that extended beyond its own ethnic community, Leeds's new restaurant attracted many local businesses to buy advertising space in the newspaper that day. Relf Plumbing and Heating Ltd., G.T. Smith and Sons Ltd. Licensed Electrical Contractors, and the Williams Restaurant Supply Ltd. in Winnipeg all wished him well in his new business venture. Leeds had strong economic, political, and social networks that enabled him to succeed in Chinese and non-Chinese circles. Not one to remain in a business venture very long, ten years later he was president of a group of men who owned and operated the Kam Lung Restaurant. This new enterprise had an auspicious Chinese name, Kam Lung, or *jinlong,* meaning Golden Dragon. It was also designed to emphasize a "Chinese atmosphere."[14]

For elderly research participants who grew up with a restaurant in their rural town or village, it was not the Chinese Canadian food – chop suey, chow mein, egg foo young, fried rice, hamburgers – or even the decor that they recalled. Their memories focused instead on the adventure involved in going to the cafe to see the Chinese man who had the candy. Some of the bachelors, kept from their own families by racist immigration laws, must have relished the moments when children came to them for candy. And, when the bachelor packed an order of food for delivery, he never forgot the children. As Gerald Friesen comments, "he always put a bag of candy for the children with an order."[15] One elderly woman who grew up in many towns and villages throughout southwestern Manitoba and Saskatchewan remarked:

> I am too young to remember much about the Chinese cafe but I do know that the community welcomed the Chinese owner and his wife. I do remember my dad buying us huge ice cream cones there and Cadbury's Caramel chocolate bar, which is still my favourite today. Although I was very young I have vivid memories of Lyleton, Pierson, and North Antler. Lyleton was always small but, like many small towns, had a great spirit. I lived in at least five if not more Manitoba towns during the 1930s and I recall a Chinese grocery or restaurant in all of them.

Other people shared this woman's view, recalling the broken pan taffy, crystallized gum drops, and, of course, the chocolate bars and the homemade ice cream and pies that could be purchased and eaten at the cafe. Some of the material we found went further, indicating that the men were not only selling candy but also manufacturing it. For instance, in Carberry, the local newspaper ran an article on the "Chineseness" of this skill:

> The Chinese are very skilful in making confectionery. They are able to empty an orange of its pulp entirely and then fill it up with fruit jelly without one being able to find the smallest cut in the rind, or even a tiny hole. Indeed, they even empty an egg in this manner and fill it with a sort of almond nougat without one being able to find the slightest break or incision in the shell.[16]

A visit to the Chinese restaurant was a decadent experience, and, when small children grew into young teenagers, they used all of their allowance for visits to the cafe. One research participant commented: "In Oak Lake I had twenty-five cents a week to spend and would go to the restaurant to have a cherry sundae and drink – I would blow the money all at once there." For many elderly Manitobans, a visit to the Chinese restaurant was their one extravagance in an otherwise modest Prairie day. And, because they offered this kind of excitement to rural children, the restaurant owners became revered grandfather-like figures to an entire generation of people – people who still favour this kind of restaurant. Although seniors still eat in Chinese restaurants today, they now order the chow mein and deep-fried shrimp and sample other items in the buffet/smorgasbord.

While candy and ice cream drew an entire generation of people to the cafe, for Ukrainian Manitobans, eating Chinese food was tied to a shared history of migration, employment, and intermarriage. Some young Ukrainian girls who ran away from home, or finished school early, went to work as servers in the local restaurant or the one in Brandon. A research participant commented:

Probably the connection started [when] the [Ukrainian] girls would have a hard time getting a job. But they could often get a job at a Chinese restaurant and serve food there. That is how [Chinese and Ukrainians] became associated and later married.

I found no evidence of sexual or other kinds of abuse to support the earlier bylaw banning Chinese men from hiring white women. However, I did encounter several Ukrainian women who had met and married their husbands through their work at a cafe. Reflecting the close connection between the two communities, when there was a high Ukrainian population there was usually a proportionately high number of Chinese restaurants (e.g., Dauphin had a population of 8,085 and three Chinese restaurants). Today, some Ukrainians include spring rolls in their New Year's celebrations, but when they are asked why, they are not sure. Still, this is one example of how Chinese Canadian food became part of local customs.

Since the early days of settlement on the Prairies, Chinese and Ukrainians have shared an underclass status, running laundries, working in restaurants, and intermarrying. Frequenting a Chinese restaurant elevated the status of the Ukrainian immigrant in much the same way as it elevated the status of New York Jews. Gaye Tuchman and Harry Gene Levine explain:

New York Jews have found in Chinese restaurant food a flexible open-ended symbol, a kind of blank screen on which they have projected a series of themes relating to their identity as modern Jews and as New Yorkers. These themes were not inherent in the food itself, nor did they arise from Chinese Americans' view of their own cuisine. Rather, Jewish New Yorkers (and, to some extent, other Americans as well) linked these cultural issues with eating in Chinese restaurants.[17]

Ukrainians in Manitoba, like Jews in New York, adopted Chinese restaurants as their own. Hanna Miller describes the fascination: "'Eating Chinese' has become a ritualized element of the ongoing acculturation process that affirms traditional values while embracing new ones."[18] Although the population had always been small in rural Manitoba, most towns had a Jewish merchant and a Chinese cafe. As Gerald Friesen observes:

> Jews began to arrive in numbers in western Canada as a direct result of pogroms in tsarist Russia in the early 1880s ... They gathered in Winnipeg, where employment could be obtained, friends of one's faith found, and a religious congregation established, but they were also to be found in the rural west, both in agricultural colonies such as those near Wapella, Hirsch, Cupar, Lipton, and Sonnenfeld in Saskatchewan; Rumsey, Alberta; and Bender Hamlet, Manitoba; and in the little towns of the agricultural region where the Jewish general store – at one time there were over 100 in Manitoba – was as common as the Chinese café.[19]

To these merchants, eating Chinese food was a custom that started early in their lives and that continues today, with weekly meals. Like the elderly residents of cities, towns, and villages throughout Manitoba, Ukrainians and Jews feel like they are at home, in a place that brings back happy memories, when they eat in Chinese restaurants. Christmas and other Christian religious holidays are marked by many Jews in rural and urban locales by a meal at the family's favourite Chinese restaurant; in Brandon, usually Kam Lung, and in Winnipeg, the Shanghai. For some, Yom Kippur (during which Jews should be fasting and praying) and other Jewish festivals are similarly observed with a non-kosher meal at a Chinese Canadian restaurant. These have traditionally been places where Jews can establish their own social heat and build relationships that extend outside of Winnipeg's large community. Food, as Carolyn Daniel writes, is about more than eating:

> Whatever the occasion, food is never just something to eat. Even when it is mundane and everyday it carries meaning. Food events are always

significant, in reality as well as in fiction; they can reveal fundamental pre-occupations, ideas, and beliefs of society.[20]

Restaurants and the food offered at them provide opportunities for people to gather and eat with others. As long as you can pay (and wear shoes and a shirt!) you are welcome to eat at a Chinese restaurant. Seen from one perspective, Chinese cafes and their owners had agency because they provided commodities at reasonable prices and had little competition. Yet, the success of bachelors who became cafe owners was due to much more than economics. I think that the success began with food and the way in which food breaks down barriers between people. People who share a meal are doing something that is both ordinary and universal. Everyone has to eat. And in order to eat something, you usually have to come into contact with someone who provides one or more of the ingredients, makes the food, or serves it. Very few people are entirely self-reliant when it comes to eating. Food, then, requires relationships. Men like Sam Wong, Buddy Leeds, Sam Dong, and Lee Low thrived in relatively isolated areas of the eastern Prairies because they had strong relationships with the people who inhabited local, provincial, national, and sometimes international Chinese and non-Chinese communities. There were three stages of integration. First, these relationships concerned the everyday needs of bachelors who had to find distributors to supply the cafe's food and be welcomed into networks. Second, over time, relationships expanded beyond the everyday economic ones as the bachelors became accepted and took on identities that overlapped with cultural, social, political, and (sometimes) religious ones. Cafes facilitated the building of bridges in and between communities, and they were used by Ukrainian and other communities to serve the same purposes. Third, as this happened, the identities of bachelors and cafes were animated and maintained by relationships that enabled them to become accepted and even embraced by the dominant society.[21]

Chinese Food and Identity

Just as there are diverse ways of being Chinese, so there are diverse ways of eating. What people eat and where they eat it creates boundaries, such as the one around the Jewish and Ukrainian communities described above and also around Chinese and Ukrainian mixed families. What and where you eat signals degrees of taste and ethnic belonging. Joining that group takes time, as does changing from being perceived as a stranger to being someone who is welcomed into the back regions of cafes and other domains that characterize private life. Food is about relationships. Emiko Ohnuki-Tierney puts it well:

> Food tells not only how people live but also how they think of themselves in relation to others. A people's cuisine, or a particular food, often marks the boundary between the collective self and the other, for example, as a basis of discrimination against other peoples.[22]

While Ohnuki-Tierney emphasizes how taste discriminates, we can also extend her comments to show how recipes or menus that combine elements from two cultures create bridges between those two cultures when the foods are eaten and shared. The "doing" of "authentic" food is amplified when it is produced, eaten, and shared in rural Manitoban settings, where there are usually only a few Chinese people.[23] That hundreds and sometimes thousands of people went to one place to prepare, serve, and eat authentic meals demonstrates the creative power of such gatherings. Events like the annual Decoration Day created social heat and, thus, became significant anchors to a shared past.[24] Food – the way it looks, smells, and tastes – mediates memory, connecting people to earlier places and times. Elderly non-Chinese settlers remember the cafe owners' candy. Chinese Canadian settlers remember the Orange Crush and crispy pork served on Decoration Day. Chinese and Chinese Ukrainian Canadians remember the foods of their homeland through their mothers' recipes for latkes, roast duck, roast pork, and southern Chinese stir-fried beef.

In addition to its strong emotional power, authentic Chinese food is economically valuable. Some people travel long distances to obtain the ingredients to make such food; others have family members who bring the ingredients back from visits to China.[25] People also often drive a half hour or more (which is considered to be quite a long time in rural communities) to privately consume authentic food or to attend community events at which it is served. The way one eats such food is also instructive. Newer immigrants consume rice a couple of times a day, use chopsticks at every meal, and, if they drink anything, it is usually a kind of Chinese soup, or tea.

The production of food on the Canadian Prairies is dynamic and requires sharing, as does *ling*, or efficacy, a concept I introduced at the beginning of this book. Efficacy undergirds all forms of everyday religious interaction and links people to each other as well as to ancestors, gods, and the spirit world.[26] In traditional religious practice, *ling* is believed to be transferred from person to person and from place to place during overtly religious events such as processions, ceremonies, and festivals. In these contexts, the transfer of *ling* (fenxiang) happens through the passing of a smaller deity's image along a route that leads to the larger deity at the main temple. As each person and place along the way encounters the deity, pathways uniting distant and originating entities are created. In the same way, the doing of food is dynamic and is constantly creating connections between people and places. Food and the events at which it is consumed vary. Sometimes events are overtly religious, requiring food offerings to establish vertical connections to a deity or ancestors; other times events simply establish horizontal connections between people and to the western Manitoba landscape. It is not difficult to see some similarities among religious practice, efficacy, and food. Meals and food offerings provide opportunities for families and friends to congregate, creating social heat. These group activities draw together both the living and the dead, and they create and sustain social and religious relationships. Timothy C. Lloyd explains the connection between foodways and the supernatural:

> The engagements with the supernatural I will discuss have to do with foodways: not simple recipes, but different aspects of the entire cycle of food generation, production, preparation, and consumption. Foodways are important in our connections with the supernatural because the food cycle itself – from seed to table and onward – is one of the very most fundamental sets of natural and social patterns, and is interlaced with others like it. In fact, neither of the examples here is focussed on cooking technique – which is usually conceived as the centerpiece of food activity – precisely because I want to show how significant the supposedly "peripheral" aspects of the food cycle are.[27]

Lloyd's comments remind us of the mundane quality of food that grows from a seed and comes to the table in various forms. But when the many acts that go into producing food and putting on events are understood together, the aggregate is far from mundane. The doing of food – from growing, harvesting, preparing, to serving – connects people and creates new traditions for the new worlds and lives that diaspora people inhabit. It connects them to the traditions of their homeland, memories,[28] and to the land where the food was grown. In these significant ways, foodways functions like *ling*.[29] But we can't forget that the chain of actions needed to produce and consume food requires people to come together. This process and the relationships and social heat manufactured through it transform the group into one community that meets human needs.

Privately, food was also valuable not only for sustaining the bachelor over the long cold winters but also for nourishing him when he attended or produced events at which meat and other calorie-rich foods (ordinarily too expensive to be eaten) were consumed. On the evening before the New Year, men would gather together and share a sumptuous banquet, thereby demonstrating the power of commensality. Emiko Ohnuki-Tierney remarks on this power during the Japanese rice-sharing rituals:

> These rituals also embody the single most important social role of rice – its use as food for commensality at both a cosmic level between deities and humans ... and among the folk ... In fact, the symbolic power of rice derives to a large degree from the day-to-day sharing of rice among the members of a social group and its uses in the discourse.[30]

But food also requires people to acknowledge its source and, in so doing, to become rooted there. Buddy Leeds's annual duck-hunting trips not only connected him to Manitoba parks but also to the white people with whom he hunted and the Chinese people who tasted that duck (an important meat) at many events, especially those pertaining to the New Year. Leeds was very assimilated for a Chinese man of his time and place: this was because he created relationships not only with people but also with the land (when he hunted) and the water (when he fished). These everyday leisure activities were ritual acts in which he used food to produce a trans-national identity.[31]

Food links people to each other and to the places where it grows. But it also links them to the memories and places from whence they emigrated. Here, I return to the work of Lily Cho, who emphasizes the roles played by nostalgia, collective memory, and food in the creation of diaspora communities: "I suggest that we must think of diasporic community as constituted not in history but in memory."[32] Bachelors constructed the decor of their restaurants based on their memories (or their parents') of traditional culture. When customers became more receptive to Chinese Canadian foods, they reinvented items to suit the diners' idea of what Chinese food should taste like (and, as mentioned, cafe owners remembered their customers by their tastes). Residents who moved away for a number of years before returning to visit the cafe in their home town remembered its Chinese owner in and through the food he served. Memory and food worked together to construct images that were Chinese, non-Chinese, and in-between.

Avtar Brah describes the two ways in which diaspora communities imagine home and identity: first, identity is based on the nation (this is the floating aspect of identity); second, identity (and longing for one's homeland) is rooted in the specific locality from which one emigrated. According to Brah:

> Home is a discourse of locality, the place where feelings of rootedness ensue from the mundane and the unexpected of daily practice. Home here connotes our networks of family, kin, friends, colleagues and various other "significant others." It signifies the social and psychic geography of space that is experienced in terms of a neighbourhood or a home town. That is, a community "imagined" in most part through daily encounter. This "home" is a place with which we remain intimate even in moments of intense alienation from it. It is a sense of "feeling at home."[33]

Chinese cafes scattered throughout the Prairies helped to root Chinese men and to make them feel at home. I was told how Toisanese men received free meals at some rural restaurants because of their shared ethnicity with the owner. The cafes became sites of and connections to home – both the imagined one and the new Chinese Manitoban one. The social and psychic transformations of geographic spaces took place through the doing (the making, serving, sharing, and eating) of food.

Restaurants serving "authentic" Chinese food are chosen to make the cakes for the Moon Festival and to provide items for New Year celebrations. They are also places in which to host major milestones, such as the full-month party for a newborn child or eightieth and one hundredth birthday parties. The menus for these events differ and include things not associated with one's home country. Such events also have a guest list that reflects the different setting. In some cases, only co-ethnics are invited. For newer immigrants, non-Chinese friends and co-workers are invited, along with a small number of close co-ethnics. These events and their foods provide connections to home and reinforce a feeling of community. For new Chinese immigrants today, food continues to play an important role in connecting them to their homeland. One young student from China remarks:

> I really struggle with English and the culture and the dialogue ... And also I cannot forget about the Chinese events and the food, I mean I cannot forget about Chinese people, but I speak English with English people ... It is hard for me because I am an individual, you are by yourself ... so that is why I sometimes feel emptiness in my heart.

The doing of food repositions traditional events within the Prairie landscape. Ingredients for dishes must be obtained, cleaned, seasoned, and prepared with specific cooking utensils. For the many who left China to do migrant work here, food produced and shared during these events reflects their hybrid identity.

If we examine food habits, ethnic restaurants, and events in the history of migration to western Manitoba, we are able to see a long chain of association. But the identity and the customs associated with the cafe are not located in one place. The population is too small for that. They are found among and across family networks that have developed for over a century as people and communities intersected and produced food through village, town, and city nodes. Henry Yu argues for the need to move away from discussing a migration that begins in one place in China and ends in one place in North America; rather, he suggests that we examine migration through locations:

> It would be more interesting to talk about locations, about points between which people move. Getting away from the metaphors of homeland and destination that make America the end of long journeys, this story is about various sites. These places were the central nodes for the production and distribution of knowledge, the founts for creating the forms of consciousness that result from contact.[34]

To understand the nature of food customs and identity we need to consider all the various locations, nodes, and hubs of identity.

At first, it was an all-male community that celebrated events at laundries, at KMT offices (after 1912), and at restaurants. When women and children came over after 1947, visits no longer had KMT politics as their focus. Every week people took turns travelling along the highways to eat meals and to socialize at each other's houses. In the summer, the visiting and social heat became more intense, and people got together at picnics, lakes, and fairs. Co-ethnic children in the region spent most summers playing with each other. One research participant elaborated:

> When I was a kid my dad would take us around the Parkland to visit with others who ran Chinese restaurants. In the summer for six weeks we would do that. We would drop in and say hello, spend most of the day, and have a meal and then go home. That is how all the Chinese in the area got to know each other. When we were growing up all the kids spent the summers together ... Family became the people from the home country.

Food customs in western Manitoba developed through the institutional assistance of clan associations and, most notably after 1912, through the KMT. The 1911 opening of the Winnipeg Chinese Masonic Lodge (a front for the Chinese United League, which would later become the KMT) was marked with a grand traditional Chinese meal. The *Winnipeg Free Press* reported as follows:

> At the conclusion of the celebration many of the members of the [Chinese Masonic] lodge betook themselves to dinner. And a dinner it was. There was Li Tung Chang, extra fine; there was Chow Gui Fan, fried with chicken; there was Ye Foo Yong Dan, which means eggs; Yan Wor Chow Mein, which being interpreted means noodles fried with birds nests; Mi Lee Li Chee nuts; Pow Chong tea, and there were all other dainties dear to the Celestial palate. And it was all done beautifully and to the king's taste.[35]

The variety of foods served at the event represented the complexity of Chinese identity on the Canadian Prairies. The food was complex because the ingredients were hard to obtain, and the dishes were hard to make, hard to explain, and hard to write about in English. From 1911 onward, small-town newspapers showed that men from Baldur, Carberry, Dauphin, and Brandon were travelling to Winnipeg to celebrate the New Year. Although these accounts tell nothing of the KMT as the site of New Year festivities, other archival material recounts the KMT's central role in hosting and organizing such events.

Food was often the focus of how the KMT chose to mark its events and festivities throughout the year. In addition to hosting annual New Year celebrations, the Manitoba KMT held festivities for Double Tenth Day (10 October marks the anniversary of the Wuchang Uprising, which led to the fall of the Qing dynasty) at prominent restaurants in Winnipeg's Chinatown:

> During the war years (1941-45), banquets were given on the Double Tenth National Day in restaurants in Chinatown. These banquets were attended by representatives of the provincial government, the city council, the bench, as well as representatives from the Chinese associations in Winnipeg ... [O]n October 10, 1944, a banquet was given by the Winnipeg Patriotic League, a front organization of KMT at the New Nanking Restaurant. It was a banquet to celebrate the 33rd anniversary of the new Chinese republic.

At the banquet were governmental representatives and guests of honour including Hon. R.F. McWilliams, Lieutenant-governor and Mrs. Williams, and Winnipeg's first Chinese consul, Wen Tao Weng, and his wife. (He was the only Chinese consul ever posted in Winnipeg, established in 1945 and ended in 1950.) The Double Tenth National Day was then such a glittering occasion.[36]

Life was better for some men than it was for others. Those who had a large network of friends and who owned prosperous businesses had the most money and the most active social lives. They had the finances and connections to be able to spend half a day travelling to Winnipeg (by train or by car) for grand banquets and other events. Spring and summer involved visiting with friends at picnics and swimming parties at Clear Lake, Twin Lakes, Lake of the Woods, and other places. Sometimes men went to the movies, fishing in Flin Flon, or hunting for deer, goose, or duck in season. In 1905, the *Boissevain Globe* reported the success of Lee Ming's goose-hunting trip on page one: "Lee Ming, of Treherne, came over to the district for a goose hunt. He intends to camp on the north side of the lake. Lee succeeded in bagging 150 ducks a few days ago near Belmont."[37] In the winter, the men went to hockey games in Brandon and Winnipeg. As one research participant notes, they formed close family bonds:

> Basically, at that time, because the Chinese here have no family, they worked eighteen hours a day, seven days a week. They got together to help one another and play some games and socialize and keep each other company ... There were a couple of houses in the downtown [Brandon] area and most people went there to read the [Chinese] newspaper and do a little gambling and talk to each other. They worked hard and saved as much as they could and then they sent the money home to support the family. It was a very hard life.

Almost one hundred years later, food and the events at which it is served still display the many layers and kinds of contemporary Chinese identity. When the KMT branch office closed and families were reunited after the repeal of the Chinese Immigration Act in 1947, people congregated at Winnipeg's New Nanking and, later, at Chan's Cafe. Today they gather at Kum Koon Garden.

Representative of the tradition of contemporary private food in western Manitoba is a restaurant known for serving Chinese Canadian as well as authentic dishes. Newly arrived immigrants, and the executive of the

Brandon University Chinese Students and Scholars Association, rave about the authenticity of the food served at this restaurant. They try to eat there once a week and organize and host their special events there. The owner's wife will also prepare special foods for different festivals.[38]

Real soya sauce, as opposed to China Lily, sits on the tables of this restaurant. There are three menus from which to choose (not including the unwritten specials offered only to people who ask): two menus are written in English – one for Chinese Canadian and one for authentic Chinese food; and one is written in Chinese. The owner is a bit like Sterling Lung of David Louie's 1991 novel *The Barbarians Are Coming*, who refuses to offer what most people expect to eat at Prairie restaurants.[39] Chinese tea is served in Chinese teapots with Chinese cups. Decorations are limited to historical reproductions of Tang and Song dynasty landscapes, along with Beijing 2008 Olympics curtains that the owner's wife found in China. Some Chinese restaurant owners construct their spaces so that they conform with customer expectations of a Chinese Canadian cafe. This owner has not. He has attempted to distinguish himself from others by combining elements from his own impression of modern China with a traditional impression. For this reason, there are no lanterns, altars, lunar calendars from Manitoba Chinese food distributors, lucky cats, or framed pictures of birds and flowers. The same is true with regard to the food.

When I get to the restaurant I scan the three menus to find the whole yellow fish that is deep fried with scallions and cilantro. This dish has been recommended to me by a friend who is picky about food because her parents used to own and operate a restaurant in a large North American city. I don't find it. I ask the owner if he can make this for me. He can, but he's curious how I heard about the fish. I tell him, and I also ask for green tea, mapo tofu, and gailan. The food arrives and tastes as good and as authentic as anything I have ever eaten in China.

In one of the last interviews I completed for *The Way of the Bachelor*, I met with the family of an early rural restaurant owner over dim sum in Vancouver. It was one of the most memorable interviews among the hundreds I conducted in the writing of this book. This friendly and kind family taught me many things about Chinese culture and food during our hours and conversations together. For instance, they told me that when the teapot at dim sum is poured and you receive a top-up, you tap your finger on the table to indicate thanks. The table was filled with all kinds of wonderful and authentic southern Chinese food. We had braised chicken's feet, pork dumplings, bread dumplings, shrimp dumplings, *joongzi* (packages of bamboo leaves with glutinous rice inside), gailan, tofu skins wrapped up with pork and beef, and other delicious foods. We talked and ate and then talked some more. They said that their favourite dishes were southern Chinese. They said, over and over again, that their family events always centred around food – New Year celebrations, Qingming, and all kinds of gatherings with Chinese and non-Chinese friends and family. But they were not religious.

Post-1947 brought new diaspora female and male roles to Manitoba, and these developed in and through food customs and rituals. Men continued to make the food in restaurants but women now made it in the home and during the festivals. In addition to the events that take place in restaurants, private celebrations also occur in homes above or beside the restaurants. And it is here that people come from up to five hundred kilometres away to eat and to celebrate events with family and others with whom they share fictive kinship. In spite of the itinerant Chinese restaurant owner population in western Manitoba, diaspora identity has remained strong. Here, identity is related not to specific rural towns or cities but to the Prairies. Families tell how they often visit with friends and relatives who own rural Prairie restaurants in Manitoba and Saskatchewan:

> At Chinese New Year, [my mother] would have the fish and the chicken and the pork, that was a basic requirement for doing the offering, so she would do that for Chinese New Year and then for my dad's birthday what we would do is have a big party and invite all the Chinese people, the relatives [who] were really stretched all along the Yellowhead route [throughout Manitoba and Saskatchewan].

There are rules that people must follow when cooking the food and setting it out in the prescribed combinations. There are two bowls with six dumplings each for lower-ranking gods; for the six ancestors there are six bowls with six dumplings in each bowl. A research participant explains:

> Six dishes and that includes the fish, the chicken, and the crispy pork, and then mushroom, dried bean curd, and then the black moss and then the noodles. But it is always set out in six different dishes ... We also have this sweet soup dumpling for the Heavenly God *(Tianshi)* ... two bowls with six dumplings in each with the syrup ... And then for the ancestors and great-grandfather, it is six with six in each.

Instructions must be followed exactly, and it is a very stressful time – a time in which relationships between the older women (who know the traditions) and the younger women (who do not) become tense. On New Year's Day, people drink alcohol, which symbolizes happiness, and eat hard filled candies in circular and octagonal shapes, which symbolize together-ness. One research participant explains the significance of food and its ef-ficacious power during New Year's celebrations:

> Food means you do well. It is a sign of prosperity and success so that is why you always bring [it] out [during the events]. There are all the different dishes and always the best quality and especially for New Year because it is the final event [and it shows] that you are doing well and I think it is also a guarantee that you are giving the very best when you make the offering to the gods. And then with the ancestors there is the guarantee in return of the same, you know, in the New Year.

Most often, men (usually the father, then the eldest son once the father has died) are responsible for the ancestral offerings. They set up the table, which functions as an altar, in front of the window. Sometimes the names of ances-tors (up to four generations) are written on wooden plaques or are repre-sented by pictures placed near the window. The men might be responsible for lighting the incense and pouring out the wine (or whisky and tea for the non-drinkers) for each ancestor and deity. As one research participant explains:

> On special occasions I pray to my [deceased] father and give offerings in the evening. There are oranges, fish, barbecued pork, rice, wine, whisky. I am in charge of pouring the whisky, the good stuff. Yeah. My father likes to drink Canadian whisky [laughing].

It is the women who are in charge of the food that is offered to the deities and ancestors on the altar table, and then put on the family dinner table and eaten after about half an hour. The women know the food preferences of each ancestor and deity and make sure to provide what is appropriate. One woman elaborates on foods given during the festivals, noting that fruit (especially apples and oranges) is eaten at all of them. Another woman adds that Chinese in western Manitoba eat sweet dishes typical of southern Chinese cuisine in mainland China, as well as savoury foods, during the festivals. A third woman explains that the reason Chinese offer duck during Ghost Month is that, if they offered a rooster, it would make too much noise and scare the ghosts away from the offerings. Other women suggest that offerings need to be made in the morning. They told me the stories and foods associated with each of the festivals that are marked throughout the year, such as sticky rice and the dragon boat festival, which occurs in the fifth month of May according to the lunar calendar and is observed in June according to the Western calendar.

Besides these overt food offerings there are more subtle ones. Chief among them is that which occurs at the annual Decoration Day, which was started by clan associations and the KMT to unify the Chinese community and to help people remember the contributions of early laundrymen and later male and female settlers. Whether intentional or not, Decoration Day has transformed certain individuals into Manitoban Chinese ancestors. My desire to record and recount the history and religion of Chinese people in western Manitoba was sparked during a visit to my dentist's office when I first arrived in Brandon in 2000. In the dentist's chair, I learned that the local community had recently attended the annual Decoration Day. Years later, when I was considering directions in which to take my research, I followed up on this information and arranged to attend the event with a colleague at Brandon University and her friend. In the past, only the men were welcome to participate, but this unwritten rule had changed in recent years to include women.

We drove to the gravesite one week after Father's Day and parked the car. Both of the people I accompanied to the event had graves of family members and non-Chinese friends that they wanted to visit, and we went to these first, cleared the debris away from the graves, and made offerings of fresh-cut flowers. My colleague's friend brought with her three bouquets of peonies and roses from her garden. There was one large bunch and two smaller ones. Then we walked over to visit with the others who had come to the cemetery. They pointed out the places where the various laundrymen and other early settlers (including Chinese, Chinese Ukrainian, and Ukrainian men and women) were buried. We went to the graves of Bing Woo (1894-1982) and others and bowed.

Every grave we visited had between one and three sticks of incense that had been placed before it, except for George Chong's, which had not been cleaned for a long time and had no incense. I was told that you placed three sticks of incense for someone whom you remembered and one stick for someone whom you did not. At one time, people used to light the incense and make offerings of food and wine, but this ended when officials from the City of Brandon complained. Many of the graves also had fresh and plastic flowers. As we walked from grave to grave and paid our respects, many of the men in our crowd of ten people (there were several groups in our vicinity of between five and ten people) told stories about the settlers, recounting where they worked, what they did in their spare time, and sometimes how they died. The early settlers were revered and remembered in much the same way as were the ancestors who were buried in the surrounding graves. After about an hour, the cemetery portion of the custom was completed, and everyone returned to a large Chinese Canadian restaurant for a meal.

The restaurant was closed for the event and people who came had to pay for the meal in advance. I paid fifteen dollars to attend, and I was told that others paid more. A portion of the money went toward the offerings that were placed in front of the graves, while the rest went toward the food. While this was a buffet-style meal, there was a clear seating plan, which reflected the hierarchy of the Chinese community in the region.[40] The southern elders of the community, the male old-timers, sat at one table. The southern women who met weekly at the downtown mall for coffee sat together. And families, relatives, and other friends from southern China, Taiwan, and Hong Kong were similarly grouped.[41] Likewise, there was an established routine for access to the buffet table. The male old-timers and the women from southern China went first, followed by everyone else. There were long strips of crispy pork, chicken, and fish dishes, noodles, dumplings, soups, Chinese vegetables, dainties, and Chinese tea. The most important food was crispy pork.

Crispy pork represents the nostalgic southern identity that is associated with the earliest settlers and the time when the KMT was most active. It also establishes a bridge between that group and the one that joined it after 1947, when wives and families arrived to change group dynamics and identities.[42] The crispy pork, which is purchased in Winnipeg and driven two hundred kilometres back to Brandon, is heated, cut up, and served as the sign of an identity that exists in collective memory, As Lily Cho notes:

> Diasporic communities are formed through the processes of memory that bind vertically through generations and horizontally across individuals. Diasporic subjectivities emerge not simply from the fact of geographical displacement, but also from the ways in which forgotten or suppressed pasts continue to shape the present.[43]

The Chinese diasporic community in western Manitoba has been created in precisely the manner that Cho describes. Vertically, people are linked through the generations back to the first bachelors who settled in the region; horizontally, people are united by the common experience of coming together each year to remember and tell the stories of the region's first settlers. While the earliest settlers were male, the women and children who came later (and the Ukrainian wives of Chinese men) are also acknowledged on Decoration Day. In this way, the community encompasses first-generation immigrants from China, Taiwan, and Singapore; second-, third-, fourth-, and fifth-generation Chinese from Toisan Province; and Ukrainian, half-Chinese, and half-Ukrainian offspring born on the Prairies. Different members of the community are assigned to the fundraising, buying, cooking, serving, and cleaning up associated with the grand event. Someone is also assigned to pack up the leftovers and send some home with each guest. Southern Chinese male elders and women go home with crispy pork in their packages.

Since the time of the KMT, Sun Yat-sen, and the laundrymen, food prepared and served at Prairie events such as Decoration Day has become emblematic of a hybrid western Manitoba Chinese identity. According to Roland Barthes: "When he buys an item of food, consumes it, or serves it, modern man does not manipulate a simple object in a purely transitive fashion; this item of food sums up and transmits a situation; it constitutes an information; it signifies."[44] To borrow from Barthes, food "signifies" the hybridity and fluidity of identity. My findings are consistent with much of the literature on the correlation between food and ethnic affiliation.[45]

The annual Decoration Day, organized by the elders, commemorates the region's first settlers, and it is here that Bing Woo's story is told and retold in a fitting tribute to him as an ancestor and forefather. Bing Woo was born in southern China in 1894 and immigrated to Canada with his father and younger brother when he was an eleven-year-old child. He attended Central School for a time and then joined his family in the laundry business. In the late 1940s, the popularity and need for laundries was eclipsed by Chinese restaurants, and 1949 saw Woo enter the restaurant business. He remained a bachelor and worked as a waiter until he retired in 1965. During his life, Bing Woo became known for his facility in both English and Toisanese. He responded to census questions by saying that he was a Presbyterian, and, when he died, a United Church minister officiated at his funeral. May Yoh supplies the details of the remainder of Woo's life:

> In the early 1970s, by then retired and quite frail looking, Bing Woo was frequently seen, in the summer months and early autumn, sitting on a bench in the park at the site of the old city hall on Princess Avenue between Eighth and Ninth streets. A lone figure now, having long outlived his father and even his younger brother, Bing would look at passersby, giving a nod or a smile to whomever he recognized. Sometimes he simply dozed off in the

warmth of the sun. Did he dream of China and the little village where he was born? Or would he have dreamed of his mother, whom he never saw again after he left China as a child? Blind and in a wheel-chair, he was later cared for at the International Home on Eleventh and Lorne. When he died in 1982, in his eighty-eighth year, his estate was bequeathed to the Brandon General Hospital. Wes and Helen Wong, the son (and his wife) of his former restaurant employer, arranged for his burial.[46]

The arc of Bing Woo's life reflects the pattern of those Prairie settlers who never returned to China to see their families or to have an arranged marriage. He arrived in Manitoba with male family members and received very little formal education; he worked as a laundryman and then as a waiter. Many, like him, came as poor migrant workers from southern China and self-identified as Christian. They could not afford to return to China for an arranged marriage. And, being restaurant labourers, they often lacked the status to form relationships with Ukrainian women who worked in the restaurants as servers and cashiers. In the early period, men lived mostly in groups, ranging from three to eight people, in laundries, restaurants, Brandon's tiny Chinatown boarding houses, or in nearby Chinese dormitories. This group of men bonded and became like family to one another. They worked at the same jobs and slept, ate, and socialized together, playing mahjong, pai gow, and fan-tan for small amounts of money. As one person explained: "They all were free and they had no families and this was camaraderie. They would play mahjong and they would all be there and go out for a meal, everybody would go ... a big table, maybe two tables and they would have very traditional things to eat."

The doing of food defines the nature of identity and belonging. It ranges from the organizing and hosting of simple events (such as the get-togethers of elderly first- and second-generation individuals) to the more elaborate events of new immigrants through to Decoration Day festivities. Like the images that carry the *ling* of the smaller temples in China and Taiwan on annual visits back to their originating home temples, food carries with it important global, spiritual, and social meanings.

5
The Religion of Chinese Manitobans and KMT Confucianism

What started as labour practices to enable bachelors to feed, clothe, and house themselves; send money to families at home; and contribute to the Kuomintang and local communities turned into strategies to ensure their success. Neither laundries nor restaurants were ever only about the money. They were about human beings trying to figure out ways to exist in foreign places where they were forced to live apart from their kin because of racist immigration laws. And, most often, businesses thrived or failed to thrive because of the relationships that did or did not support them. These relationships intersected, overlapped, and attended to cultural, social, political, religious, and economic needs. They allowed the global flow of people, ideas, commodities, and culture. They were the means by which people contributed to local economies as well as to war efforts both in Canada and in China. And their own taste for sweet southern Chinese food shaped rural tastes and culture. These relationships most often entailed involvement in Chinese political groups such as the KMT and religious groups such as (after 1925) the United Church. Relationships and group involvement often entailed overlapping identities and, thus, were frequently ambiguous. In this chapter, I examine the way in which this ambiguity gave rise to new forms of Chinese religiosity and efficacies in western Manitoba.

The way of the bachelor emerged for many reasons. Chinese bachelors in western Manitoba lived without women and families for thirty-three years. They started laundries and found themselves battling stereotypes that portrayed them as "filthy heathens." Rural missionaries, churchwomen, and ministers who visited the laundries and whom these men encountered in English classes became their friends. Then, a few years after the turn of the last century, the men saw opportunities in the restaurant business. While cafes were cleaner than laundries, and friendships with non-Chinese people had already started to form, Chinese restaurant owners still had to over-come preconceptions that they served barbarian foods such as dog, cat, or even rat. Although these preconceptions still lingered, my informants gave me the impression that they were less predominant than they were when Chinese were predominantly laundrymen. This is because the phenomena associated with food differ from those associated with laundry. In order to live, people had to buy what the bachelor made and sold. They depended on him for food and so, through constant association, eventually became his friends. But it wasn't just non-Chinese and Christian relationships that were part of the way of the bachelor: Chinese relationships were part of it, too.

When the earliest Chinese settlers arrived in western Manitoba, they found Chinese friends through clan associations. In western Manitoba, men from a few families, such as the Mas, Lees, Choys, and Wongs, got together. These men came from the same area in China (usually Toisan) and generally lived together in KMT dormitories when they first arrived. They would gather when laundries (and, later, restaurants) were closed. When the KMT opened its Brandon outpost in late 1912, everyone met there. Eventually, the KMT united the fragmented groups into one Chinese identity that was modelled after Sun Yat-sen. As Allen Chun explains, this identity was chiefly Nationalist:

> The transformation of Chinese overseas into "overseas Chinese" (hua-ch'iao) was, then, an expansion of Chinese nationalism abroad that attempted to galvanize Chinese identity from what was once kin-centered, dialect groups into a radically new "imagined community" reeducated in standard Mandarin and the orthodox teachings of Chinese civilization.[1]

This "imagined community" was also modern, Western, and ambiguous.

In the introduction I explain that the "way of the bachelor" enabled new immigrants to flourish in Canada. In Manitoba, the way of the bachelor expressed itself, as one research participant put it, a desire to "just be normal." Or, as others put it: "We just want to fit in"; "We are Canadians." These comments represent the continuation of a trend that began when, in 1911 (just a month before Sun Yat-sen visited Manitoba), men like George Chong and his "brother" Tom cut their hair to show that they were modern and that they belonged. In photographs, oral history accounts, and interviews, the appearance of the early Chinese settler was a consistent one. A research participant explains:

He would have his suit and tie on if he was going anywhere special. Fitting in and making appearances counted. It was important to be seen as assimilated. What[ever] they did in the community they had to [be seen to] fit in. What they did behind closed doors was something else. He wore short hair – quite short. And he wore Western clothing – always a buttoned shirt. Regular pants.

In Canada, Christian identity was normative. So most (but not all) Chinese men became nominal Christians. To some extent, KMT membership was also normative. If you were Chinese and living in Manitoba, you became a KMT member because it was socially accepted and expected. As one man who followed his father and grandfather to Manitoba put it: "I wanted to get a job, and all the men told me that I needed to become a [KMT] member to get one." KMT membership linked newcomers vertically to Sun Yat-sen and horizontally to the broader KMT governance structure.

Men who eventually joined the KMT were first attracted to it through Sun Yat-sen, who visited Canada one time. When branch members responded to central party fundraising requests, they received all kinds of KMT and Sun Yat-sen propaganda, including letters and telegrams sent in his name. In his correspondence, he empathized with the men who had mortgaged their buildings and "lived difficult lives."[2] KMT leaders were aware of Sun Yat-sen's personal appeal and worked hard to maintain allegiance to him among overseas Chinese communities. They sent things that reminded Chinese settlers of him, such as revolutionary dollars with the twelve-pointed star (later they sent one-, five-, and ten-dollar bills, all of which bore the picture of Sun Yat-sen), and bonds that bore his Chinese signature "Sunwen" (made with his personalized Chinese chop or stamp). KMT offices in China (and later Taiwan) sent other things, too: copies of his will, his three principles, couplets, and building signs written in his own calligraphy and all signed "Sunwen." These mementoes were in addition to the oil paintings, photographs, and reams of cheaply printed posters of Sun Yat-sen that adorned office walls and filled drawers. His image was also on local KMT office stationery. What began as a top-down effort to inculcate party loyalty in KMT members turned into a grassroots movement that transformed Sun Yat-sen into a god.

Robert Orsi writes about the power of media, such as rosaries, to make the Virgin Mary present in everyday lives. More than a reminder of Mary, he notes, this medium showed the daily interactions on earth with someone residing in heaven.[3] While Sun Yat-sen died from liver cancer in 1925, he continued to inspire and to be present through pictures and other media that the faithful had collected over the years. For some, these possessions and the transnational relationships they represented were among what was most valuable to them when they died.

Sun Yat-sen's charisma, Christian rhetoric, and the efforts of his circle transmogrified him.[4] Those who had faith in him came to feel as though they had special access to his vision for a new nation. Although he was a trained medical doctor, he was neither an intellectual nor a classically trained scholar. Still, Sun drew on what he knew about traditional thought and culture (and Christianity) to write speeches that were evocative of the master-retainer relationship in Chinese history. If Sun was loyal and sincere and tried to provide the men with a new nation, they would believe in and support him. For these men, Sun's behaviour was efficacious. With Sun Yat-sen as their leader, overseas Chinese men continued to feel connected to China and to make financial contributions to the growing movement there.[5] Laundry and restaurant work was difficult and tedious, but life was made bearable during the many events that were hosted and organized throughout the year. A blusterer who earned the nickname "the Big Gun" for audacious proposals like the multi-billion-dollar Chinese railway (which was to be financed through the contributions of foreign dollars), Sun Yat-sen was nevertheless adored even after his brief period as provisional president ended in 1912. Following his death in 1925, he continued to be remembered and revered through his picture, his will, and the toasts given in his honour. To many of western Manitoba's earliest settlers and their descendants, Sun Yat-sen became a god-like figure during his lifetime and was worshipped after his death. Other new forms of efficacy were reflected in the importance of relationships with both Chinese and non-Chinese people and organizations. This Nationalist identity was defined by homosociality and loyalty to Sun Yat-sen and (later) Chiang Kai-shek, and it was intricately connected to a Christian identity.

Front-Stage Christian Behaviours
In census surveys, assessment rolls, and in other public ways bachelors told people that they were Christians. This Christian identity was nominal as most of them neither converted nor accepted baptism, and most combined Christian and Chinese beliefs. In the earliest period of settlement, Chinese bachelors used Christian public spaces to partake in the activities of the dominant society, to learn Canadian customs, and to establish their own networks.

The earliest Manitoba Chinese missionary work coincides with the arrival, in November 1877, of Charley Yam, Fung Quong, and an unnamed woman

FIGURE 21 Methodist funeral of Chin Ping, with Chinese KMT,
Chinese Freemasons, and CBA, YMCA, and Chinese Young Men's Christian
Association of Winnipeg leaders and members in attendance.
Winnipeg, Manitoba, 1920.
Source: United Church Archives.

by stagecoach from the United States. From that time forward, Baptist,
Methodist, and Presbyterian men and women began to visit Winnipeg and
rural Manitoba laundries and cafes. They invited the mostly male labourers
to churches for Christian lessons on Saturday evenings (when bachelors
were most in need of being distracted from the vices of gambling, drinking,
and smoking opium) and on Sundays (after the regular morning services).
Missionaries also ran the soup kitchens in Winnipeg.[6] In 1894, Reverend
Bethel Argue established the Bethel Mission, which provided legal, medical,
financial, religious, and social counselling to non-English-speaking Winnipeggers and newcomers living beyond the perimeter of the city. By the
early 1900s, very small groups of Winnipeg Chinese were converting to
Christianity, being baptized, and participating in church-run English classes.
In 1911, John Maclean (1851-1928), a Methodist minister known for his work
with First Nations people in Alberta, Saskatchewan, and Ontario, took over
the operation of the mission, then located at 719 Pacific Avenue in Winnipeg.
Seven years later, Bethel Mission was renamed the John Maclean Mission

to reflect his leadership.[7] By 1933, the mission had five hundred men under its care within Winnipeg and in rural towns and villages.[8] In their spare time, bachelors went to church services as well as to the Bible study groups and the ice cream socials and picnics they organized. Ministers performed marriages and funerals.

Christians expected a certain degree of indifference from Chinese bachelors. These men were strangers who needed to be "civilized." As the eighty-fourth annual report of the Missionary Society of the Methodist Church notes:

> The Orientals are here, and a time will come when they will be here in larger numbers. How shall we deal with them? Shall we regard and treat them as barbarians, a menace to society, to be mobbed, boycotted, driven out of the country? That were only to proclaim that we are barbarians ourselves ... Surely there is "a more excellent way." These strangers from the Far East are human beings like ourselves, of the "one blood," and just as capable, under proper leadership, of rising in the scale of civilization and becoming a useful element in our cosmopolitan population as are the immigrants from other countries. In proof of this we need only cite results already accomplished, showing what is possible on a larger scale.[9]

In 1887, in addition to the Bethel mission, a Chinese Sabbath school was started by St. Andrew's Presbyterian Church.[10] It was located on the corner of Ellen Street and Elgin Avenue in Winnipeg,[11] and, a decade later, was offering Chinese classes:

> A new branch of Sabbath school work is taken up after our Sabbath evening services, namely the Chinese Sabbath school, which is attended by from twenty-five to thirty Chinamen who take a deep interest in the teaching that is imparted to them by the young people who so cheerfully give their services. The seed thus sown may yet bring forth fruit even to the hundred fold.[12]

These classes were often taught by missionary women. Through these classes, Chinese men received "Christian instruction" and learned how to read and write in English. From the beginning, the work was challenging. Missionary workers continually encountered indifference and syncretism (the tendency to blend Christian ideas with Chinese ideas). According to a report from 1900: "If these men are to be taught the English language, the principles of Canadian citizenship, and, above all, a saving knowledge of Jesus Christ, the task requires the faithful efforts and prayerful co-operation of Christian workers."[13] It was hard for the missions to employ Chinese Bible teachers for long periods of time. Most of the early teachers quit out of frustration because the bachelors continued their customs and would not convert.

Once KMT offices opened in Winnipeg and Brandon in 1912, Chinese Christian institutions, the first being the Chinese YMCA in 1913, started to take root as well. KMT and Chinese Christian organizations had overlapping membership and governance structures. By 1915, there were twelve Winnipeg churches that offered Toisanese Christian services and Bible study classes.[14] And, two years later, native-born Chinese-speaking ministers were recruited to teach the bachelors. In 1917, Reverend Mar Sheung and Reverend Wong Soonghong founded the Presbyterian and Methodist Chinese Christian Association, which was located in the Chinese Mission on Logan Avenue.[15] The mission was close to the Winnipeg-based KMT office, where men would come after meetings to attend Bible classes and church services. Those without a mailing address would use it as a Chinese post office.[16] On the weekends, children attended morning Mandarin lessons taught by old-timers at the KMT office and then spent the afternoon at the Bible study classes run by Daisy Ross and her sister. Members organized annual picnics and sporting events.

We know less about what kinds of missions and churches were available to bachelors living in western Manitoba around the turn of the last century. St. Paul's Church in Brandon offered Chinese Bible classes that were attended by George Chong and many other early bachelors and KMT members. The Women's Missionary Society, associated with St. Paul's Church, attended the funeral of Wong Au, western Manitoba's first Chinese woman, and we may presume that they were actively ministering to the Chinese community at the time. And United Church ministers married Chinese men to non-Chinese women and presided at Chinese funerals. Others, who lived too far away, attended regular services in their own communities and relied on the help of local female missionaries to learn English. Some young boys, orphaned through migration, said that they would have "died if it were not for the church lady who took care of [them] when [they were] young." Ling Lee, who was a popular bachelor and cafe operator in Neepawa and had also lived in Winnipeg briefly, had the same name as a founding member of the Winnipeg Chinese Christian Fellowship.

Relationships began to form when the earliest settlers came to Manitoba in the late 1870s and missionaries started to visit and minister to them in their laundries. As I have mentioned, most bachelors did not convert. This, however, did not dissuade missionaries, who set up Saturday evening Bible classes to keep Chinese and other lone bachelors out of gambling dens and away from other "vices." Negative attitudes towards the Chinese bachelors began to change once the last Chinese dynasty fell in 1911 and the KMT opened branches in Manitoba (and in many overseas settlements). Sun Yat-sen and others within the KMT saw Christianity as the doorway to the West and encouraged religious encounters. By the end of the First World War, Manitoba's Christians had started to notice that bachelors were providing free meals to enlisted men, sending them care packages with cigarettes, chocolate bars, and letters, and helping them in other ways when they returned home. Bachelors were welcome at church services and were extolled for their generous contributions to the church. For instance, Lee Chee, who lived in Estevan, Saskatchewan, was noted in the local paper for his donation of Easter lilies to the church in April 1920: "Lee Chee of the Victoria Cafe is a good soul; he finds joy for himself in making those around him happy. Attendants at the Easter morning services will find their pleasure enhanced through the timely generosity of Lee Chee's beautiful Easter Lilies for all the churches."[17] Although Lee Chee lived in Saskatchewan, he did what others were doing in Manitoba. He was active not only in his own Chinese community but also in the Christian community. In rural communities, where one might find three Chinese men at most, settlers had to learn English and make friends with their customers in order to make a living. People had to be more accepting of one another in rural areas than they did in larger places, where there were Chinatowns and other kinds of ethnic enclaves to house Chinese businesses and activities.

By the end of the Second World War, missionaries were still attempting to convert the men and still finding their efforts met with indifference. By now, Christians were, for the most part, very accepting of Chinese immigrants in rural western Manitoba. They invited the men to Sunday school, Bible study groups, ice cream socials, and picnics while, at the same time, accepting their ambivalence. Churches provided English lessons and strategies for learning about Western customs and making friends. Moreover, since these settlers had no priests or religious functionaries of their own to preside over funerals and marriages, using a Christian minister was clearly efficacious. Carolyn Chen notes that church congregations "ground religious experience in the practical, everyday needs of immigrants, primarily the need for community."[18] In 1947, the Chinese United Church was formed, symbolizing the nearly three-quarters of a century that Chinese and Christian communities had shared institutions, identities, and events.

One of the main reasons for the success of the Chinese-Christian relationship and the acceptance of Chinese indifference and nominal Christian identity had to do with the similarities between Christian moral teachings and the values of Confucianism.[19] Confucian texts (such as the Analects) contain discussions between Confucius and his disciples regarding the merits of virtuous behaviour, which would establish harmony between human relationships and those in Heaven (Heaven and Human are one – *tianren heyi*). Gradually, as relationships between Chinese and non-Chinese communities became stronger, the bachelors became more aware of the global significance and agency of polite behaviour, or propriety *(li)*, which is a key aspect of Confucianism.

Two of the most notable virtues that govern global social interactions are benevolence *(ren)* and loyalty *(zhong)*. Such virtues direct behaviour in both public and private settings, allowing men to form bonds and establish *guanxi* (personal connections) inside and outside their ethnic group and, most significantly, to draw on civilized codes of conduct to make friends with Christians. Mayfair Mei-hui Yang links *guanxi* to Confucian ethics and *li*. In this way she maps the manner in which *guanxi* straddles the boundaries between religious and social domains.[20] *Guanxi* presupposes that when people behave according to these virtues they and their relationships will be empowered and transformed. As a result, in a small community in which few if any people are related, being from southern China becomes reason enough to justify treating another person as "fictive" kin.[21] Something else made ritualized relationships and their Confucian underpinnings crucial. Here, I am referring to a new identity that was perpetuated and constructed by the Nationalist Party in China (the KMT) and in overseas communities.[22] In this new Nationalist identity, emerging concepts of the nation-state were associated with the Chinese Han race, which, historically, has been considered to be China's elite ethnic group. Although Confucianism has been associated with Han culture (considered by traditional Chinese to be elite and pure), many aspects of it were rejected by Nationalists, who wanted Chinese people to be free from autocratic rule and costly imperial rituals.[23]

Rural churches have provided "boundary resources," a phrase used by Tony Carnes and Fenggang Yang to describe the spiritual, therapeutic, social, and practical services offered by religious institutions. Although churches could easily be understood to provide spiritual resources, it is harder to see the religiosity of social resources (e.g., organizing dances and picnics).[24] Yang and Carnes describe the boundaries that are created through the many acts in which we "do" religion. They note that "immigration is not only a crossing of national boundaries but also a mixing of the way boundaries are organized and implemented."[25] With this in mind, we can see that, when new settlers attended and were "doing" religion in a Western context, they were crossing cultural, economic, social, linguistic, and other boundaries.

Before I discuss KMT Confucianism, I would like to delve into the ideas that disappeared (or were erased by those in positions of power in the KMT and Christian organizations) when beliefs and practices from Chinese, Nationalist, and Christian texts were combined. These included everyday religious practices that did not fit with the new image of a Western, educated Confucian elite. From this modernist perspective, the burning of incense and paper money, and other traditional customs, had to be pushed to the innermost regions of the back stage.

These ritual actions now took place behind bedroom doors, in garages, and in the deepest recesses of backyards. They also had to be balanced by other, more traditional behaviours, such as the reading of Confucian and Nationalist texts (especially those written by Sun Yat-sen). Most of the backstage everyday customs that I describe below were related to me by women (rarely by men) and were most often performed by women.

Backstage Everyday Customs

Over the years, hundreds of people talked to me about their lives and the lives of their parents, grandparents, and friends in Manitoba. While some people entirely avoided questions about religious practice, others gave detailed answers. Very elderly informants told me about 1920s Prairie towns in which a bachelor lived and died alone. Within a few days of his burial, a group of bachelors would arrive, congregate at the gravesite, burn incense, and later soak it with an offering of whisky. People were guarded in their discussion of these kinds of everyday beliefs and practices. They feared that those with a modernist point of view might perceive them to be superstitious and, hence, unacceptable to the dominant society. Their fear of being perceived as superstitious had been inculcated in both China and in Canada. As one person explained: "We go out of our way to avoid a lot of the Chinese customs, or the worship of ancestors, because we don't want to be termed superstitious. So when I was growing up we didn't have the couplets in the home at all. This was viewed [as] maybe bordering on superstition." This view grew out of the anti-superstition campaign conducted in China in the post-1911 period, and it was perpetuated by both Christians and Nationalists.

What follows amounts to a summary of some of the everyday religious customs that continue even today. One research participant makes offerings of three cups of tea and three sticks of incense for the ancestors on the first and the fifteenth of every month. She also has an altar for ancestors, consisting of a simple wooden memorial tablet, in her home. This person recognizes four generations of ancestors, including great-grandfather and great-grandmother, grandfather and grandmother, mother and father and husband (if he is deceased). Another research participant varies her offerings, giving six sticks and sometimes nine on the first and fifteenth of the month, and twelve sticks on odd-numbered days. This person does things according to Chinese geomancy. Other research participants were more opaque: "I just look up and pray to the sky ... on special occasions." Over a year later, I learned that the "sky" to which prayers were offered was actually the name of the traditional deity *Tianshi* (天師) (in Daoism, *Tianshi* is often translated as "Celestial Master"). This research participant explained that *Tianshi* is the Heavenly God.[26]

Some research participants explained that offerings are an excuse to have an excellent meal and some dainties. These people make offerings to ancestors on their birthdays and during the different festivals throughout the year. Another person said that, in Brandon, there is a new custom, according to which the hearse drives past the house of the deceased one last time on the way to the cemetery. Others claimed that everyday rituals in western Manitoba are hybrid: "We've become really practical here now. Like a different culture. You can see a lot of change here. Lots of old Chinese customs are not being practised now." One person added that her family still continues a tradition her mother taught her when she was young and growing up in western Manitoba:

> When you move you take water from [the] old house and mix it with water from [the] new house. You also bring a flashlight and keep it on when you move from the old house to the new one. You keep it on during the drive and only turn it off after you turn on the light at the new house and say some prayers. At the new house you eat a chicken with its head.

At the core of all these everyday customs were food and relationships. But they were also ambiguous displays, hidden in the back regions so that Chinese settlers could be socially accepted among Christians and Nationalists. One research participant noted:

> Whatever customs we have, we try to keep it to ourselves. We don't expose our customs to anyone else. We try to live like a Canadian. Like anyone else. Except that we go to the cemetery [to celebrate the Decoration Day] with lots of people.

When I asked if people had a religion, respondents almost always remarked that they did not: "I am not religious"; "I have no religion." Often, when interviews took place in a group setting, various individuals would interrupt and try to clarify what someone else had just said. In response to someone's answer to my question as to whether he/she was atheist, someone asked: "[Do] you have a buddha in your house?" The person replied, "No I don't." Then another person offered: "You don't? We do. We have two or three of them. I like those guys. I don't pray to them. They have a nice smile."

At other times, the mention of the word "religion" was met with the shaking of a head or the waving of a hand, both gestures urging me to move on to the next question. One research participant elaborated:

Religion as such, with a name on it, I can't give you. When Mr. Kee was a child his family used to go to the Salvation Army and they would have their own beliefs, too ... This isn't something that I ever talked to them about but they would, you know they lived, they were very good people.

Another research participant explained that his grandfather was not very religious:

Grandfather did not encourage me to go to church. But he also did not discourage me. His view of the United Church was neutral. Religion was not a big thing. He observed a few Chinese events – New Year's, for example, when he would cook a meal and ask friends to come and share. These friends were customers and no relations at all.

When I asked research participants if they went to a temple or church, almost everyone said no. When they were asked if they had altars in their homes or businesses, most of them said yes. A few of them had these altars in their kitchens. Some even allowed us to photograph the altars, which always featured *Guangong* (the Daoist god of war) or, occasionally, *Guanyin* (a Buddhist goddess associated with salvation).[27] One research participant provided very clear details regarding the offerings that were made:

We have an altar in the restaurant kitchen as well as in our home. It faces the door and the god [i.e., the god of wealth or the kitchen god] looks after business. We offer one stick of incense each morning. On the first and fifteenth of each month we offer three sprigs of incense and burn paper money on special occasions in a metal pail. In China we used a porcelain pail – all the ashes remained there.

The doing of more everyday forms of religion told me two things. First, these forms of religiosity were constantly evolving. Second, when people explained these more traditional behaviours they assumed I shared their view that these customs were in some way illicit (and, by implication, exotic and exciting). Explanations were followed by awkward silences. These accounts did not fit with the modern sensibilities of immigrants who "only wanted to fit in." Sometimes informants tried to assure me that these were old-fashioned customs that were no longer practised. They explained: "It's just important to belong to Canadian culture. That's why we are not that religious."

Reflecting this reserved behaviour, research participants rarely described the choice to erect an altar to ancestors or other deities as their own. Usually, it was someone else's choice: "My mother-in-law wanted it"; "It was put there by my wife." Another explained: "We have an altar for *Guanyin* upstairs, which my mom gave me. Sometimes we make offerings of oranges, apples, and other fruits, and incense. My mom got it for us to keep there when my dad passed away a few years ago." Ambivalence pervaded these explanations of the doing of religion in the back regions. Over time, I came to see that, for many research participants, it would take much longer than an afternoon or two to get to know me and, thus, not have to treat me as a stranger whose impressions needed to be controlled.

Everyday behaviours and identity were ambiguous; thus, initially, results varied and patterns were difficult to perceive. One family would be adamant about one practice, such as, for example, the burning of paper money at Qingming. Many families in Manitoba observe Qingming once the snow has melted and during Chongyang in September before the snow comes. Several families go to family gravesites at other times of the year. As one informant remarked: "Mom [deceased] doesn't drink. We don't give her whisky. She likes chicken legs and barbecued pork. But mostly we burn spirit money. We go there quite often and burn tens of thousands of dollars and paper television sets and other things to send to her. Mom is really rich now." Another family would explain that money is no longer burned at gravesites. As one person explained: "We don't burn money any more because it will make the ghosts greedy and they will not agree to do what they say they will do so. [Instead of burning paper money] we just keep praying." In this response, I began to notice new understandings of efficacy. Some research participants had sincerely given the requisite foods and other items to ancestors, ghosts, and spirits, yet their gifts had not been reciprocated. Instead, there had been a rupture in the understanding of *ling*, or efficacy, the result being that, for some, the custom had to be adjusted. If ghosts and spirits could no longer be counted on to do the things needed of them, who could? Efficacy, I would argue, changed in frontier regions where normative identity and behaviours were required to survive. People (mostly men) became more connected to everyday relationships and the events that maintained them and, in the process, became less traditionally spiritual.

Religious Ambivalence and the Straddling of Chinese and Western Religiosity

R. Stephen Warner's proposed theory of religious ambivalence enabled me to see the modern sensibilities of research participants who prayed at home with "an image of the Buddha beside them" but who were otherwise not part of a religious congregation.[28] They could wear *Guanyin* amulets and prayer bracelets, but these behaviours did not conflict with their attending church on Sundays. Statues of Confucius, beautiful bound copies of the *Analects*, and Zhu Xi's *Four Books* decorated their homes. But were these anything more than decoration? For some, these items hinted at a Confucian identity; for others, they were just attractive things that reminded them of life before the Chinese Communist Party ruled China.

Initially, I was concerned that, by calling my research participants ambivalent, I would be perceived to be criticizing them. I was worried that people would presume I thought that they were not committed to being religious, were deceitful, or, worse, were not religious at all. What I failed to realize at the time was that Chinese immigrants, like everyone else, sometimes experienced conflicting feelings. I began to see that "religious ambivalence" was one of the strategies that early Chinese immigrants used in order to cope with life in western Manitoba. They had mixed feelings, and they felt displaced. They had overlapping identities in Canada as laundrymen, restaurant owners, or peasants, and in China as distant fathers, providers, and perceived members of the overseas gentry.

Warner's theory of religious ambivalence is influenced by Neil Smelser's ideas about the ambivalence of people who are in dependent relationships. The Chinese men who were forced to live apart from their wives and family relied on Western institutions, customs, missionaries, Christian religious spaces, and people in order to gain economic, social, and political capital. These men were not free to come and go as they wished.[29] They had to behave publicly in ways that were socially acceptable, while keeping their traditional customs hidden from view. The notion of religious ambivalence helped me understand the data I had collected from people who, as Karl Mannheim wrote in 1928, lived in the same "historical social space."[30] It enabled me to see that, for first-generation immigrants, identity was and continues to be amorphous, ambiguous, idiosyncratic, nuanced, and in-between. This identity was efficacious and, if held sincerely, resulted in this-worldly benefits. For second- and later-generation Chinese Canadians, however, this attitude of ambivalence was neither necessary nor efficacious. They were unlike their parents and other family members who had lived here before 1947 (the year of the repeal of the Chinese Immigration Act) and 1949 (when the KMT was most active and membership in it was normative). Some of them were now actual baptized Christians; others were atheists. These second-generation Chinese Canadians had been raised by parents who spent their time working to pay for their education and their ability to have a better life. Many did not know (or care) about the traditions that had once been practised away from the public eye. For them, there was little or no dislocation between their front-stage and back-stage religiosity. They did not have to rely on people outside their family and they had personal freedom. Their boundaries did not need to be as porous as did those of their forebears. Social acceptance and life in present-day Manitoba is more complicated than it was in the Manitoba of their parents and grandparents. And, in many ways, it is easier.

I have been examining the role of religious ambivalence in enabling Chinese immigrants to integrate into Canadian society and to create opportunities for themselves and their family members. I have called the dynamic and multivalent three-staged process through which they became 1) welcomed, 2) accepted, and sometimes 3) embraced "the way of the bachelor." Their religious ambivalence guided them through the complex negotiations that enabled the formation of relationships with those inside, as well as, outside their group. Non-normative private customs were practised first behind screens in laundries, later after hours in the back of restaurants, then at KMT offices, and, after 1947, mostly in private homes. Normative public customs were nominally Christian and Nationalist.

We are only now beginning to see studies that examine the relationship between religion and migration. My study of Chinese communities in Manitoba brings us one step closer to understanding how religion operates in frontier regions. It also tells us why Japanese immigrants in Canada,[31] as well as those in the United States, were able to set up Buddhist institutions,[32] while comparatively few Chinese immigrants did so.

Although there are no Chinese Buddhist temples in western Manitoba, there is one in Winnipeg. Established in 1998, the Chinese Buddhist Association of Manitoba's headquarters is the Pure Land Huaxing (Huasing) Temple at 585 Cumberland Avenue outside of Chinatown. The temple offers

Cantonese services Sunday mornings from 9:00 a.m. to 11:00 a.m. to a mostly Chinese Vietnamese congregation of several hundred. These services incorporate chanting, singing, and a dharma talk by visiting abbots brought over from Malaysia, Vietnam, and China. These abbots serve for a term and then return to their host temples in Asia. Following the large service is a free community vegetarian meal. Temple women hand out plates of food, and people sit at long tables in the basement. While they eat, people chat with friends and family, watch Cantonese programs on the large flat-screen television, or read Buddhist books from the library on the adjacent wall. The library includes a full set of the Mahayana Canon in classical Chinese as well as other books provided at no cost by Buddha's Light International Association (Foguangshan) based in Taiwan. Ming, a Vietnamese Canadian, gives English lectures at the temple. In these lectures he describes Buddhism as an "education that is compatible with everyday life." He further notes that its values are not in conflict with those of Christianity. The temple's purpose is to help native Chinese newcomers learn about Western values and to adjust to life in Canada. While this Winnipeg temple offers Buddhist services, it is not widely known or used by my research participants, who live in more rural areas. Only one participant had ever been there.

Western Manitoba has at least two Chinese acupuncturists whose methods draw on traditional Daoist theory. Tsu Hua Daoist Temple in Winnipeg is the only Daoist temple in the province, and it was opened in June 2007. Its members belong to Yiguan Dao or the Way of Unity sect. Elijah Siegler has noted that native temples have not developed in many communities outside the Chinese cultural sphere because they are lineage-based priestly institutions that rely on local organization.[33] Siegler's remarks describe the situation in Manitoba, where not even the twenty thousand Chinese Canadians estimated to now reside in Winnipeg are enough to sustain more than one native Chinese Daoist and Buddhist institution. There are, however, tai chi, qigong, and other Daoist types of exercise groups in the region. Most of the Brandon-based and more rural groups are operated by Westerners, often in church basements, community centres, and parks. A British Columbia-based Daoist qigong master named Master Michael J.C. Shen is president of the International Qi Gong Association, Canadian Chapter. Master Shen visits Clear Lake, Manitoba (a resort town), Brandon, and Winnipeg a couple of times each year and, for a fee, meets with mostly white seniors, offering full-day level one and two qigong classes as well as one-on-one sessions.[34]

Because the Manitoba Chinese population is small and relatively young, native religious institutions have not been able to take root here until very recently. However, I think the absence of these native religious institutions has also been influenced by the absence of women and the KMT.[35] Because KMT branches and membership performed the same functions as religious congregations in the early period of settlement, there was no felt need to create others.[36] Until families were reunited in 1947, and the KMT retreated to Taiwan two years after that, KMT offices were available as a place to congregate. Once the KMT no longer had its headquarters in China, branches and members started to disappear. What sustained the group of people who ended up with no KMT locations at which to congregate was a dispersed form of religiosity that I refer to as KMT Confucianism. In returning to the discussion of the KMT and Sun Yat-sen, I hope to show the patterns that moored the men to both home and host nations.

KMT Confucianism

It is far from accepted that Confucianism is a religion, although, for over a hundred years, scholars in the West and missionaries have described it as such.[37] One of the first places where Confucianism was described as a religion was in Qing dynasty gazetteers.[38] In Manitoba, it emerged as a category of religious identity in the 1911 and 1921 Canadian census surveys. While both Chinese and Japanese settlers could have self-identified as Confucians (and presumably as Christians) on census surveys, the number of Japanese living in the region was very small.[39] During this period, the number of Confucians in the province jumped from 15 percent[40] in 1911 to over 50 percent[41] in 1921.[42] In Western Manitoba, in 1911, at least three Chinese men self-identified as Confucian. One person lived in Elkhorn, near the Saskatchewan border, and was the only Chinese man in that location. The other two Confucians lived in Carberry. These new "Confucians" must have surprised the census takers, who likely had never heard of the term (although editors and readers of the *Baldur Gazette* were aware of it in 1900). By 1921, however, the category of Confucianism had become well established. Then the population of Confucians in the City of Brandon stood at 12 percent (5/41), and, in the province as a whole, roughly 50 percent of the Chinese population self-identified as Confucian.

What were the causes of this new acceptance? Although there were some Confucians in the 1911 Canadian census, just ten years later there were large numbers. This happened not only in Manitoba but throughout Canada. In western Manitoba, the recognition of Confucianism as a religion occurred after the First World War, during which the Chinese community had given generously to soldiers and had become friends with those in the non-Chinese community. It also occurred because, by that time, the KMT, having had offices in Manitoba for nine years, was well established and respected. With two branch offices and hundreds of members, KMT leaders hosted and organized numerous events throughout the year. Chinese men ate with, played football and basketball against, and got to know Christian, Jewish, Ukrainian, and other European settlers at picnics and other events. Now the men felt comfortable self-identifying as Confucian as they were able to do so in the company of many others. All of these factors had an impact on the rise in the number of Confucians in Winnipeg and in Manitoba generally.

Still, one has to wonder how these Chinese settlers themselves came to see Confucianism as a religion. Some must have grown up learning that Confucianism was an autocratic system of values, that it was associated with imperialism, and that they should have rejected it on voicing their support for the KMT and Sun Yat-sen. Indeed, the KMT would have rejected such aspects of Confucianism as imperial rites, sacrifices, and notions regarding the Mandate of Heaven (i.e., the idea that emperors ruled because they had been chosen to do so by gods and spirits). Natural omens and uprisings were seen to portend the end to a period of rule. The end of Imperial China in 1911 was believed to herald a modern republic. However, despite modernist views that traditions such as Confucianism should be eschewed in favour of a republic that favoured the people, many older traditions continued. Veneration of deities such as Laozi (believed to be the earliest ancestor of the Lee clan) still occurred before clan association altars throughout Canada. From 1916 until it became an official holiday in China, Confucius' birthday was, at the behest of the Chinese Freemasons and the Chinese Benevolent Association, celebrated by the closing of KMT and other offices, laundries, and cafes, and the holding of teas and banquets. But, in China, this day only became known as Teacher's Day in 1931.

In the first fifteen years of the twentieth century, a movement led by Kang Youwei sought to transform Confucianism into a national religion in which offerings and sacrifices would be made to both Confucius and Heaven.[43] Other influences included Yuan Shikai, who was president of the new republic until his death in 1916. He was not a Christian, but he was well-versed in Confucian thought and culture. Even though its rituals had been discontinued in the new republic, he resurrected some in 1914. During the Constitutional Conference, held on 26 January 1914, Yuan drew on his understanding of classical texts to make the role of the president equivalent to that of an emperor,[44] thereby reinstating some of the formerly disallowed Confucian rites. When Yuan Shikai died in 1916, these rites died with him. It would be easy to attribute KMT Confucianism to the later efforts of Chiang Kai-shek (1887-1975), who became leader of the Nationalist government of the Republic of China after Sun Yat-sen's death. Chiang founded the New

Life Movement *(Xin Shenghuo Yundong)*, which was based on YMCA doctrine and designed to further Sun Yat-sen's goal of a new modern China and to elevate the value of Confucian virtues. But years before the creation of this movement in 1934, there was already a fully formed version of Confucianism here in Manitoba. Like its eventual counterpart in China, Confucianism was efficacious as a form of social, as opposed to spiritual, religiosity, emphasizing the importance of virtues such as benevolence, loyalty, and sincerity in creating connections and relationships and in supporting nationalism.

As Lionel Jensen remarks, the Confucianism and Confucius we in the West know today were invented by sixteenth-century Jesuit missionaries and reinvented by Europeans.[45] The Canadian reinvention involved a complex transnational process, with Chinese immigrants playing a part in negotiating and transforming Confucianism as a brand of Christianity. How they did this had a lot to do with the KMT. This kind of KMT Confucianism combined aspects of China's Nationalist policy towards religion. Rebecca Nedostup explains:

> During [the late 1920s and 1930s] ... the KMT leaders launched a variety of "anti-superstition campaigns" meant to radically redefine the meaning of religion, restrict its practice, and ultimately subordinate it to the needs of the nation. At the same time, however, they recognized the importance of myth and ceremony to the age of mass politics, and tried to create a repertoire of secular, civic performances meant to foster a sense of national unity and political allegiance among China's citizens.[46]

Nedostup goes on to present examples of hybrid rituals that emerged as a result of these campaigns in Nationalist China. At the same time that these hybrid rituals were surfacing in China, they were also appearing in western Manitoba. Like Sun Yat-sen, many of the early leaders of the revolutionary movement had a knowledge of life beyond China, having been schooled by missionaries and having later converted (at least outwardly) to Christianity. As the movement grew, it came to encompass other less orthodox religious elements as it gained new members who belonged to Chinese triads (i.e., criminal organizations).[47]

Blending Christian beliefs and values with Chinese beliefs and values, KMT Confucianism encouraged the sentiment that the veneration of deities with incense, spirit money, the use of mediums, and so on was a blight on the image of the modern educated gentleman.[48] While such private rituals and customs could be tolerated in the back regions, they had to be supported by a deep understanding of more orthodox tradition. To accommodate these goals, the KMT leadership encouraged its members to read the classics, to venerate Confucius as a teacher, and to impart this understanding to their children. As one research participant explained:

> I didn't really know about Chinese festivals until I started to study Chinese, and then I recognized the things that people did all through the years that would be traditional things. And they carried those on but a name was never put on it as far as I was concerned.
>
> There was a Chinese school in Winnipeg. It was organized by the Chinese community and it was held in the KMT building ... We used to have to go for two hours after school every day and two hours on Saturday, Saturday afternoons. And actually it wasn't a real teacher, they were fine men but all they did was read from a text, and, you know, for those who didn't understand anything, you would get up and you would have to read, so it was hard.

As a result of the developments in China and in Manitoba, we begin to see new rituals, which represent the new hybrid identity (such as the one to celebrate Sun Yat-sen's death in 1925 and the one to celebrate the anniversary of the KMT twelve years later).

In addition to the events that transformed Sun Yat-sen into a god-like figure, there is Decoration Day, which continues to celebrate the lives and accomplishments of the early Manitoba laundrymen. And there are more subtle moments that we might include under the rubric of hybrid, everyday KMT Confucian ritual. For example, the old-timers in Brandon gather in the mornings, while a younger group gathers late Friday night. Not many of these people would say they are religious. However, when they speak about Sun Yat-sen they do so proudly. In an interview, the grandson of an early settler commented: "My grandfather admired Sun Yat-sen and regarded him as one of the greatest minds of his time. He admired him for having attained higher education outside of China and his efforts of travelling all over the world meeting with Chinese elders to gain their support for his cause."

Between 1884 and 1911, Chinese men commonly identified as Methodist or Presbyterian on census surveys, in assessment rolls, and in public. Between 1911 and 1921, the number of Christians declined and the number of Confucians jumped from 12 percent to over 50 percent. I would explain this change by pointing to the KMT. Over time, events served to perpetuate what I call KMT Confucianism, in which ethics, rationality, education, and social harmony are most important. KMT Confucianism was the most readily apparent layer of a hybrid religious identity. There may be many layers and kinds of religiosity in Manitoba, but, historically, the most remarkable of them may well be KMT Confucianism.

Conclusion

When I began writing *The Way of the Bachelor* five years ago, my goal was to tell the stories of early Chinese settlers in Manitoba. I knew that the histories would be loosely organized around labour patterns in laundries and restaurants. I also anticipated that food ideas and customs would be central themes that would help me understand and convey the link between Chinese religiosity and immigrant success and integration. Chinese religious practices and beliefs in China and in Canada were controlled and regulated by the Kuomintang. The new Chinese Canadian gods (Sun Yat-sen and the earliest settlers), created by top-down efforts, put power and money (donated at events held in their honour) into KMT and Nationalist hands. As for the old Chinese gods such as *Guangong, Mazu,* and *Guanyin,* there were very few native places of public worship, with the exception of a few offering halls in which one could pray and make donations before altars in CBA buildings. Over time, the few men who continued to acknowledge these gods did so in private in their homes or cafe kitchens. For the most part, leaders weren't concerned if a few men converted to Christianity (rather than just being nominal Christians) and worshipped its god. Involvement in Christianity was regarded positively because it furthered Nationalist goals, creating social and business connections and international networks. Religiosity was linked to Chinese and Canadian patriotism, morality, and citizenship. As Chinese Canadians became more modern, they didn't necessarily become less religious. In many ways, because moderns were Western they became more religious and, at least on the surface, Christian. What I was not aware of, in the initial stages of research, were the global dimensions of political and other networks built by involvement in the KMT, the CBA, and the Chinese Freemasons on the Prairies. I had some early inkling that men like Sam Wong were special, but I had no idea why. It was only when I started to look into early Chinese political history in Manitoba that

FIGURE 22 China, 1954. Inky Mark's sister June and her children Albert,
Mary, and Scott, along with Inky's mother Winnie with Inky and Debbie.
In 1950, June and Winnie escaped from China to Hong Kong with their young
children. One year later, when Inky, Debbie, and Winnie came to Canada,
Winnie was reunited with her husband (whom she had married in 1926),
and the children finally had a chance to know their father.
Source: Inky Mark

I discovered that merchants like Wong came to Brandon because of KMT
connections that they had made elsewhere in Canada. Discovering the
important role of the KMT and other political groups in this province required me to re-interview several groups of men and to ask them about
their involvement. It also prompted me to investigate their links to KMT

offices in Winnipeg, Toronto, and Montreal, among other cities. While I have been able to present some of my findings, many of them will appear in later works.

As I considered what to write about in this conclusion, I reflected on all the people with whom I'd talked since 2005, when I first mused about a project that would look at the history of Chinese settlers in Manitoba through focusing on food. I wanted to be able to tell all of the stories that were recounted to me and, just as important, to be able to display all of the wonderful photographs that people had given me. Unfortunately, I had to make choices. I also reflected on themes that I have not discussed at great length and that now seem important to put into global contexts: race, gender, economics, and sports.

The Way of the Bachelor reveals the hidden lives of Chinese Canadian men who lived in Manitoba. Scholars before me have expertly recounted the myriad ways that Chinese were discriminated against by governments in New Zealand, the United States, Canada, and Australia. Others have written about the racist ideas perpetuated by Christian ministers and missionaries as well as by businesspeople and communities who both loved and hated Chinatowns. I did not want that to be my focus, but it was difficult to strike a balance between telling people's stories and recounting the barriers posed by sixty-two years of institutionalized racism (from 1885 to 1947). While racism was not my primary focus, it was certainly a concern because it shaped so many dimensions of Chinese Canadian life on the Prairies, especially gender patterns. I also had to emphasize that there was considerably less racism in Manitoba and Saskatchewan within a four-hundred-kilometre radius of Winnipeg. I was attentive to the ways bachelors conformed to normative white social and religious behaviours. I was also conscious of research participants who were careful to omit details of discrimination or who had me turn off the tape recorder or delete a sentence from my notes. As the years passed, interviews turned into conversations and informants became friends. As I wrote these stories, I tried to show the resilience of men who encountered racism but who flourished in spite of it. When I showed some informants (now friends) their own stories, most wanted me to emphasize what was constructive about their experiences on the Prairies. They didn't want me to highlight the abuses or the obstacles that had been overcome.

And so *The Way of the Bachelor* is about the first Chinese who lived in Manitoba. It is mainly about men because there were so few Chinese women here. The first Chinese woman in Manitoba, Wong Au, died in childbirth because Brandon's Chinatown (unlike most Chinatowns in Canada) didn't have a Chinese midwife, and there was no doctor present during the birth. The first Chinese resided in what were called "bachelor societies," which existed outside of traditional family structures. Bachelor societies were filled with many married men who were effectively single because they had been forced to come to Canada alone. They were identified as "bachelors" on immigration documents. This appellation, though largely inaccurate, was used to refer to Chinese Canadian men in the early period of settlement. Omitting a larger discussion of gender presented me with a challenge because, although these bachelors were discriminated against in Canada, in China they occupied privileged gender roles. People who heard me give presentations said that they wanted to hear more about the women who had been left behind.

According to Chinese tradition, and in wealthier households until 1911, boys and girls were separated as children. Boys were taught to read and write as well as about music and poetry. They also learned that their everyday lives were located in the public sphere, tilling fields, studying for state examinations in order to become officials, and/or endeavouring to become merchants. Women and girls, by contrast, were usually responsible for sewing, weaving, cooking and cleaning, and other aspects of life that were contained in the private sphere. Some of these ideas persisted in Canada after 1911. Chinese Canadian women who didn't work alongside their husbands in cafes could often find employment in sewing factories. As it did for the bachelors, life in Canada transformed Chinese female roles from traditional to more modern ones.

Mention of wives and mothers was almost always omitted in the accounts Chinese men related to me. This was not an attempt to silence or erase the women from their lives: racist legislation had done that. Informants were protective of their mothers, whom they cherished. Like the bachelors, first wives in China lived very difficult lives and crossed gender boundaries: they raised children on their own, held jobs outside the home, farmed, ran their own households, and frugally invested the remittances sent to them by their husbands. They lived with and took care of their own, and occasionally their absent husband's, parents, and remained loyal to spouses who sometimes remarried in Canada. While in many ways a husband's absence further degraded a wife's already low social status in China and increased her suffering, in other ways her position was elevated because her husband was perceived to be part of the overseas Chinese gentry. And she only had to serve him when he visited, which was no more than every few years. When family photographs were taken in China, the women would arrange for a friend who was the approximate size of the absent father or grandfather to sit with the family and possibly even wear the man's suit. The women would then literally cut the face of the absent man out of a photograph that had been taken in Canada and paste it into a family photograph that had been taken in China. This way, men continued to be in family photographs.

But the story in this book is not the story of these women; rather, it is a story about manhood and the bachelor. It is about how frontier Canadian life produced novel male subjectivities that enabled Chinese men to succeed. Their ability to relate with others provided Chinese men opportunities to become politically involved nominal Christians and businessmen, and it changed perceptions that they were heathen homosexuals who worked and lived together without women. When men joined groups they formed friendships with Chinese and non-Chinese men, and these relationships took on significant religious dimensions – dimensions that had been missing in China. Members of these groups appeared to work harmoniously together to host and organize events, to fundraise, and to put on plays. Beneath the surface, however, men competed for positions and status within hierarchies that were in the process of being conceived.

The image of new Chinese Canadian male subjectivities was not defined by a muscular male body; rather, it was defined, at first, by the "Chinaman's" queue, clogs, baggy pants, and tunic. Dominant society in the earliest period regarded the "Chinaman" as an alien, feminine, and weak creature. Then, in early 1911, the bachelor changed his appearance, cutting his hair short and adopting modern western clothing.

The new modern Western image of the bachelor was encouraged by the KMT and produced in a public front-stage setting. This was balanced and rendered ambiguous by the image of a more traditional man still lurking in the private back-stage setting. All Chinese male relationships were triangulated with Sun Yat-sen, whom most men emulated and revered as the father of modern China. Those men who became KMT members after the death of Sun Yat-sen in 1925 identified more closely with Chiang Kai-shek. Allegiance to Dr. Sun and General Chiang fortified homosocial relationships on the Canadian Prairies.

Male subjectivities in Canada sometimes became refined, or more civil (*wen*), especially in the period from 1912 to 1925. In this period, men identified with Sun Yat-sen, whom they perceived to belong to the traditional male category of the good fellow (*haohan*). Many of the men in this group, such as Sam Wong (from Brandon) and Lee Wee Foon (from Baldur), had been wealthy enough to bring wives to Canada and had been associated with restaurant work and Chinese Canadian food. Living with a Chinese wife gave them status as well. Other men, such as Buddy Leeds (from

FIGURE 23 A white man dresses up as a stereotypical "Chinaman." "Hop Sing
Laundry" – An Act performed by Denney Brook's Vaudeville Company.
Source: Brandon Daily Sun, 15 August 1916

Brandon) and Charlie Foo (from Winnipeg), who rose to positions of power
later, became rougher (more traditionally *wu,* or martial) because they identified with Chiang Kai-shek, who took over as leader of the Nationalist Party
once Sun Yat-sen died in 1925.[1] For Leeds, Foo, and others, Chiang Kai-shek

was a brave and courageous hero *(yingxiong)*. The KMT fundraising strategies and tactics employed in Canada and China during the Generalissimo's leadership were considerably more aggressive and punitive than those employed during the time of Sun Yat-sen, and before the war and Japan's invasion. Many (but not all) of the courageous hero types of men in Manitoba were orphans or from poorer backgrounds and had intermarried with Ukrainian or British women. For some of the men in these two nationalist groups (Sun Yat-sen's and Chiang Kai-shek's), political community always came before family. Male subjectivities were not restrained by this refined/ rough binary. They were also influenced by involvement in Chinese dramatic troupes and other organizations. Canadian dramatic troupes were founded by early settlers who came to Canada to tour with Cantonese operas in the mid- to late 1800s – one of the earliest ones being in Barkerville, British Columbia. At the time, Chinese populations were small and scattered, so the men travelled from city to city entertaining audiences by playing the roles of both men and women. There was not much money to be made, and some men didn't make enough to be able to return home. They became stranded in various cities throughout Canada. And these men, who were neither religiously nor politically inclined, enjoyed working in new Chinese dramatic troupes that had formed in Canada. These troupes were regularly engaged to perform traditional southern Chinese operas and Lion Dances at KMT and other Chinese events.

The last two themes that I leave largely unexplored are economics and sports, which always seemed to be part of the stories told to me. It was not until I was editing the manuscript that I came to see the significance of banking networks and sports in normalizing Chinese behaviours. I have not presented much detail on the remarkable role played by economic networks with regard to influencing the formation of an iconic Chinese Canadian man: the modern Western gentleman. Making connections with bank managers and banking networks was very important to bachelors, especially once Japan invaded the Chinese province of Manchuria in 1931 and during the Second Sino-Japanese War, from 1937 to 1945. The KMT, the CBA, the Chinese Freemasons, and the Chinese Patriotic League (formed in 1937) needed their Prairie members to collect donations from other bachelors and from their small communities. There were always fundraising campaigns, and KMT members were expected to contribute, even in 1911, when they were asked to buy revolutionary ten-dollar bills for five dollars each. Fundraising was the raison d'être of events held by the KMT. Member donations were posted on the walls of the KMT building along with photographs (in varying sizes, depending on how much was given) and printed in Chinese and English newspapers, giving men status and agency. Most men who owned Chinese restaurants or laundries had business accounts with local banks and sometimes, as in the case of Buddy Leeds, Lee Wee Foon, and Sam Wong, they had strong ties to bank managers and others within the larger non-Chinese community. That economic relationships and connections were key is not news. Men needed to make enough money for themselves, their wives and families in China, and sometimes for another wife and family here. In one interview, the son of an early restaurant owner explained that, when he was growing up, his father reminded him that he had to attend to practical concerns first. There were only so many hours in a day, and, since most of them were spent working, a social life came at the expense of sleep. If you did not get enough sleep you risked getting sick. He remembered his father's constant refrain: "You can die but you cannot get sick." There was no money to pay for a doctor or medicine. Beyond everyday needs, men also had to be able to make donations to Chinese political organizations, to the KMT, and to home associations. But the idea that banking networks connected rural men to global economic, political, and social channels is significant. Economic networks enabled the flow of global capital, commodities, people, and ideas into and out of the rural Prairies.[2]

Sports and other recreational activities were also significant. KMT picnics, first organized in 1918, always featured football matches, three-legged races, and tag. From 1914 onward, Chinese YMCA members played in basketball leagues against members of the KMT, the CBA, and the Chinese Freemasons. Team sports enabled the more fit, stronger but less connected men to compete against the less fit, weaker but better connected and higher-ranked men. Men came to have power in other ways. Involvement in sports diffused tension and created bonds. Men also became prominent businessmen by sponsoring hockey and curling teams, attending local games, and speaking at banquets. Sports helped men to integrate, to develop new masculinities, and to become modern.

The Way of the Bachelor tells the story of the earliest Canadian ancestors of families who have lived on the Prairies for a hundred years and more. The bachelors were able to live here because they continued their customs back stage, adopted nominal Christian identities front stage, and contributed to the KMT from 1912 to 1949. These behaviours and the relationships formed through them display the enduring power of *ling* (efficacy) in Chinese thought and culture. *Ling* continued to motivate men in frontier regions of Chinese settlement both to adapt to modern Western life and to maintain a connection to a pre-1911 life.

As Chinese settlers adapted to life in Manitoba, new efficacies and rituals were developed. For the bachelors, it was no longer socially appropriate (or efficacious) to worship traditional Chinese deities who could provide little assistance in Canada. Instead, Sun Yat-sen became a god-like figure, and the earliest settlers became ancestors who were to be acknowledged in a special annual funerary festival known as Decoration Day.

Quotidian rituals changed as well, and this is where the discussion returns to friendship. In China, everyday life and the festivals that punctuated it were organized according to male and female roles within the family and, to a much lesser extent, by district magistrates. In Manitoba, Chinese people seldom lived near family, and there were very few women until after 1947. Under these circumstances, homosocial relationships took on religious dimensions, connecting men vertically and horizontally: to each other, to local KMT leaders, to Sun Yat-sen, to the Canadian landscape, and to China. It makes sense that, as a new alienated minority community developed in western Manitoba, new articulations of efficacy evolved to replace those that had been available at home.

The new forms of hierarchy that developed in Manitoba produced the structures for both vertical and horizontal relations as well as the foundations for the building of bridges between Chinese and non-Chinese communities. New rituals developed to solidify the position of Sun Yat-sen at the top of the hierarchy. These rituals distinguished Sun Yat-sen as leader and others as his followers, who bowed once toasts were given in his name and (after his death in 1925) when his will was read. His supremacy in the KMT was also enforced by his portrait's being consistently placed on a table with fresh flowers at every KMT event. Provincial members who were chairmen, and English and Chinese secretaries, would be in charge of the reading of the will and the toasts. They would also sit in the centre of the group, along with Nationalist Chinese and non-Chinese leaders and dignitaries who were invited to the event. Below Sun Yat-sen and the Nationalist and provincial leaders, but still holding an honoured place within the organization, were the loyal KMT members and merchants who donated the food for every event. The final KMT ritual act at picnics and banquets was the singing of the Nationalist anthem. While new ritual actions such as toasts, the placement of Sun's photograph, and the reading of the will assigned and reinforced roles within hierarchies, the musical performance of the Nationalist anthem united and bound KMT members (from different villages, families, and trade associations and guilds) together.

Frontier life transformed vertical and horizontal Chinese relations in remarkable ways. Relationships between men and within governance

FIGURE 24 "Forever China" embroidered on a pillow held by
Moon Dong, 1948. This was a sofa pillow from Sam Dong's residence on
Brandon's Tenth Street, where many western Manitoban Chinese gathered.
Source: Moon Dong

structures were ranked, were no longer voluntary, and had become the
heart of KMT Confucianism. In China, a man would have had a specific
place within the social, political, and economic networks as defined by
education and family. In Canadian settlements men were inventing their
own hierarchies, and social mobility was relatively easy, especially for successful business owners. If one got involved in major organizations such as
the KMT, the CBA, or the Chinese Freemasons, and in any Christian organization, one could easily succeed. Homosocial relationships and connections
were the key to doing well. KMT members drew on relationships with non-
Chinese ministers, Methodist and Presbyterian missionaries, and businessmen to establish themselves in society. Over time, KMT, CBA, and Chinese
Freemason members also became members of Christian organizations.

Without cafes, however, and the physical spaces and businesses that
bachelors transformed in remarkable ways, there would have been far fewer
opportunities for relationships to form between Chinese men and the dominant society. Through the doing of food a bachelor made the transition from
"Chinaman" to modern Western gentleman. And, as he became known for
Orange Crush, broken pan taffy, and halibut steaks that "hung off the plate,"

he became part of rural Prairie life and culture. He introduced this community to global commodities and new cuisines, and, in return, it cared for him. When he took trips away, the people in the community missed him. Newspaper reporters mused about how long he would be away this time, and whether he would come back with a wife or child. Few of these community friends had intimate knowledge either of the scope of this man's hardships or of the breadth of his Chinese involvements. The way of the bachelor was admirable. It was quietly noble and historically meaningful. In this book, I have attempted to convey some of what I have learned about it.

Notes

Introduction

1 Compared to other Chinese Canadian settlements, the western Manitoban one was tiny. In the 1901 census, Manitoba had a population of just 206 (all male) Chinese, in contrast to the 14,885 male and female Chinese who lived in British Columbia. For this number I rely on the table in Con et al., *From China to Canada*, 301. See also "Table XII – Nationalities," in *Census of Canada, 1901* (Ottawa: S.E. Dawson, 1902), 1:406. The information from this table may be misleading because, in 1901, it combined Chinese and Japanese population figures. By the 1911 census, that number had grown to 885. See "Table VII – Origins of the People by Sub-districts," in *Census of Canada, 1911* (Ottawa: C.H. Parmelee, 1913), 2:173. The number of Chinese people living in the Brandon District (the largest area in western Manitoba and the second largest city after Winnipeg) more than tripled in the period from 1901 to 1911, growing from thirty to ninety-seven.

2 The KMT, which was known in the West as the Chinese Nationalist League, opened offices in Brandon in late 1912 or early 1913. It was the sole political association in the region until the 1950s, when the Chinese Canadian Citizens' Association formed. Although group clan associations consisting of Lees, Wongs, Yuens, Mas, Choys, and others may have existed before 1912, there is no evidence that there were ever enough people from one clan to have a branch of the Lee or Wong family associations (Wong Wun Sun Association) in this part of the province, though there were such groups in Winnipeg. Likewise, the Chinese Benevolent Association and the Chinese Freemasons never had branches outside of Winnipeg. For information about the Winnipeg CBA, see Du, *Mr. Hung Lee and Winnipeg Chinatown*.

3 The KMT was the core of Brandon's early Chinatown and was located on Twelfth Street, several blocks away from the Canadian Pacific Railway (CPR) station. So-called prairie Chinatowns like this one were not ghettos in which men were forced to reside and run businesses. For its part, Brandon's Chinatown was an extension of China – a place where you could find a small house that functioned as the KMT hall and dormitory. There would also be a Chinese laundry, where you could play games; and, for many years there was also a Chinese grocery store where you could pick up a few traditional spices, vegetables, cooking utensils, and other items. Unlike early Vancouver, Victoria, and Winnipeg Chinese settlements, those in western Manitoba had to form outside of large Chinatowns and ethnic enclaves. See Lai, *Chinatowns*. See also Lai, "Transformation of Chinatowns."

4 Here I follow Kam Louie's definition of the beginning of modern Chinese culture. See Louie, "Defining Modern Chinese Culture," 5.

5 Men came alone partly because Qing dynasty policy did not allow women and children to leave China. After 1893, when the policy changed, many families were reunited. For some, however, families remained apart because the wages earned in Canada were too low to support a Chinese family and the head tax was too high. See Mazumdar, "What Happened to the Women," 58-76; and Lin, *Surviving on the Gold Mountain*, 25-28.

6 Norman Kutcher, "The Fifth Relationship: Dangerous Friendships in the Confucian Context," *The American Historical Review* 105, 5 (December 2000): 1615-29.

7 Although Chinese men were able to live and work with family in larger Chinese communities, such as those in British Columbia, in Manitoba the Chinese population was dispersed. One or two Chinese men worked together to operate rural laundries and cafes. In the earliest period of migration, from 1884 to 1911, very few men would have resided with kin. As time progressed and immigration to the area increased (between 1910 and 1912 and again between 1920 and 1922) more men lived near or with kin.

8 In recent years there have been numerous studies of modern Chinese religiosity, including: Yang, *Chinese Religiosities*; Clart and Jones, *Religion in Modern Taiwan*; McLellan, *Many Petals of the Lotus*, chap. 6; Miller, *Chinese Religions in Contemporary Societies*, chaps. 1 and 2; Heine and Prebish, *Buddhism in the Modern World*, chaps. 4 and 5; Tan, "Modernizing Confucianism," chap. 7, 135-54; Chen, *Getting Saved in America*; and Bell and Chaibong, *Confucianism for the Modern World*.

9 The Chinese Communist Party (CCP) recognizes five religions: Buddhism, Daoism, Islam, Roman Catholicism, and Protestantism.

10 Efficacy has always been more important than belonging to one religion or church, acknowledging one deity, or restricting oneself to one piece of scripture.

11 In western Manitoban communities, the divine element seemed, at least to non-Chinese outsiders, to be completely absent.

12 In the first of the *Nine Songs*, "Lord of the East – the Great Ultimate," mediums dance in order to cause the god to descend and possess them. See Hawkes, *Ch'u Tz'u*, 36.

13 Chau, *Miraculous Response*, 2.

14 Today, *Guangong* is known by many names and is a ubiquitous figure in China, with strong connections to war, revolution, and migration history. The loyal, courageous, fierce-looking *Guangong*, also known as *Guandi* or *Yunchang*, has been linked to General Guan Yunchang, who served the warlord Liu Bei during the latter part of the Han dynasty (206-20 CE) and afterwards. Most people today know about him from the fictionalized account known as *Romance of the Three Kingdoms (Sanguo Yanyi)* and popularized through Chinese novels and televisions series. Around 1762, an early Chinese brotherhood, or triad, known as the Heaven and Earth Society, was founded and worshipped *Guangong*. New members were initiated into the society by drinking blood, offering incense, and swearing allegiance to *Guangong*, whom they recognized as the God of Righteousness. Early Chinese Canadian revolutionary groups, such as the Chinese Freemasons and Chinese United League (forerunner to the KMT), have been associated with this early Chinese brotherhood and the worship of *Guangong*. *Guangong* was one of the three sages in the offering hall of the Chinese Benevolent Association building in Victoria. It is not uncommon to find images of this martial god representing loyalty and courage in police stations in Taiwan, to which the KMT fled after 1949. He continues to be a fearsome guardian figure in North America as well, where he may be found in Chinatown police stations. *Guangong* is also a common sight in many Chinese Canadian restaurants, where he often

shares an altar and receives offerings of incense and food items along with the friendlier-looking Buddhist *Guanyin*, Goddess of Compassion. *Guangong* also holds a place of honour in Daoism as *Guandi*, or *Guanyu*, who becomes a god during the Sui dynasty. See also Duara, "Superscribing Symbols."

15 Decoration Day was also observed by the white Christian community in Winnipeg. In honour of soldiers, Winnipeggers held a parade on Sunday, 28 May 1922, to remember those who died in the First and Second world wars. See "Go to Sunday School Plans Upset by Parade," *Winnipeg Free Press*, 27 May 1922.

16 I have been told, however, that even in the 1960s there were still few women in the Manitoba Chinese community.

17 I am grateful to Glen Peterson, who reminded me of the need to emphasize this point.

18 For a discussion of the complex nature of dispersed and mobile transnational Chinese identity, see Hsu, *Dreaming of Gold*.

19 See Lai, *Chinatowns*, 276-77.

20 Chinese Immigration Act, 1923, S.C. 1923, c. 33, s. 5.

21 Some of the excellent studies on Chinese settlements in, and Chinese immigration to, British Columbia include: Roy, *White Man's Province*; Roy, *Oriental Question*; and Anderson, *Vancouver's Chinatown*.

22 Con et al., *From China to Canada*; Lai, *Chinatowns*; and Li, *Chinese in Canada*.

23 Chen, "Chinese Minority and Everyday Racism"; Chan and Lam, "Chinese in Timmins"; and Chiang, *Chinese Islanders*.

24 Baureiss and Kwong, *History of the Chinese Community of Winnipeg*; Huffman and Kwong, *Dream of Gold Mountain*; Chow, "Chinese Community in a Prairie City"; Millien et al., *Winnipeg Chinese*; Manitoba Chinese Historical Society Oral History Project; Wilder, *Read All about It*. See also Seng, "Adaptive Change and Overseas Chinese Settlements." During a telephone conversation with me in April 2007, Frank Quo said that, when he conducted his study of Prairie Chinese life and culture in 1977, he did not examine any of the smaller cities or rural areas outside of Winnipeg, Regina, and Saskatoon. See Quo, *Chinese Immigrants in the Prairies*. See also Li, "Chinese Immigrants on the Canadian Prairie."

25 MacDonald and MacDonald, "Chain Migration Ethnic Neighborhood Formation."

26 Kellee S. Tsai describes the long history of the rotating credit association in China: "The [hui] ... dates back to the third century in China when the Seven Worthies of the Bamboo Grove (zhulin qixian) established cooperative loan societies consisting of seven members. This is, however, subject to debate among sinologists. It is better established that Buddhist monasteries ran cooperative loan societies called "sher" during the Tang dynasty (618-907 AD). Monks originally created these societies to finance religious activities, but they also took on the function of extending credit to members to pay for funerals and travel expenses." See Tsai, "Circle of Friends," 82-83.

27 University of British Columbia Archives, Edgar Wickberg Fonds, Chinese in Canada series, Lai Man Cheung interview, vol. 8-28, 1984, Winnipeg, 3 October 1983, 4.

28 *Report of the Royal Commission on Chinese and Japanese Immigration* (Ottawa: House of Commons Journals, 1879).

29 Siu, *Chinese Laundryman*, 294 and 299.

30 Siu, "Sojourner," 34. Hoe Ban Seng explains that, in Canada, Chinese immigrants were sojourners in the early period of migration before their families arrived. In particular, he notes, "they seldom developed personal friendships with either clients or neighbours" (Hoe, *Enduring Hardship*, 46). Patricia Roy, in her research on BC settlements, adds that the sojourner mentality may have been the result of "racist rejection" (Roy, *Oriental Question*, 31). She reasons that, since the white people did

not want them in their communities, the immigrants never tried to assimilate. There is no question that life was arduous for Chinese immigrants in western Manitoba and elsewhere as they moved from place to place in search of work, all the while suffering from racism. Interviews with elderly Chinese Canadians who have lived here all their lives suggest that scholarly theories about racism in Canada have been somewhat imbalanced. This is because they have not compared the lives the men had in Canada with those they would have had in southern China during the same time period. Edgar Wickberg, in his state-of-the-field review in 2002, notes that Canadian studies have seldom looked beyond victimology to consider transnationalism's effects on migration and settlement patterns. See Wickberg, "Overseas Chinese." Several of my research participants were third-generation migrant workers who had left their villages to escape poverty. Had they remained, they would have worked longer hours, in poorer working conditions, and for a fraction of the pay. Wives, children, and extended families would not have benefited from the remittances sent home. Interview subjects emphasized that their fathers,' grandfathers,' or uncles' lives as laundrymen or restaurant owners were arduous, but they were still better than they would have been had they laboured in their homeland.

31 See Chan, "Myth of the Chinese Sojourner."

32 Quo, *Chinese Immigrants in the Prairies*, chaps. 1, 2, and 4.

33 Here I use terms defined in John Berry's acculturation model (see Berry, "Acculturation and Adaptation of Immigrants"). For example, in Davidson, Saskatchewan, between 1903 and 1919, oriental masquerading (along with other racist types of masquerading) was a preferred form of entertainment during long winters. Churchwomen and schoolchildren dressed and were dressed for these racist moments, which functioned to marginalize and/or separate non-Chinese society from Chinese society.

34 The term "Celestials" was commonly used in North America and Australia in the nineteenth century and early twentieth century to refer to Chinese immigrants. The moniker was derived from the religious and political importance of Heaven (or the Celestial Realm) in Chinese civilization. Beginning in the Zhou dynasty (1045-1256 BCE), Heaven *(tian)* was the name of the main god, to whom sacrifices and offerings were made at the Temple of Heaven *(tiantan)* during the Ming (1368-1644) and Qing (1644-1912) dynasties. The emperor was believed to be the son of heaven *(tianzi)*, who had the mandate of heaven *(tianming)* to rule all those under heaven *(tianxia)*.

35 Beginning in 1931 (when the Japanese invaded the Chinese province of Manchuria) and from 1937 to 1945 (during the Second Sino-Japanese War), Chinese men collected money from local communities throughout Manitoba and the rest of Canada. This fundraising effort was organized by political groups, most notably the Chinese Patriotic League (operated by the KMT), but it also required the assistance of Canadian banks and their managers.

36 I am aware that, though the KMT unified men, there continued to be factionalism, intergenerational conflict, and resentment of its apathy (especially under the leadership of Chiang Kai-Shek) towards overseas Chinese.

37 McGuire, *Lived Religion*, 185.

38 Chinese religions, like other Asian religions, provide what Tony Carnes and Fenggang Yang refer to as "boundary resources." See Carnes and Yang, *Asian American Religions*, 13-15.

39 This is the traditional understanding of gendered division of labour in early China. There is evidence, however, that house boys worked in kitchens, as is indicated by the famous story of Cook Ding in the *Zhuangzi* (c. third century BCE).

40 See Smith, "Women, Class and Family," 1-44.

41   Goffman, *Presentation of Self in Everyday Life*, 35.

42   Seligman et al., *Ritual and Its Consequences*, 44.

43   Anderson, *Food of China*, 199. See also Chang, *Food in Chinese Culture.*

44   Threadgold, "When Home Is Always a Foreign Place," 203.

45   Chau, *Miraculous Response*, 149.

46   The number is estimated to be over two hundred and continues to grow as people become familiar with my research and contact information through local television, radio, newspapers, and others who have spoken to me. As a result, because I live where I conduct fieldwork, I have continuously received unsolicited information by telephone, e-mail, from strangers on the street, at banquets, and other events.

47   I also interviewed restaurant owners. For a study of Chinese restaurant owners in Alberta, see Smart, "Ethnic Entrepreneurship."

48   See Hannerz, "Being There."

49   Gerald Berreman discusses the natural impulse of informants to control strangers' access to their back regions. See Berreman, *Behind Many Masks.*

50   Thompson, *Voice of the Past*, 8-9.

51   Rural Municipality of Pipestone, comp., *Trails Along the Pipestone*, 501.

52   General Register of Chinese Immigration, 1911, serial number 66722.

53   Before the United Church formed in 1925, Chinese immigrants usually self-identified as Methodist or Presbyterian. Although there have continued to be congregations of the Presbyterian Church of Canada throughout the Prairies, most Chinese people have belonged to the United Church.

54   *Baldur Gazette*, 22 September 1910.

Chapter 1: Christianity and the Manitoba Kuomintang

1   The relationship between the KMT, churches, and missionary groups has been well documented. See Lutz, *Chinese Politics and Christian Missions*, 47-51; Lancashire, *Chinese Essays on Religion and Faith*, 5-10; and Nedostup, "Civic Faith and Hybrid Ritual."

2   While I have found references to Chinese Bible study classes in Brandon, I have not found any evidence that Chinese Christian church services were offered in Cantonese, Toisanese, or Mandarin before the 1980s.

3   De Certeau's notion of the everyday provides a useful framework for understanding the complex range of factors that influences actions in Chinese settlements. Following de Certeau, I highlight the agency of relationality in transforming religious behaviour, individual male bonds, and new immigrant hierarchies. According to him, agency is achieved through alienated minority group tactics and larger dominant-society strategies. Where de Certeau's interpretation differs from the one presented here is in its dualistic structural assessment of power relationships. Such neat dualistic categories of doing are entirely absent here because the particular modalities of everyday religion are rooted in ambiguity. Sometimes people are in positions that enable them to use strategies, for instance as KMT leaders. These same party leaders held concurrent overlapping positions as laundry workers and labourers in cafes, and this required certain tactics. In these positions, they had no authority and stood outside of the boundaries of the larger dominant society. A set of strategies and tactics emerged as intercultural bridges and relationships formed among, across, and through Chinese and non-Chinese communities. The boundaries between secular life and religion, Christianity and Confucianism, and China and Canada were blurred. See de Certeau, *Practice of Everyday Life.*

4   Ward, "Oriental Immigrant and Canada's Protestant Clergy," 44.

5   See Con et al., *From China to Canada*, Table 9, 305.

6   See Lancashire, *Chinese Essays on Religion and Faith*, 4-6.

7   Reinders, *Borrowed Gods and Foreign Bodies*, 22.
8   See Lutz, *Chinese Politics and Christian Missions*, 3:2.
9   Jose Cabezon identifies this as the first of three stages of the Christian encounter with non-Christian cultures. See Cabezon, "Discipline and Its Other," 23.
10 Ward, "Oriental Immigrant and Canada's Protestant Clergy," 46.
11 See Osterhout, "Our Chinese Missions in British Columbia," 499-500; and Ward, "Oriental Immigrant and Canada's Protestant Clergy," 40.
12 Mrs. Culbertson of the Presbyterian Women's Foreign Missionary Society, who had lived in China for twenty years, gave a public presentation on Chinese life and customs in August 1888. See *Brandon Sun Weekly*, 9 August 1888; Dr. Hart, who had also lived in China for twenty years, spoke at a missionary service before his return to China in September 1891. See *Brandon Sun Weekly*, 24 September 1891.
13 *Carberry News-Express*, 11 September 1919. The Imperial Order of the Daughters of the Empire was associated with evangelical Christian groups in Canada that were actively involved in trying to help Chinese immigrants integrate into society. See Pickles, *Female Imperialism and National Identity*, 23.
14 See Lutz, *Chinese Politics and Christian Missions*, 47-51. See also Lancashire, *Chinese Essays on Religion and Faith*, 5-10.
15 Nedostup, "Civic Faith and Hybrid Ritual," 2.
16 Wang, "Organised Protestant Missions," 712.
17 *Manitoba Northwest Gazetteer*, 1901, 26; Baureiss and Kwong, *History of the Chinese Community of Winnipeg*.
18 Millien et al., *Winnipeg Chinese*, 17-18. See also Baureiss and Kwong, *History of the Chinese Community of Winnipeg*, 98-103. While there were no Chinese churches in western Manitoba, people could travel to Brandon to attend activities at the YMCA. See *Brandon Sun Weekly*, 27 April 1911, pt. 1. They could also go to Winnipeg to attend the Chinese Christian Fellowship (later known as the Chinese United Church), which opened in 1917.
19 Huffman and Kwong, *Dream of Gold Mountain*, 32.
20 For a discussion of some of the more negative Christian views on mixed marriages between whites and Chinese, see Roy, *Oriental Question*, 33.
21 Officially, Chinese Canadians (even those who were born in Canada) had to register with the government between 1923 and 1947. Very few of them were able to become naturalized, or Canadian, citizens until 1947.
22 Spirit money comes in different colours with different deities and different denominations. The idea is that ancestors, deities, and ghosts inhabit a world in which they need money to buy things. By torching these and other symbolic offerings, one is transporting them to the world in which spirits live. By providing ancestors and deities with money you help them and show your gratitude, with the sincere wish that they will help you in return.
23 Although the organization was founded in Winnipeg in 1910, it has been in Canada since 1863.
24 A minimal number of Chinese characters are used in this book. When available, Chinese characters are provided only for English names. Chinese characters are also provided for Chinese political organizations and key ideas.
25 Millien et al., *Winnipeg Chinese*, 20. See also Quo, *Chinese Immigrants in the Prairies*, chaps. 3 and 2; and Baureiss and Kwong, *History of the Chinese Community of Winnipeg*, 29.
26 "Lovell's Classified Business Directory," 846. See also Yee, *Chinatown*, 67.
27 Baureiss and Kwong, *History of the Chinese Community of Winnipeg*. See also Millien et al., *Winnipeg Chinese*.

28 The Chinese United League was a secret society that had been set up in 1905 to raise money to overthrow the Qing dynasty. It lasted until 1911, when it merged with the KMT. Sun Yat-sen was the director of that new society. Jay Taylor notes that, even in this early period of Chinese nationalism, Sun advocated the three principles (nationalism, democracy, and livelihood). See Taylor, *Generalissimo,* 17.

29 The KMT was one of many political organizations that emerged in Canada between 1911 and 1923. As Edgar Wickberg notes:

> The decade 1911-23 witnessed a proliferation of organizations probably unmatched in any previous decade. The reasons were many: the appeal of Chinese politics; the opportunity to participate in the economic and educational modernization of China; the growth in size of various Chinese communities in Canada; the new occupations into which Chinese had begun to move; and the new leadership emerging in these communities. All of these developments produced a number of organizations whose reference was China and several others that were responses to restrictions on the opportunities of Chinese in Canada.

See Con et al., *From China to Canada,* 106.

30 Wilder, *Read All about It,* 56.

31 See Millien et al., *Winnipeg Chinese,* 25; and Baureiss and Kwong, *History of the Chinese Community of Winnipeg,* 37. Sun Yat-sen's trip to Manitoba took place during fifteen months that he spent fundraising in Canada, the United States, and Hawaii. This occurred in the two years leading up to the fall of the Qing dynasty. See Wilbur, *Sun Yat-sen,* 72-73.

32 All of the accounts of this visit come from interviews with old-timers who consistently note that Sun Yat-sen came to Winnipeg in April 1911. Thus far, I have been unable to corroborate this with photos or other documentation. In an e-mail dated 22 June 2009, Charles Wong, great-grandson of Sun Yat-sen, indicated that Sun Yat-sen likely visited Winnipeg in 1911. He wrote: "I do not have any specific information about Sun Yat-sen in Manitoba during April 1911 ... Sun widely travelled from coast to coast in both the United States and Canada raising funds amongst overseas Chinese communities in order to support his revolution. Practically every major overseas Chinese community in North America was visited by Sun. However, records of his visits have been passed down as family stories, rather than clearly recorded and documented events ... Sun travelled and lived on three continents in Asia, North America and Western Europe for more than 20 years of his life in exile, always on the go and always on the run ... Sun often described himself as a vagabond without a home."

Sun Yat-sen is known to have arrived in Vancouver on 8 January 1911 and to have given speeches there; he is also known to have spoken in Toronto on 29 March 1911. One old-timer in Montreal explained that, during his visit to Canada, Sun Yat-sen had spent a lot of time with a friend in Calgary and had used his home as a base, suggesting that he may have returned to Calgary before heading east to Winnipeg and then to Chicago in April 1911. While I am not able to produce them here, I have seen photographs of Sun Yat-sen's son, Sun Fo, whom I was told visited the Winnipeg KMT branch in the 1960s, a sign that his father had indeed been there. See Harry Con et al., *From China to Canada,* 101-3. See also Li, *Jianada Huaqiao shi,* 301-2.

33 Nedostup, "Civic Faith and Hybrid Ritual," 35-44.

34 See Duara, *Rescuing History from the Nation.*

35 Here I follow Jason Knirk's interpretation of the response to the new Irish nationalism during the Easter Uprising. During that uprising, Catholicism played a large

role in shaping the new nation. Women could not do anything about the suffering they felt when their husbands, fathers, or brothers died, but they could martyr themselves in protest. See Knirk, *Women of the Dail*, 169-70 and chap. 4.

36 *Brandon Daily Sun*, 23 November 1911, pt. 2.

37 Con et al., *From China to Canada*, 101.

38 See Lai, Hongmen yuanliu zhi chuanshuo yu kaozheng 洪門源流之傳說與考證. See also Con et al., *From China to Canada*, 102-3n5. For American figures and accounts, see Bergère, *Sun Yat-sen*, 191. See also Wilbur, Sun Yatsen, 42-43.

39 *Brandon Weekly Sun*, 19 January 1911, pts. 1-4; ibid., 16 February 1911, pt 1; ibid., 30 November 1911, pt 2; ibid., 24 August 1911, pt. 2.

40 Ibid., 23 March 1911, pt. 1; ibid., 5 October 1911, pt. 1; *Baldur Gazette*, 16 May 1912.

41 *Brandon Weekly Sun*, 18 May 1911, pt. 2.

42 Ibid., 14 September 1911, pt. 1. ibid., 21 December 1911, pt. 1.

43 Ibid., 19 October 1911, pt. 1; ibid., 26 October 1911, pt. 1; ibid., 9 November 1911, pt 1; and ibid., 16 November 1911, pt. 2.

44 Ibid., 4 January 1912, pt. 1.

45 In the 1960s, Charlie Foo, as leader of the Manitoba branch of the Chinese Anti-Communist League, organized and hosted an exhibition of 264 photographs to depict the poor conditions of life in Red China. See "Photos Tell of Life under Communism," *Winnipeg Free Press*, 22 May 1961.

46 At this time it had five hundred members. See Chow "Chinese Community in a Prairie City," 107-8. See also *Manitoba Free Press*, 23 August 1915. The Winnipeg branch was one of the key branches in Canada. Like those in Vancouver and Montreal, it aimed to help the overseas Chinese community maintain customs and ties to their homeland.

47 Photographs of the Brandon branch members did exist at one time. In 1967, behind an old photograph, Tom Robinson discovered fifty-three pictures of its members and executive from 1917. He placed an advertisement in the *Brandon Sun* for someone from the local Chinese community to claim the pictures. Unfortunately, I have been unable to locate either Tom Robinson or the pictures. See *Brandon Sun*, 19 August 1967.

48 Wong, comp., *International Chinese Business Directory*, 1383.

49 Con et al., *From China to Canada*, 313.

50 *Brandon Daily Sun*, 15 April 1916.

51 Wong Higgins likely adopted the nickname "Higgins" after Higgins Street, which is located north of Winnipeg's Chinatown. Scores of men named Wong were active in the Winnipeg KMT, and, thus far, I have been unable to determine his Chinese name.

52 Wong, *International Chinese Business Directory*, 1383.

53 *Henderson's Directories*, 1913.

54 Edgar Wickberg has identified six ways to imagine Chinatowns, and Brandon's Chinatown exhibited two of them: it was an "extension of China" and an "organizing point." See Wickberg, "Vancouver Chinatown."

55 On 16 February 1916, the *Brandon Daily Sun* reported that fifty members of the Regina branch of the KMT attended an event at 1812 Osler Street, at which its leader, Alex Getyee, addressed the group and appealed to them to donate to the Red Cross and Patriotic Funds. Even though some of the men attending the event were out of work, the branch managed to raise forty dollars to help with the war effort. See *Brandon Daily Sun*, 16 February 1916.

56 Library and Archives Canada (hereafter LAC), RG 13, correspondence 163/19, Deputy Minister of Justice to L.S. Quong, 22 January 1919.

57 Library Archives of Canada, RG 13, Justice, series A-2, vol. 1940, file 1919-1947, L.S. Quong to Department of Justice, 5 May 1919.

58 There continues to be a close relationship between Chinese community organizations in Montreal and Winnipeg.

59 Charlie Foo's English name was derived from the sound of his given name, Fu, and not his clan name, Au (*Ou* 區).

60 It declined after having increased steadily for many years following 1911. In 1915, when the Brandon KMT announced its branch in the local paper, it claimed to have between 150 and 200 members. This figure represented a significant jump from the ninety-seven individuals reported on the 1911 census.

61 Paul Yee notes that, in the 1930s, the Winnipeg "Chinese population shrank by a quarter." See Yee, *Chinatown*, 73.

62 KMT members have always been encouraged to donate to the party by purchasing revolutionary dollars and party bonds, but fundraising efforts and leader strategies became much more aggressive after 1937, when China was at war with Japan. By 1940, Winnipeg KMT leaders interrogated party members who did not contribute a dollar to the Chinese relief fund or buy KMT party bonds. While exceptions were made for those who were poor or out of work, those who had the funds but failed to donate were questioned, and if they still failed to pay they would be photographed wearing dog tags. The photograph would be sent to the local press and central party headquarters in China. See *Canadian New Nationalist Press (Jianada Xinminguo Bao)*, 29 May 1940, KMT Archives, Taiwan. I found no evidence that this happens.

63 Similarly, Rose Hum Lee remarked that, in the 1930s and 1940s, the rise in "voluntary taxes" imposed by the KMT kept many Chinese out of the organization. See Lee, *Chinese in the United States of America*, 150-55.

64 *Province* (Vancouver), 8 December 1977.

65 Citizenship was a dominant theme within the Chinese community long after it had fought for the repeal of the Chinese Immigration Act. Representing the Winnipeg Chinese community, the Chinese Benevolent Association, and Freemasons, Charlie Foo went to Ottawa thirteen times during his life. The purpose of most of these visits was to lobby for the repeal of the Chinese Immigration Act, which finally occurred in 1947. On Saturday, 18 November 1961, John Maclean, along with Foo, Reverend Alan Lam (a Baptist minister), and Pat Low (president of the Chinese Canadian Citizens Association of Manitoba) had a breakfast meeting with Prime Minister John Diefenbaker in his personal car at the train station in Winnipeg, where they complained about human rights violations during the RCMP investigation of Chinese immigration to Canada. The prime minister promised the delegation that he would take a personal interest in the matter, and he called off the investigation of Chinese immigration (and the interrogation of new immigrants) soon after that meeting. See Diefenbaker Archives, University of Saskatchewan, document 036485, confidential memorandum 036473 re conversation between Diefenbaker and John Maclean, Andrew Cam, Mr. Charlie Foo, Rev. T.P. Low, Winnipeg, 18 November 1961. See also Roy, *Triumph of Citizenship*, chap. 7.

66 The several hundred Chinese Canadian citizens throughout Manitoba now have an organization of their own. Sunday night at an organizational meeting, Pat Low of Brandon was elected first president of the Chinese Canadian Citizens' Association of Manitoba. Purposes of the association are to enable members to become better Canadian citizens; to promote closer ties between Chinese and other Canadians, and to help new Chinese Canadians become acclimatized to new surroundings, Mr. Low said.

See *Winnipeg Free Press*, 20 July 1953.

67 While the aim to maintain pre-existing ties and to create new intercultural ones with non-Chinese communities became the main focus of groups after 1950, it had always been desirable. Today, the Chinese community (led by Dr. Joseph Du in Winnipeg [through the Winnipeg Chinese Cultural and Community Centre] and Kenny Choy in Brandon [through the Westman Chinese Association]) continues to organize and host cultural and historical events that create intercultural bridges. In Winnipeg, this happens through the annual Chinatown Street Festival, in which hundreds of Manitobans converge in Chinatown for two days of events sponsored by the Province of Manitoba, the City of Winnipeg, the Royal Bank, the United Way, and various Chinese individuals and businesses. The popular Lion Dance opens and closes the festival. People come to see more than twenty acts, which include the Winnipeg Symphony Orchestra, the Shriners, First Nations traditional dances and songs, and Chinese music, tai chi, kung fu, and dance.

68 *Province* (Vancouver), 8 December 1977.

69 Chinese Canadian communities celebrate New Year's and other festivals with traditional Lion Dances. The southern style Lion Dance has two different religious dimensions: bringing good luck and exorcizing malevolent influences. It is an important component of Chinese Canadian history. Most festival processions and events open with the Lion Dance performed by martial arts groups. A Chinese band with cymbals, gongs, drums, and horns introduces the lion as it approaches the crowd.

70 Edgar Wickberg presents ten categories of Chinese communities that are prevalent in Canada. The clan association and the fraternal-political association are two of these. He notes that "even small Chinese communities without any other organizations would often have either a Freemason branch or a KMT branch, or both." See Wickberg, "Chinese Associations in Canada," 28.

71 I have been told, however, that while KMT leaders performed this role, other clans (the Wongs and Lees) had representatives greet trains and discourage those who were not from their clans from coming to Winnipeg.

72 Historically, associations have helped new Chinese immigrants find sponsors, housing, schools, communities, and translators. They have organized Chinese banquets and other cultural, religious, and educational events, and have put on plays for Chinese audiences. See Willmott, "Some Aspects of Chinese Communities," 31.

73 Offices provided free language texts and philosophy books to their members, and they sponsored the printing of Chinese newspapers such as the *People's Outlook*. The *Manitoba Free Press* described the paper's inaugural printing in 1915: "'The People's Outlook' ... is to be printed on wax paper and rolled up on a stick. The printing will all be in Chinese characters. In politics it will support Dr. Sun Yat-sen." See *Manitoba Free Press*, 10 November 1915. There are no extant copies of this paper.

74 University of British Columbia Archives, Edgar Wickberg Fonds, Chinese in Canada series, Lai Man Cheung interview, vol. 8-28, 1984, Winnipeg, 3 October 1983, 9.

75 *Brandon Daily Sun*, 12 February 1917.

76 Ibid., 16 February 1917.

77 There were no further stories about these men and their gambling in the 1917 *Brandon Daily Sun*. The paper reported a raid on a gambling and opium "joint" down the street from the branch on Monday, November 1917. However, none of the men listed in the previous raid was mentioned in the article, and there is no evidence to suggest that Brandon KMT members were ever involved with opium. See *Brandon Daily Sun*, 5 November 5 1917.

78 *Brandon Weekly Sun*, 8 June 1916.

79 Anderson, *Imagined Communities*, 6.

80 Perry, "Chinese Conceptions of 'Rights.'"
81 Each KMT branch had a local commissioner who was elected from among the ranks of the elders. He was charged with the tasks of writing monthly reports, ensuring the officers were elected, being a mediator, and generally taking care of the overseas men in his community. See Quo, *Chinese Immigrants in the Prairies,* chaps. 3, 4.
82 *Winnipeg Free Press,* 23 November 1974, 6.
83 The relationship between China and Canada strengthened in 1943 and 1944 when British prime minister Winston Churchill, US president Franklin Roosevelt, Canadian prime minister William Lyon Mackenzie King, and others met twice in Canada. The first of these meetings was called the First Quebec Conference and took place between 17 August 1943 and 24 August 1943 in the City of Quebec to discuss Allied forces' military strategies. These were communicated to Chiang Kai-shek as well as to the Soviet Union.
84 University of Manitoba Archives, Stubbs Fonds, Mss 188, P.C. 180, A 96-94, fol. 17.
85 *Winnipeg Free Press,* 7 July 1936.
86 Ibid., 27 August 1935.
87 The Chinese Dramatic Society was started in Winnipeg in 1921 by two laundrymen named San Wei (Sun Wei) and Hok Sam (He Can), and it operated out of the City Cafe at 236 King Street. Two years later, the Chinese Dramatic Society had outgrown the cafe and now held smaller opera performances at 258 King Street and larger ones at the Columbia Theatre, which it rented at 604 Main Street. Chinese movies were shown at the Fox Theatre. About thirty male actors and musicians gathered there many nights a week to rehearse the musical scores and arias in order to put on the operas that the society offered twice a year on Saturday and Sunday evenings. There were additional performances to mark New Year's, the Moon Festival, Nationalist Day (10 October), and the victory celebration party on 15 August 1945. The performances, which were derived from traditional operas and other dramatic stories that depicted different periods of Chinese history, provided much-needed entertainment for the lonely group of (mostly) men in the city. Because of the scarcity of women, the men played both male and female parts and were costumed in appropriate traditional robes and dresses. Admission was free, but donations were expected and, up to 1945, were used to fund war relief in China. See Yee, *Chinatown,* 71; Baureiss and Kwong, *History of the Chinese Community of Winnipeg,* 46; *Manitoba Free Press,* 10 March 1924; *Winnipeg Tribune,* 15 August 1945; *Winnipeg Free Press,* 12 March 1955; and Chow, "Chinese Community in a Prairie City," 107.
88 While the Chinese Freemasons were seen to be the earliest provincial association, the Chinese Benevolent Association (founded in Victoria in 1884) had always been recognized by the Canadian government as the face of the Chinese community in Canada. This, however, had not been the case in Winnipeg, where the CBA often operated in the shadows of the more powerful KMT. Led by Mah Yuk, it opened an office in Winnipeg in 1914. See Chow, "Chinese Community in a Prairie City," 110. The office reopened in the early 1920s after having been shut down for six months between 1918 and 1919. Like the KMT, the CBA charged no membership fees, but everyone was a member and was expected to contribute. As a rule, the CBA had eight people on its executive, and they were usually involved in the restaurant business and with other Chinese associations in the city. The CBA continues to be somewhat active in the province.
89 *Manitoba Free Press,* Winnipeg, 13 April 1925.
90 Chinese Patriotic League of Canada (Winnipeg branch) (Mandarin: *Jianada Wen(nipei) Diqun Huaqiao Kangri jiuguohui yongjian* 加拿大溫地群華僑抗日救國會用箋).

91   *Winnipeg Free Press,* 13 July 1937.
92   Joining other communities and businesses that took part in the parade along Win-nipeg's Pacific Avenue and Main Street, the Chinese Nationalist League organized the Manitoba Chinese parade for the celebration of Winnipeg's seventy-fifth anni-versary in June 1949, with the assistance of the Chinese Benevolent Association, Chinese Freemasons, Chinese United Church, and the Chinese Dramatic Society. Mah Ming 馬明, a prominent Chinese studio photographer of the 1940s, documented the celebration and the interior of several Chinese businesses that were open for the event.
93   "Banquet Held for Chinese Minister," *Winnipeg Evening Tribune,* 8 June 1943.
94   "Chinese Hold Their Annual Decoration Day Services Sunday," *Winnipeg Free Press,* 9 June 1936.
95   The grave custom procession symbolically marked the territory inhabited by Chinese Canadians, from Chinatown to the gravesites and back. It united those who were at the centre of power (Sun Yat-sen and KMT leaders) with those who existed on its periphery (deceased Chinese settlers and the places where their families lived).
96   I have been told by old-timers in other parts of Canada that this custom is observed throughout the country.
97   Brandon Cemetery Transcript, section 16, block E, plot 25, sub-plot 1. Wing Lee had been a laundryman in 1899, working in Dauphin, Manitoba. See Peel's Prairie Prov-inces, Peel 2449, Dauphin, Manitoba, Municipal Office, list of electors of the Village of Dauphin, Province of Manitoba, 1899 (available at http://peel.library.ualberta.ca).
98   *Brandon Daily Sun,* 31 December 1917.
99   Brandon Cemetery Transcript, section 16, block B, plot 24, sub-plot 1. For over one hundred years there have been many connections between families and businesses in Saskatchewan and Manitoba. I have interviewed two people who had family members who ran laundries and restaurants along Highway 18 (and before that, along trails and branch lines) that connected Frobisher, Oxbow, and Gainsborough to the Manitoba border. The family members eventually retired to Brandon, where they died and were buried.
100 The Winnipeg branch of the KMT used to arrange with the Red Cross to ship bones back to China. I have not heard of such a practice in Brandon, however. See University of British Columbia Archives, Edgar Wickberg Fonds, Chinese in Canada series, vols. 8-39, n.d.
101 Madeline Y. Hsu echoes this thought, explaining the draw of Toisanese Chinese men to the nationalist cause of the KMT. See Hsu, "Migration and Native Place," 326.
102 See Stanley, "Chinamen."
103 When Saskatchewan lawmakers moved to ban white women from working in Chinese restaurants, Yee Clun sought the help of Frank Yee, who was then leader of the Chinese Masonic Order in Manitoba. Frank Yee, in turn, wrote to Sun Yat-sen on behalf of Yee Clun and requested his assistance. Excerpts from Sun Yat-sen's response to Frank Yee were then published in the *Regina Leader.* In his comments, Sun promised Canada Chinese trade and shipping restrictions if the act went forward. See "Dr. Sun Urges Fight against White Help Law," *Regina Leader,* 13 May 1912. The act was eventually passed, and Sun seemed to forget about the issue.
104 I have not been able to ascertain the exact amount of donations sent by the Manitoba branch. I do know that the branch sent thirty dollars for the fundraising campaign in September 1917 and another thirty dollars in June 1920 to contribute to the revolu-tion. A further thirty dollars was sent in March 1937 by the Revolutionary Fund Commission. Canadian contributions in 1922 were second only to those given by

the San Francisco community. See Con et al., *From China to Canada*, 101-3. See also Wilbur, *Sun Yat-sen*, 42-47, and 307n51.

105 The building, which has not changed much since 1933 when the group moved into it, is expensive to heat and maintain. The KMT party in Taiwan no longer provides financial support to any of its overseas branches. Manitoba KMT executive leaders have worked hard to rent out unused portions of the building to cover the mortgage and other expenses, but without central party contributions and a larger membership base renovations have been minimal. I understand that the Manitoba executive has recently started to fully renovate the building.

106 Bergère, *Sun Yat-sen*, 6.

107 *Brandon Sun*, 19 June 1934.

108 Http://multiculturalcanada.ca/.

109 See Con et al., *From China to Canada*, Table 8, 304.

110 Chinese were classed as aliens and could become citizens through a petition. After the Canadian Citizenship Act of 1 January 1947, Canadian citizens were no longer considered to be British subjects. And, that same year, Chinese received the right to vote in federal elections.

111 Chinese were expected to contribute to the Chinese War Relief Fund beginning in 1937, when China was at war with Japan. Donations (and lightly used clothing) were collected by the Chinese Patriotic League (which also formed in 1937) and sent to China to buy medical supplies, food, and clothing for the wounded, sick, and or-phaned. Wives of members were asked to knit and sew clothing to send to China.

112 Sam Dong purchased this shop from its former owner and his life-long friend Harry Chan.

113 *Winnipeg Free Press*, 19 December 1960.

114 Ibid., 2 April 1962.

115 Sun Yat-sen has become a saint in at least one other religion, namely, the Vietnamese religion of Cao Dai.

Chapter 2: The Western Manitoba Laundry

Epigraph: Manitoba Provincial Archives, Manitoba Chinese Historical Society Fonds (2005-54), box 1 [F1], file 24, Chinese poetry collection.

1 *Report of the Royal Commission on Chinese and Japanese Immigration* (Ottawa: House of Commons Journals, 1879).

2 Lai, "Home County and Clan Origins," 18.

3 *Manitoba Free Press*, 5 and 12 November 1931.

4 Ibid., 16 November 1931.

5 In addition to the obvious racism inherent in the way that Chinese names were re-corded in census data, it is also important to remember that Chinese often did not put their original Chinese names on Canadian birth certificates and other important documents.

6 *Census of Canada, 1901*, indexed census, Brandon District (available at http://automatedgenealogy.com/).

7 *Census of Canada, 1911*, indexed census, Brandon District (available at http://automatedgenealogy.com/).

8 Hoe, *Enduring Hardship*, 19.

9 *Brandon Daily Sun*, 26 September, 1916.

10 Ibid., 20 May 1917.

11 For a description of the life and interior of a Manitoba Chinese laundry, see *Winnipeg Free Press*, 19 January 1988. See also *Western Report*, 8 February 1988; University of British Columbia Archives, Edgar Wickberg Fonds, Chinese in Canada series; Quo,

Chinese Immigrants in the Prairies; Manitoba Provincial Archives, Manitoba Chinese
Historical Society, oral history project; Cheng, Oriental Immigration in Canada, chaps
1 and 2; and Seng, "Adaptive Change and Overseas Chinese Settlements."

12 See Paul Crowe's discussion of the Lee family altar in "Chinese Religions in British
Columbia."

13 I am grateful to Henry Yu, who during a conversation mentioned that he thought
Gold Mountain (variously used to refer to Canada, the United States and other
Western places of Chinese settlement) was not a geographical place but, rather, an
idea associated with opportunity.

14 Huffman and Kwong, *Dream of Gold Mountain*, 25.

15 See McKeown, "Conceptualizing Chinese Diasporas," 310.

16 *Brandon Daily Sun*, 10 April 1913, pt. 2.

17 For a discussion of the way American public health officials spread the notion that
Chinatowns were dirty and, hence, breeding grounds for cholera, smallpox, and
bubonic plague, see Shah, *Contagious Divides*.

18 *Brandon Daily Sun*, 8 August 1917.

19 Ibid., 11 August 1917.

20 See Ward, *White Canada Forever*, 7.

21 Kay Anderson notes: "Other evidence reveals that the 'bias of the municipal authorities' attention to sanitary matters in Dupont Street stemmed from their respect for,
and manipulation of, the race idea." See Anderson, *Vancouver's Chinatown*, 86.

22 *Brandon Daily Sun*, 17 July 1917.

23 See the discussion in Backhouse, "White Female Help and Chinese Canadian Employers." See also "An Act to Prevent the Employment of Female Labour in Certain
Capacities," Statutes of Saskatchewan 1912, chap. 17.

24 See Dyzenhaus and Moran, *Calling Power to Account*, 50-51n47.

25 *Brandon Daily Sun*, 15 June 1911, sec. 11.

26 Siu, "Sojourner."

27 Peel's Prairie Provinces, Peel 714, Peter O'Leary, *Travels and Experiences in Canada,
the Red River Territory, and the United States* (London: J.B. Day, 1876), 191 (available
at http://peel.library.ualberta.ca).

28 Chan, "Myth of the Chinese Sojourner."

29 The material in this section on early western Manitoba Chinese laundries is based
on combined oral histories and interviews as well as on data found in Hoe, *Enduring
Hardship*; and McLeod, *Pigtails and Gold Dust*, chap. 8.

30 Chow, "Chinese Community in a Prairie City," 67.

31 May Yoh Archives, Brandon University, Manitoba, oral history interview, 1987.

32 *Minnedosa Tribune*, 29 August 1895.

33 May Yoh Archives, Brandon University, Manitoba, oral history interview, 1987.

34 Wilder et al., *Read All about It*, 56-57.

35 University of British Columbia Archives, Edgar Wickberg Fonds, Chinese in Canada
series, vols. 8-28 (see two interview transcripts, Winnipeg, 1984).

36 Pettinger, *Shoal Lake Businesses*, 15. See also Deloraine History Book Committee,
Deloraine Scans a Century, 231 and 221.

37 *Manitoba Daily Free Press*, 19 November 1877.

38 Ibid., 29 January 1878.

39 Brandon Tax Roll, 1884, Assessment Roll Book 1, 120 and 4223.

40 Con et al., *From China to Canada*, 36.

41 *Brandon Sun Weekly*, 5 June 1884. As Gerald Friesen notes: "By the end of 1881 the
prairie line had reached Oak Lake, near Brandon; by the end of 1882, it was past
Swift Current, over 575 miles west of Winnipeg, and trains were covering the

Winnipeg-Regina run regularly; by the end of 1883, the end of the track had passed Calgary and was near the summit of the Kicking Horse Pass, 962 miles from Winnipeg." See Friesen, *Canadian Prairies*, 179.

42   *Brandon Sun Weekly*, 10 July 1884.

43   Peel's Prairie Provinces, Peel 1407, Robert Miller Christy, *Manitoba Described: Being a Series of General Observations upon the Farming, Climate, Sport, Natural History and Future Prospects of the Country* (London: Wyman, 1885), 154 (available at http://peel.library.ualberta.ca).

44   On 1 December 1900, the *Brandon Daily Sun* ran a story about three men in Montreal who cut off their queues a decade before men would do it en masse in Manitoba and elsewhere in the world. By cutting their hair, they showed themselves to be supporters of the growing revolutionary movement, thereby being ostracized by those who supported the Manchurian government. While it may be true that many Chinese immigrants in Canada cut off their queues at least a decade before 1911, in western Manitoba, there is ample evidence that Chinese men were still wearing the queue in 1910 and 1911. The *Baldur Gazette* ran a news item from San Francisco on 10 November 1910, which indicated that the Chinese consul-general Li Yun and others had been seen without their queues. See also *Baldur Gazette*, 26 January 1911; *Brandon Daily Sun*, 19 January 1911, pt. 2; and Barker, *Brandon*, 134.

45   *Brandon Weekly Sun*, 16 February 1911.

46   *Brandon Daily Sun*, 9 January 1884. There was another man with a similar name: W.H. Johnstone (with an "e"). He is listed as working for the firm Sovereen and Johnstone. See *Henderson's Directories*, 1883, 194.

47   *Brandon Daily Sun*, 28 August 1884. Wah Hep may have chosen the name "Johnson" because it was the surname of many residents in the city at the time, including a prominent businessman named J.A. Johnson who owned fifteen hundred lots of land in the downtown area. See Steen and Boyce, *Brandon*, 17.

48   In his account of travels across the Prairies, Robert Miller Christy describes these trails, or "prairie roads," which had "two narrow wheel-marks with grass growing between (the team running in the wheel-tracks." See Peel's Prairie Provinces, Peel 1407, Christy, *Manitoba Described*, 25 (available at http://peel.library.ualberta.ca). During many months of the year, travel was difficult along these routes. Often large amounts of wind and snow made the trails invisible. See *Brandon Daily Sun*, 10 December 1900. Even as late as 1926, these trails and branch lines were the only transportation channels for settlers in places like Carberry. See Goldsborough, *With One Voice*, 52.

49   A search of voters' lists in the City of Brandon and *Henderson's Directories* from 1883 to 1925 reveals that no one by the name of Wah Hep was registered as a voter or listed as a laundryman. Unfortunately, there was no directory for the year that Wah Hep operated a laundry in the city. For this entire period, there was a man known by the common name of John Johnson, sometimes spelled "Johnston," who, for thirty years, operated a laundry first on Sixth Street and then on Seventh Street. The 1901 census listed him as laundryman who came from Iceland.

50   City of Brandon Assessment Rolls, 1885 and 1886. *Brandon Sun Weekly*, 18 February 1886.

51   *Brandon Sun Weekly*, 1 January 1891, and 2 April 1891.

52   City of Brandon List of Electors, 1896 and 1897.

53   Ibid., 1898.

54   Ibid., 1899 and 1900. Unlike Wah Hep and Kee Lee, only 10 percent of the men who came between 1884 and 1905 were Protestant Christian. The largest category of

religion for this period was "other religion" (69 percent), followed by "religion not indicated" (21 percent).

55 That George Chong is assumed to be Long Gee Lan is based on information provided in the General Register of Chinese Immigration, 1892, serial no. 14328.

56 *Brandon Sun*, 6 August 1940.

57 Although George Chong's obituary mentioned a brother, it is uncertain whether Tom was his sibling, cousin, or just another Chinese man. The term "brother" was used quite casually to refer to men who were Chinese. There is no record of a Tom Chong in *Henderson's Directories*, voters' lists, or 1911 census.

58 A memorial is a formal essay that politely articulates recommendations to the emperor and his advisors.

59 See Rhoads, *Manchus and Han*, 163-64.

60 *North-China Herald and Supreme Court and Consular Gazette* (weekly edition of the *North-China Daily News*, Shanghai), 5 August 1910, 309-10.

61 Harrison, *Making of the Republican Citizen*, 20.

62 *Brandon Sun Weekly*, 5 February 1911, pt. 3.

63 Ibid., 19 January 1911, pt. 2.

64 *Birtle Eye-Witness*, July 1911. Quoted in Abra, *A View of the Birdtail*.

65 Barker, *Brandon*, 134.

66 Lai, *Chinatowns*, 60.

67 The second largest early group of Chinese settlers came to Manitoba between 1920 and 1922. The dominant age group to arrive was between eleven and seventeen years old, followed by the eighteen- to twenty-five-year-old age group. Henry Yu and Peter Ward, principal investigators on a Social Sciences and Humanities Research Council-funded research project, provided me with not yet publicly accessible data, with geographic coding produced by Edith Tam. I am grateful to Sarah Ramsden, who provided the Manitoba statistics based on the Chinese Canadian data.

68 *Brandon Daily Sun*, 6 August 1940.

69 *Winnipeg Free Press*, 23 November 1974.

70 Beginning in the 1920s, the idea that short hair conveys a modern, Western appearance is also reflected in the image of the "modern girl," whose short bob, Western clothing, and makeup was used to sell all sorts of products throughout the world. See Weibaum et al., *Modern Girl around the World*. Sam Dong used an image of the modern girl on the door knocker he left with people as a token when he was a travelling salesman.

71 See Ward, *White Canada Forever*, 5 and chap. 1.

72 *Brandon Weekly Sun*, 10 April 1913, pt. 1.

73 Ibid., 17 April 1913, pt. 1.

74 Ibid., 31 July 1913, pt. 2.

75 *Report of the Royal Commission 1885*, lvii.

76 Gray, *Booze*, 43.

77 *Henderson's Directories*, 1883, 56; *Brandon Sun Weekly*, 2 January 1889.

78 City of Brandon List of Electors. See also *Brandon Sun Weekly*, 3 September 1896.

79 *Census of Canada, 1901*, indexed census, Brandon District, 6, line 4 (available at http://automatedgenealogy.com/).

80 *Henderson's Directories*, 1909.

81 Ibid., 1911.

82 *Brandon Weekly Sun*, 18 May 1905.

83 Ibid., 15 September 1910.

84 While there was no *Henderson's Directories* for 1910, they listed eight Chinese laundries in 1909 and thirteen in 1911.

85 Quoted in the *Brandon Weekly Sun*, 23 November 1911, pt. 1.
86 Cartoons with the Yellow Kid were used to sell all kinds of construction and gardening supplies in hardware companies throughout North America. See Blackbeard, *R.F. Outcault's The Yellow Kid*, 131.
87 I am grateful to my department chair and colleague Kurt Noll, who recognized the Yellow Kid from his days in advertising. See Blackbeard, *R.F. Outcault's The Yellow Kid*, 135.
88 Richard Felton Outcault, "Li Hung Chang Visits Hogan's Alley," *New York World*, 6 September 1896.
89 *Brandon Weekly Sun*, 25 May 1913.
90 *Henderson's Directories*, 1913. See also *Brandon Daily Sun*, 6 February 1918.
91 *Henderson's Directories*, 1917, VII.
92 Fen Lee opened the laundry in Baldur in April 1899. See *Baldur Gazette*, 27 April 1899.
93 *Baldur Gazette*, 19 April 1900.
94 Ibid., 27 February 1902.
95 Ibid., 17 August 1908.
96 Ibid., 15 November 1901.

97   In discussing the recent murder by torture of the Rev. Mr. Brooks, Ho Yow, the Chinese consul general at San Francisco deplores the event and gives assurance that the Chinese government is anxious to protect Christian missionaries ... [T]here is another side to the condition, and it is this which concerns us in the Brooks incident. The work of the missionary is primarily aimed against the religion of China. Now, it is all right for the missionary to carry his doctrine in among the savages of the mountains of Luzon or among the natives of Borneo ... They have no religion and are therefore open to the reception of one. With China, however, religions are most pronounced and most confirmed. The chief body of religious belief is Confucianism ... I have always thought that if it is desired to make Christianity an influence in China it should not be made the pioneer influence. It should properly follow, not precede, the introduction of the improvements and advancements of western science.

        (*Baldur Gazette*, 5 July 1900)
98 Ibid., 30 June 1904.
99 Ibid., 25 December 1908.
100 Ibid., 24 April 1902.
101 Ibid., 19 January 1905.
102 Ibid., 8 February 1912.
103 Ibid., 21 October 1909.
104 Fifth Census of Canada, 1911, district 23, Souris, enumeration no. 58, township 5, range 14, west 1st, 6, line 3.
105 *Baldur Gazette*, 20 April 1911.
106 Ibid., 28 October 1909.
107 Ibid., 29 April 1911.
108 Ibid., 23 November 1911.
109 Ibid., 16 May 1912.
110 "Local News," *Baldur Gazette*, 30 September 1909.
111 *Baldur Gazette*, 17 April 1913.
112 Ibid., 28 November 1912.
113 Chinese New Year fell on 6 February 1913 that year. In the two-week period of Chinese celebrations that normally follow this date, Tom went to Winnipeg. See *Baldur Gazette*, 13 February 1913.

114 *Baldur Gazette,* 6 April 1916.
115 Ibid., 12 October 1916.
116 Ibid., 30 August 1917.
117 Oral history interview.
118 Ibid.

Chapter 3: The Western Manitoba Restaurant

 1 In rural Chinese settlements in western Manitoba, in which populations were small and connections were essential to success, the restaurant offered a way to become a social capitalist. See Li, "Social Capital and Economic Outcomes," 181-83.
 2 This information has been gleaned from many fieldwork visits to rural towns and villages in western Manitoba as well as from oral history accounts. See also Huffman and Kwong, *Dream of Gold Mountain,* 12-13.
 3 Levenstein, *Revolution at the Table,* 190.
 4 This information has been compiled from oral history accounts and interviews.
 5 People did not understand these, to them, unusual behaviours and living arrangements and so assumed that at their root were "immoral" and "un-Christian" influences such as homosexuality. See Shah, *Contagious Divides,* chap. 3. None of the research participants mentioned having male sexual partners, although it should be noted that I did not ask this question. I also did not delve into court records and other archival material to determine whether this was a practice in the area.
 6 This information has been compiled from oral history accounts and interviews.
 7 *Carberry News Express,* 16 June 1921.
 8 Ibid., 2 September 1920.
 9 Ibid., 10 April 1919.
10 For instance, see the story in ibid., 1 April 1920.
11 We have encountered several restaurants that have been in business for twenty, thirty, and (rarely) forty years. Currently the common ownership pattern in smaller rural communities seems to be characterized by a high rate of turnover.
12 Family members could be relied on to work very long hours, often with no vacations, year after year. See Gabbacia, *We Are What We Eat,* 87.
13 See Steinberg, *Ethnic Myth.*
14 *Henderson's Directories,* 1905.
15 City of Brandon Assessment Roll, 1904, no. 7455, ward 3, sec. 23, block 77, book 2, 30.
16 Buddy's family members have disappeared from the area, with the result that we were unable to discover any other details of his life, such as when he died.
17 Available at http://www.collectionscanada.gc.ca/.
18 *Winnipeg Free Press,* 30 July 1960.
19 Daly House Museum, scrapbook, *Brandon Daily Sun,* 3 July 1961.
20 Ibid., 22 December 1973.
21 In 1919, Lee Foon, then living in Baldur, brought his wife and brother to Canada. This makes his wife, See Yee, the first Chinese woman in western rural Manitoba.
22 In larger areas of settlement and Chinatowns, there were Chinese midwives and even doctors (e.g., in Vancouver) who could assist with births, but Wong Au was the only Chinese woman in western Manitoba and suffered because of it.
23 The details of Wong Au's life are compiled from a number of sources, including oral histories, obituaries, and discussions with May Yoh. I also consulted materials she collected in the late 1980s. See May Yoh Archives, notes, correspondence, newspaper clippings, and photographs, n.d., Brandon University, Brandon, Manitoba. See also Brandon History Book Committee, *Millennium Memories,* 396-98.

24 This information has been compiled from obituaries, oral history interviews, field-work conducted at the KMT office, and some material in the May Yoh Archives. See also *Brandon Sun,* 6 June 1959.

25 This information has been determined by a search of *Henderson's Directories* and interviews with research participants

26 Brandon History Book Committee, *Millennium Memories,* 397.

27 See Daly House Museum, Brandon, obituary scrapbook, *Brandon Sun,* 3 December 2000, Brandon, Manitoba.

28 Choy's retirement to his homeland in 1939 represented a major trend, beginning in the 1930s and ending in the late 1950s, of return migration for Manitoba's Chinese Canadians.

29 See Newdale Historical Society, *Newdale,* 54 and 57.

30 Much of the information in this section has been compiled from interviews, oral histories (given as part of the Manitoba Historical Society Oral History Project), family stories in local history books, and obituaries in the *Brandon Sun.*

31 *Brandon Sun,* 9 September 1965.

32 Daly House Museum, Brandon, scrapbook, *Brandon Sun,* 20 April 1976, August 1979.

33 Events continue, but they are no longer organized by the KMT. The Winnipeg CBA and elders organize that city's Decoration Day, and the old-timers in Brandon organize the event there. More often, ethnic events are hosted by groups such as the Winnipeg Chinese Cultural and Community Centre (headed by Dr. Joseph Du) and the local Westman Chinese Association (headed by Kenny Choy).

34 The information on Baldur has been compiled from fieldwork interviews and oral histories as well as from data contained in Rural Municipality of Argyle, *Centennial History of Argyle,* 527-28. See also *Baldur Gazette,* 15 November 1917.

35 *Baldur Gazette,* 13 June 1918; 5 December 1918; and 9 October 1919.

36 Ibid., 15 September 1921.

37 Ibid., 1 June 1922.

38 Ibid., 13 March 1924.

39 Ibid., 27 January 1921.

40 Ibid., 10 July 1924; 24 July 1924.

41 Information in this section has been gleaned from oral history interviews conducted in January and February 2008. See also Rural Municipality of Argyle, *Centennial History of Argyle,* 159; and Rural Municipality of Argyle, *Come into Our Heritage,* 527; and Jean Lee, Manitoba Chinese Historical Society, Oral History Project, tape C-1148, 17 July 1988.

42 Brenda History Committee, *Bridging Brenda,* 693.

43 Binscarth History Committee, *Binscarth Memories,* 33.

44 Neepawa History Book Committee, *Heritage.*

45 Ling Lee lived in Winnipeg briefly and was a founding member of the 1917 Chinese Christian Fellowship.

46 *Neepawa Free Press,* 16 January 1959.

47 Ibid., 16 January 1959. See also Neepawa History Book Committee, *Heritage.*

48 *Neepawa Free Press,* 16 January 1959.

49 Neepawa History Book Committee, *Heritage.* See also *Neepawa Free Press,* 29 November 1968.

50 Only a handful of women had come to western Manitoba before 1923, when the Chinese Immigration Act came into effect. Therefore, until 1947, most men who had the means in the region went to China to obtain an arranged marriage.

51 Carberry Plains Archives, scrapbook, "Local News," *Carberry News Express,* 11 September 1891.

52 *Carberry News Express*, 4 February 1910.
53 *Census of Canada, 1911,* vol. 2 (Ottawa: C.H. Parmelee, 1913).
54 *Carberry News Express*, 4 February 1910.
55 *Census of Canada, 1921,* vol. 1 (Ottawa: F.A. Acland, 1925), 575, Table 35 (Male population classified according to religious denominations by provinces, 1921).
56 Carberry Plains Archives, scrapbook, *Carberry News Express*, 25 October 1907.
57 Carberry Plains Archives, Carberry businesses, 1913 advertisement for King's Restaurant.
58 "Police Court," *Carberry News Express*, 20 June 1913.
59 Carberry Plains Archives, scrapbook, "Advertisement," *Carberry News Express*, 29 October 1915.
60 Ibid., 17 May 1923, 6 December 1923, Carberry Plains Archives, scrapbook.
61 *Carberry News Express*, 1 April 1920.
62 Ibid.
63 Ibid.
64 Ibid., 13 May 1920.
65 Ibid., 6 May 1920.
66 General Register of Chinese Immigration, 1911, Low Kon Lee, serial no. 66722.
67 Oral history interview.
68 *Carberry News Express*, 9 February 1922.
69 Oral history interview.
70 Carberry Plains Archives, notes, research report, "Chinese Population and Immigration in Prairie Towns," September 2008.
71 *Carberry News Express*, 9 February 1922.
72 "New Carberry Luncheonette and Cafe to Open Thursday, November 7th," *Carberry News Express*, 30 October 1940.
73 Bergère, *Sun Yat-sen*, 209.

Chapter 4: Chinese Food and Identity

1 Cho, "On Eating Chinese," 46.
2 Penfold, "Eddie Shack Was No Tim Horton," 49.
3 See Newton, "Jell-O Syndrome," 255.
4 Mannur, "Model Minorities Can Cook."
5 Ferrero, "Comida Sin Par Consumption," 197.
6 Yung, *Cult of Dr. Sun,* 6. The entire first chapter of Sun's work is devoted to a discussion of the Chinese diet and its medicinal properties, and how this diet reflects China as a civilized nation.
7 *Minnedosa Tribune,* 9 January 1908.
8 *Brandon Daily Sun,* 23 December 1916.
9 Ibid., 2 January 1917.
10 Many parallels may be seen in Harvey Levenstein's description of the way in which negative American attitudes towards Italian immigrants changed once they tasted their food. See Levenstein, "American Response to Italian Food."
11 Srinivas, "Everyday Exotic," 94.
12 Bronner, *Grasping Things,* 196.
13 *Brandon Sun,* 22 July 1964.
14 Ibid., 27 February 1974.
15 Friesen, *Canadian Prairies,* 272.
16 *Carberry News Express*, 22 January 1920.
17 Tuchman and Levine, "New York Jews and Chinese Food," 385.
18 Miller, "Identity Takeout," 430.

19 Friesen, *Canadian Prairies*, 262-63.
20 Daniel, "Without Food," 276.
21 I am grateful to Meharoona Ghani, manager, Anti-Racism and Multiculturalism Unit, Settlement and Multiculturalism Branch, British Columbia, for introducing me to these three stages of integration.
22 Ohnuki-Tierney, *Rice as Self*, 3.
23 See Auletta, *Underclass;* and Morris and Irwin, "Employment Histories."
24 Feeley-Harnik, "Against the Motion."
25 As I became more familiar with research participants at restaurants, I was offered food from the back regions. At one rural restaurant I was treated to *baozi* (steamed buns made with chicken, Chinese mushrooms, and onions) and *mochi* (coconut-sprinkled dainties made with rice flour dough and containing peanut filling). These "authentic" foods had been made by a visiting family member who had brought the ingredients from China. *Baozi* and *mochi* pointed to a range of authentic foods that were hidden from the gaze (and palates) of most non-Chinese patrons.
26 For a discussion of the role of *ling* in religion, see Sangren, "History and the Rhetoric of Legitimacy," 684. For a discussion of the application of *ling* to other religious and cultural contexts, see Marshall, "Moving the Spirit on Taiwan," 86-87.
27 Lloyd, "Folklore, Foodways, and the Supernatural," 61.
28 Ang-Lygate, "Everywhere to Go but Home," 379.
29 The recent migration of large numbers of northern Chinese from mainland China is only now beginning to pose an alternative to the southern Chinese culture that has dominated the region.
30 Ohnuki-Tierney, *Rice as Self*, 9.
31 Here I draw on the insights of Emiko Ohnuki-Tierney, who notes the power of harvest rituals and rice to renew and reproduce the soul. See Ohnuki-Tierney, *Rice as Self*, 56.
32 Cho, "How Taste Remembers Life," 82.
33 See Brah, *Cartographies of Diaspora*, 4.
34 Yu, *Thinking Orientals*, 5.
35 *Manitoba Free Press*, 20 February 1911.
36 Chow, "Chinese Community in a Prairie City," 108-9.
37 *Boissevain Globe*, 26 October 1905.
38 For a description of Mid-Autumn Festival celebrations in New York and the secularization of the event and its food, see Langlois, "Moon Cake in Chinatown."
39 On the menu, many Chinese Canadian restaurants describe their food as a "Canadian Chinese Food Experience." See Wong, *The Barbarians Are Coming*.
40 Jack Goody discusses the role food plays in creating class and social distinctions. See Goody, *Cooking Cuisine and Class*.
41 Nobody from northern China came that year, but I have been told by research participants from both southern and northern China that people from northern China are now invited and attend.
42 Tulasi Srinivas, in her discussion of the relationship between food and identity in Bangalore, India, refers to a narrative of nostalgia: "The narrative of nostalgia invests the food and emphasizes the history of the dish, the authenticity of the process and ingredients, and the utopian ideal of a lost time, thereby catering to the Gestalt of loss and memory that is part of the cosmopolitan's narrative." See Srinivas, "Everyday Exotic," 100.
43 Cho, "Diasporic Citizenship," 16.
44 Barthes, "Toward a Psychosociology of Contemporary Food Consumption," 21.
45 Bell and Valentine, *Consuming Geographies*. The Prairie Chinese, like other diaspora populations, have been defined by the culture of difference as one community. Even

today, Chinese are grouped with, and mistaken for, other Asians, such as Japanese and Koreans. Homi Bhabha refers to the manner in which immigrants exist in cultures of difference and have their identity defined and fixed by others. I am not suggesting that there is any kind of national Chinese identity or generalized notion of Chineseness. Yet, at the same time, I want to demonstrate the strength of competing national identities in the isolation of the Canadian Prairies. It is this isolation, in combination with a history of racism and intolerance, that has created a powerful sense of longing for the place and time of an ideal notion of China and that has made rural Prairie Chineseness different. See Bhabha, *Location of Culture,* 46-47 and 72. See also Chow, "Introduction."

46 This anecdote about the life of Bing Woo is based on information given by Wes and Helen Wong and by Walker Wong to May Yoh in 1988. May Yoh also distinctly remembers frequently seeing Bing at the site of the old City Hall in the early 1970s. This information was verified by Wes and Helen Wong.

Chapter 5: Manitoba Chinese Religion and KMT Confucianism

1 Chun, "Fuck Chineseness," 124. See also Chun, "From Nationalism to Nationalizing," 128.
2 Province of Manitoba Archives, Letter from Sun Yat-sen to Li Kimkim and Wong Oursheng, President and Secretary of the Manitoba KMT, 1917.
3 Orsi, *Between Heaven and Earth,* chap. 3.
4 Here, I draw on the insights of Michael Puett and his ideas related to self-divination in early China. See Puett, *To Become a God,* 3.
5 See Bergère, *Sun Yat-sen,* 50-52.
6 University of British Columbia Archives, Edgar Wickberg Fonds, Chinese in Canada Series, 1984, 13.
7 *Winnipeg Evening Tribune,* 2 December 1939; *Manitoba Free Press,* 7 March 1928.
8 United Church Archives, Winnipeg, All People's Mission Papers, box B, file 1; Calendar: The Missions, November and December 1933 calendar entries include information about the French and Chinese missions.
9 United Church Archives, University of Winnipeg, Woman's Missionary Society of the Methodist, Presbyterian, and United Church of Canada (annual reports), Foreign Work – "Asiatics in Canada," *The Eighty-Fourth Annual Report of the Missionary Society of the Methodist Church* (Toronto: Methodist Mission Rooms, 1908).
10 St. Andrew's Presbyterian Church Records, Winnipeg, St. Andrew's Annual Reports, 1882-1914, 1888, 8.
11 *Lovell's Classified Business Directory,* 845-46, 26.
12 St. Andrew's Presbyterian Church Records, Winnipeg, St. Andrew's Annual Reports, 1882-1914, 1897, 9.
13 Ibid., 1900, 26.
14 Yee, *Chinatown,* 71.
15 Baureiss and Kwong, *History of the Chinese Community of Winnipeg,* 43.
16 Yee, *Chinatown,* 71.
17 *Estevan-Mercury,* 1 April 1920.
18 Chen, *Getting Saved in America,* 41.
19 David Lam, British Columbia's twenty-fifth (and Canada's first Chinese) lieutenant-governor, who immigrated to Canada in 1967, expressed the connection between Christianity and Confucianism well:

   I think it is very important to combine Christian and Confucian beliefs. Christianity gave me peace of mind, confidence and a certain value system ... The

Christian work ethic says there is no limit to the amount of money you can make or how hard you want to work to achieve your goals. But Confucius says there is a limit; you've got to have a balance. It's so important to strike a harmonious balance in our thinking.

See Huang and Jeffery, *Chinese Canadians*, 65-66.

20 Yang, *Gifts, Favors, and Banquets*, chap. 6.
21 Ibid., 112-14.
22 According to Wang Gungwu, the term "overseas Chinese" *(huaqiao)* was first used by Huang Tsun-hsien in the 1880s. See Wang, "A Note on the Origins of Hua-ch'iao," 7.
23 In her work Diana Lary includes many traditional couplets and sayings that point to the importance of Confucian thought and culture in the new republic. Some of these have been repeated to me in conversations about Sun Yat-sen and descriptions of his contribution to China. The Manitoba KMT office also displays many similar (though not identical) couplets on its walls. See Lary, *China's Republic*.
24 See Carnes and Fenggang, *Asian American Religions*, 13-15. See also DeVries et al., *Asian Religions in British Columbia*, Introduction and Conclusion.
25 Carnes and Fenggang, *Asian American Religions*, 10.
26 Several elderly Chinese-speaking research participants throughout Manitoba told me that the name of their main god, which they defined as the Heavenly God, was *Tianshi* (天師). Some had home altars dedicated to this god.
27 *Guanyin*, who resembles the Virgin Mary, is often displayed in rural restaurant altars, where, for patrons, she evokes Orientalist understandings of China and, for owners, the desired modern sensibilities.
28 See Warner and Wittner, *Gatherings in Diaspora*, 3-27.
29 Warner, "Enlisting Smelser's Theory," 113-14.
30 Mannheim, "Problem of Generations," 304.
31 There were few Japanese immigrants in Manitoba during the early period of Chinese settlement and none after the bombing of Pearl Harbor during the Second World War, when, throughout Canada, Japanese were sent to live in internment camps.
32 Mullins, "Organizational Dilemmas of Ethnic Churches"; and Kashima, *Buddhism in America*.
33 Quoted in Chen, *Getting Saved in America*, 28.
34 Master Shen was not available for an interview when he visited Brandon in the winter and the spring of 2010. Shen's website (www.qigongacademy.ca) suggests that, while he resides in Vancouver and is president of a national qigong academy, he only offers classes in Manitoba.
35 R. Stephen Warner commented on a version of this chapter and noted that the women of immigrant communities were often the ones who initiated the building of native religious institutions.
36 Warner, "Enlisting Smelser's Theory," 109.
37 See Ching, *Confucianism and Christianity;* and Kung and Ching, *Christianity and Chinese Religions*.
38 See Sun, "Confucianism as a Religion," 233-34.
39 In the 1911 census survey there were five Japanese persons (as opposed to 885 Chinese). In the 1921 census survey there were only forty Japanese persons residing in the province (as opposed to 1,279 Chinese); a quarter of these individuals lived in western Manitoba, with five living in Brandon and five living in Neepawa.
40 One hundred and thirty-three Manitobans self-identified as Confucian on the 1911 census. In total, there were 885 Chinese individuals living in the province at the time,

only five of whom were Japanese. I am assuming, since the religious data does not mention ethnicity, that all 133 Manitobans were Chinese.

41 In the 1921 census, a total of 691 Manitobans self-identified as Confucians out of a total of 1,331 Chinese. Again, because the number of Japanese persons living in the province was only forty, I have assumed that all of the Confucians were Chinese. Even if every single Japanese person had self-identified as Confucian, the percentage would still have been close to fifty. While individual census data regarding religious self-identification is available for 1901 and 1911, there is no access to individual data for the 1921 census.

42 See *Census of Canada, 1921*, vol. 1 (Ottawa: F.A. Acland, 1925), tables 25, 28, and 39.

43 See Kuo, "Redeploying Confucius."

44 See Li, *Political History of China*, 306-7.

45 Jensen, *Manufacturing Confucianism.*

46 Nedostup, "Civic Faith and Hybrid Ritual," 27-28; and Nedostup, *Superstitious Regimes*, chap. 2.

47 Bergère, *Sun Yat-sen*, 89.

48 Being modern and Western was not linked to prior knowledge or education. Early Manitoba KMT leaders were not necessarily well-educated men; however, they had powerful connections and charismatic personalities that enabled them to ascend to high positions in the party and in their professions. Wong Oursheng (Mandarin: *Huang Rongsheng*), who was local party secretary in 1917, had an elementary school education and, through a Lee clan introduction, became involved in the revolution before 1912. Charlie Foo, who was a decades-long KMT leader, had completed the upper primary grades and joined the party in 1920 through the introduction of an Au/*Ou*. He was also from the Au/*Ou* family.

Conclusion

1 Labour patterns also had an impact on food consumption and masculinity. As men became wealthier, stopped labouring in wash houses, and began working in restaurants, they had more access to better and more nourishing foods. By attending Chinese and non-Chinese events, a man also had a chance to eat high-calorie foods that would give him strength. Thus, the shift in labour patterns, coupled with new everyday and special-event food customs, contributed to an emerging stronger male persona.

2 See Chen, "Occupational Hazards."

Bibliography

Newspapers
Birtle Eyewitness
Boissevain Globe
Brandon Daily Sun
Brandon Weekly Sun
Brandon Sun Weekly
Carberry News Express
Chinese Times
Estevan-Mercury
Manitoba Free Press
Manitoba Daily Free Press
Minnedosa Tribune
Neepawa Free Press
North-China Herald and Supreme Court and Consular Gazette (weekly
    edition of the *North-China Daily News*, Shanghai)
Portage La Prairie Weekly Review
Baldur Gazette
Brandon Sun
Canadian New Nationalist Press (Jianada Xinminguo Bao)
Dauphin Press
Lethbridge Daily Herald
Province (Vancouver)
Voice (Winnipeg)
Winnipeg Free Press
Western Report

Directories
City of Brandon List of Electors, 1895 to 1925. Daly House Museum, Brandon, Manitoba.
Directory for City of Brandon. Brandon: Chas Marshallsay and Company, 1883.
Henderson's Directories for the City of Brandon, 1883-2000. Brandon Public Library,
    Brandon, Manitoba.
"Lovell's Classified Business Directory." In *Manitoba Northwest Gazetteer*, 1901.
    Legislative Library, Winnipeg, Manitoba.
Manitoba Northwest Gazetteer, 1901. Legislative Library, Winnipeg, Manitoba.
Steen and Boyce. Comp. *Brandon, Manitoba, Canada, and Her Industries*. Winnipeg,
    MB: Boyce, 1882.

Wong Kin. Comp. *International Chinese Business Directory of the World for the Year 1913: A Comprehensive List of Prominent Chinese Firms and Individuals (Wangguo Jixin Bianlan)*. San Francisco: International Chinese Business Directory, 1913.

Local Histories

Abra, Marion W. comp. and ed. *A View of the Birdtail: A History of the Municipality of Birtle, 1878-1974*. Altona, MB: D.W. Friesen and Sons, 1974.

Baldur High School Centennial Committee. *Historical Sketches of Argyle Municipality*. Baldur, MB: Baldur High School Centennial Committee, 1967.

Barker, G.F. 1977. *Brandon: A City, 1881-1961*. Brandon: G.F. Barker.

Binscarth History Committee. *Binscarth Memories*. Binscarth. MB: Binscarth History Committee, 1984.

Brandon History Book Committee. *Millennium Memories: Family Focus*. Brandon, MB: Brandon Millennium Committee, 2001.

Brenda History Committee. *Bridging Brenda: Napinka, Medora, Waskada, Goodlands*. Vol. 2. Altona, MB: Friesen Printers, 1990.

Clingan, Ida. *The Virden Story*. Virden: Empire Publishing, 1957. (Printed on the celebration of Virden's seventy-fifth anniversary.)

Dauphin Historical Society, Dauphin Valley Spans the Years. Steinbach, MB: Derksen Printers, 1970.

Deloraine History Book Committee. *Deloraine Scans a Century: A History of Deloraine and District, 1880-1980*. Deloraine, MB: History Book Committee, 1980.

Little, Adam S. *Dogtown to Dauphin*. Winnipeg: Watson and Dwyer, 1988.

Neepawa History Book Committee. *Heritage: Neepawa, Land of Plenty, 1883-1983 – A History of the Town of Neepawa and District as Told and Recorded by Its People*. Winnipeg: Inter-Collegiate Press, 1983.

Newdale Historical Society. *Newdale, 1870-1970*. Brandon, MB: Leech Printing, 1970.

Pettinger, Raymond S. *Shoal Lake Businesses, 1874-2004*. Altona, MB: Friesens Corporation, History Division, 2004.

Pipestone, Rural Municpality of, comp. *Trails Along the Pipestone*. Pipestone, MB: Rural Municipality of Pipestone Historical Project, 1981.

Rural Municipality of Argyle. *Centennial History of Argyle: Come into Our Heritage*. Baldur, MB: Rural Municipality of Argyle, 1981.

–. *Come into Our Heritage, R.M. of Argyle Addendum, 1982-2000*. Baldur, MB: Rural Municipality of Argyle, 2000.

Articles and Books

Abarca, Meredith E. "Authentic or Not, It's Original." *Food and Foodways* 12 (2004): 1-25.

Ammerman, Nancy T., ed. *Everyday Religion: Observing Modern Religious Lives*. New York: Oxford University Press, 2007.

Anderson, Benedict. *Imagined Communities: Reflections on the Origin and Spread of Nationalism*. Rev. and ex. ed. London: Verso, 1991.

Anderson, E.N. *The Food of China*. New Haven: Yale University Press, 1988.

Anderson, Kathryn, and Dana C. Jack. "Learning to Listen: Interview Techniques and Analyses." In Sherna Berger Gluck and Daphne Patai, eds., *Women's Words: The Feminist Practice of Oral History*, 11-26. London: Routledge: 1991.

Anderson, Kay J. *Vancouver's Chinatown: Racial Discourses in Canada, 1875-1980*. Montreal: McGill-Queen's University Press, 1991.

Ang-Lygate, M. "Everywhere to Go but Home: On (re)(dis)(un)location." *Journal of Gender Studies* 5, 3 (1996): 375-88.

Auletta, Ken. *The Underclass.* New York: Random House, 1982.

Backhouse, Constance. "White Female Help and Chinese Canadian Employers: Race, Class, Gender and Law in the Case of Yee Clun, 1924." *Canadian Ethnic Studies* 26, 3 (1994): 34-52.

Barker, G.F. *Brandon: A City – 1881-1961.* Brandon: G.F. Barker, 1977.

Barthes, Roland. "Toward a Psychosociology of Contemporary Food Consumption." In Carole Counihan and Penny Van Esterik, eds., *Food and Culture: A Reader,* 20-27. Reprint. New York: Routledge, 1997.

Baureiss, Gunter, and Julia Kwong. *The History of the Chinese Community of Winnipeg.* Winnipeg: The Chinese Community Committee, 1979.

Beaman, Lori G. *Religion and Canadian Society: Traditions, Transitions and Innovations.* Toronto: Canadian Scholars Press, 2006.

Bell, D., and G. Valentine. *Consuming Geographies: We Are Where We Eat.* London: Routledge, 1997.

Bell, Daniel A., and Hahm Chaibong. *Confucianism for the Modern World.* Cambridge: Cambridge University Press, 2003.

Bergère, Marie-Claire. *Sun Yat-Sen.* Trans. Janet Lloyd. Stanford, CA: Stanford University Press, 1994.

Berreman, Gerald. *Behind Many Masks: Ethnography and Impression Management in a Himalayan Village.* Ithaca, NY: Cornell University Society for Applied Anthropology, 1962.

Berry, John. "Acculturation and Adaptation of Immigrants." In Paul Crowe and Jan Walls, eds., *Chinatown and Beyond: An Interdisciplinary Examination of the Historical Development, Global Significance, Key Characteristics, Evolution and Future of the World's Chinatowns.* Hong Kong: Hong Kong Baptist University and David C. Lam Institute for East West Studies, 2010.

Beyer, Peter, and Lori Beaman, eds. *Globalization, Religion and Culture.* Leiden: Brill, 2007.

Bhabha, Homi K. *Location of Culture.* New York: Routledge, 1994.

Blackbeard, Bill, Introduction, and William Randolph Hearst III, Foreword. *R.F. Outcault's The Yellow Kid: A Centennial Celebration of the Kid Who Started the Comics.* Northampton, MA: Kitchen Sink Press, 1995.

Blanchard, Jim. *Winnipeg 1912: Diary of a City.* Winnipeg: University of Manitoba Press, 2005.

Brah, Avtar. *Cartographies of Diaspora: Contesting Identities. Gender, Racism, Ethnicity Series.* New York: Routledge, 1996.

Bramadat, Paul, and David Seljak, eds. *Christianity and Ethnicity in Canada.* Toronto: University of Toronto Press, 2008.

Bronner, Simon J. *Grasping Things: Folk Material Culture and Mass Society in America.* Lexington, KT: University Press of Kentucky, 1986.

Cabezon, Jose Ignacio. "The Discipline and Its Other: The Dialectic of Alterity in the Study of Religion." *Journal of the American Academy of Religion* 74, 1 (2006): 21-38.

Carnes, Tony, and Fenggang Yang. *Asian American Religions: The Making and Remaking of Borders and Boundaries.* New York: New York University Press, 2004.

Chan, Anthony B. "The Myth of the Chinese Sojourner in Canada." In K. Victor Ujimoto and Gordon Hirabayashi, eds., *Visible Minorities and Multiculturalism: Asians in Canada,* 33-42. Toronto: Butterworths, 1980.

Chan, Kwok B., and Lawrence Lam. "Chinese in Timmins, Canada, 1915-1950: A Study of Ethnic Stereotypes in the Press." *Asian Profile* 14, 6 (1986): 569-83.

Chang, K.C. *Food in Chinese Culture: Anthropological and Historical Perspectives.* New Haven: Yale University Press, 1977.

Chau, Adam Yuet. *Miraculous Response: Doing Popular Religion in Contemporary China.* Stanford, CA: Stanford University Press, 2006.

Chen, Carolyn. *Getting Saved in America: Taiwanese Immigration and Religious Experience.* Princeton, NJ: Princeton University Press, 2008.

Chen, Tina Mai. "Occupational Hazards: Expectations and Experiences of Chinese Businesses and their Employees during the Evacuation of Rangoon, 1942." Paper delivered at the International Society for the Study of Chinese Overseas conference, Singapore, 5-7 May 2010.

Chen Zhongping. "Building the Chinese Diaspora across Canadian Towns and Small Cities: Chinese Diasporic Discourse and the Case of Peterborough, Ontario." *Diaspora* 13, 2-3 (2004): 143-68.

–. "Chinese Familism and Immigration Experience in Canadian Towns and Small Cities: From Dual Paradigms on the Chinese in Canada to a Cross-Cultural Study of the Case of Peterborough, Ontario, 1892-1951." *Asian Profile* 32, 4 (2004): 289-312.

–. "Chinese Minority and Everyday Racism in Canada Towns and Small Cities: An Ethnic Study of the Case of Peterborough, Ontario, 1892-1951." *Canadian Ethnic Studies* 36, 1 (2004): 1-22.

Cheng Tien-Fang. *Oriental Immigration in Canada.* Shanghai: The Commercial Press, 1931.

Chiang Hung-Min. *Chinese Islanders: Making a Home in the New World.* Charlottetown, PEI: Island Studies Press, 2006.

Ching, Julia. "The Ambiguous Character of Chinese Religion(s)." *Studies in Interreligious Dialogue* 11, 2 (2001): 213-23.

–. *Confucianism and Christianity: A Comparative Study.* New York: Kodansha International, 1977.

Cho, Lily. "Diasporic Citizenship: Contradictions and Possibilities for Canadian Literature." Paper presented at TransCanada: Literature, Institutions, Citizenship, Morris J. Wosk Centre for Dialogue, Vancouver, 23-26 June 2005. Full text of paper available at http://www.transcanadas.ca/.

–. "On Eating Chinese: Diasporic Agency and the Chinese Canadian Restaurant Menu." In Maria N. Ng and Philip Holden, eds., *Reading Chinese Transnationalisms: Society, Literature, Film.* Hong Kong: Hong Kong University Press, 2006.

– "'How Taste Remembers Life': Diasporic Memory and Community in Fred Wah's Poetry." In Tseen Khoo and Kam Louie, eds., *Culture, Identity, Commodity: Diasporic Chinese Literatures in English*, 81-106. Montreal: McGill-Queen's University Press, 2005.

Chow, Rey. "Introduction: On Chineseness as a Theoretical Problem." *boundary 3* 25, 3 (1998): 1-24.

Chow Wing-Sam. "A Chinese Community in a Prairie City: A Holistic Perspective of Its Class and Ethnic Relations." PhD diss., Ann Arbor, MI, University Microfilms International, 1981.

Chun, Allen. "From Nationalism to Nationalizing: Cultural Imagination and State Formation in Postwar Taiwan." In Jonathon Unger, ed., *Chinese Nationalism*, 126-47. Armonk, NY: M.E. Sharpe, 1996.

–. "Fuck Chineseness: On the Ambiguities of Ethnicity as Culture as Identity." *boundary 2* 23, 2 (1996): 111-38.

Chung, Sue Fawn, and Priscilla Wegars, eds. *Chinese American Death Rituals: Respecting the Ancestors.* Lanham, MD: Altamira Press, 2005.

Clart, Philip, and Charles B. Jones, eds. *Religion in Modern Taiwan.* Hawaii: University of Hawaii Press, 2003.

Collier, John Jr. *Visual Anthropology: Photography as a Research Method*. New York: Holt, Rinehart and Winston, 1967.

Con, Harry, Ronald J. Con, Graham Johnson, Edgar Wickberg, and William E. Willmott. *From China to Canada: A History of the Chinese Communities in Canada*. Toronto: McClelland and Stewart Limited in association with the Multiculturalism Directorate, Department of the Secretary of Stare and the Canadian Government Publishing Centre, Supply and Services Canada, 1982.

Crowe, Paul. "Chinese Religions in British Columbia." In Larry DeVries, Don Baker, and Dan Overmyer, eds., *Asian Religions in British Columbia*. Vancouver: UBC Press, 2010.

Daniel, Carolyn. "Without Food Everything Is Less than Nothing." *Food, Culture and Society* 9, 3 (2006): 275-85.

de Certeau, Michel. *The Practice of Everyday Life*. Berkeley, CA: University of California Press, 1984.

DeVries, Larry, Don Baker, and Dan Overmyer, eds. *Asian Religions in British Columbia*. Vancouver: UBC Press, 2010.

Du, Joseph, ed. *Mr. Hung Lee and Winnipeg Chinatown*. Winnipeg: Winnipeg Chinese Cultural and Community Centre, 2003.

Duara, Prasenjit. *Rescuing History from the Nation: Questioning Narratives of Modern China*. Chicago: University of Chicago Press, 1997.

–. "Superscribing Symbols: The Myth of Guandi, Chinese God of War." *Journal of Asian Studies* 47, 4 (1988): 778-95.

Dyzenhaus, David, and Mayo Moran. *Calling Power to Account: Law, Reparations, and the Chinese Canadian Head Tax Case*. Toronto: University of Toronto Press, 2005.

Eidheim, Harald. "When Ethnic Identity Is a Social Stigma." In Frederick Barth, ed., *Ethnic Groups and Boundaries*, 39-57. Boston: Little, Brown, 1969.

Feeley-Harnik, Gillian. "Against the Motion." In Tim Ingold, ed., *The Past Is a Foreign Country: A Debate*, 11-19. Manchester: Group for Debates in Anthropological Theory, 1994.

Ferrero, Sylvia. "Comida Sin Par Consumption of Mexican Food in Los Angeles: 'Foodscapes' in a Transnational Consumer Society." In Warren Belasco and Philop Scranton, eds., *Food Nations: Selling Taste in Consumer Societies*, 194-221. New York: Routledge, 2002.

Fischler, C. "Food Habits, Social Change and the Nature/Culture Dilemma." *Social Science Information* 19, 6 (1980): 937-53.

Friesen, Gerald. *The Canadian Prairies: A History*. Toronto: University of Toronto Press, 1987.

Gabbacia, Donna R. *We Are What We Eat: Ethnic Food and the Making of Americans*. Cambridge, MA: Harvard University Press, 1998.

Goffman, Erving. *The Presentation of Self in Everyday Life*. New York: Doubleday, 1959.

Goldsborough, Gordon. *With One Voice: A History of Municipal Governance in Manitoba*. Altona, MB: Friesen Printers, 2008.

Goody, Jack. *Cooking Cuisine and Class: A Study in Comparative Sociology*. Cambridge: Cambridge University Press, 1982.

Gravetti Louis E., and Marie B. Paguette. "Nontraditional Ethnic Food Choices among First Generation Chinese in California." *Journal of Nutrition Education* 10 (1978): 109-12.

Gray, James H. *Booze: The Impact of Whisky on the Prairie West*. Toronto: Alger Press, 1972.

Hannerz, Ulf. "Being There ... and There ... and There! Reflections on Multi-Site Ethnography." *Ethnography* 4, 2 (2003): 201-16.

Harney, Robert. "Montreal's King of Italian Labour: A Case Study of Padronism." *Labour/Le Travail* 4 (1979): 57-84.

Harrison, Henrietta. *The Making of the Republican Citizen: Political Ceremonies and Symbols in China, 1911-1929.* Oxford: Oxford University Press, 2000.

Hawkes, David. *Ch'u Tz'u.* Oxford: Clarendon Press, 1959.

Heine, Steven, and Charles S. Prebish. *Buddhism in the Modern World: Adaptations of an Ancient Tradition.* London: Oxford University Press, 2003.

Heldke, Lisa M. "Recipes for Theory Making." In Deane W. Curtin and Lisa M. Heldke, eds., *Cooking, Eating, Thinking: Transformative Philosophies of Food,* 251-65. Bloomington, IN: Indiana University Press, 1992.

Hoe Ban Seng. "Adaptive Change and Overseas Chinese Settlements, with Special Reference to a Chinese Community in the Canadian Prairies." MA thesis, University of Alberta, 1971.

–. *Beyond the Golden Mountain: Chinese Cultural Traditions in Canada.* Ottawa: Canadian Museum of Civilization, 1989.

–. *Enduring Hardship: The Chinese Laundry in Canada.* Gatineau, PQ: Canadian Museum of Civilization, 2003.

Hsu, Immanuel. *The Rise of Modern China.* 6th ed. New York: Oxford University Press, 2000.

Hsu, Madeline Y. *Dreaming of Gold, Dreaming of Home: Transnationalism and Migration between the United States and South China, 1882-1943.* Stanford: Stanford University Press, 2000.

–. "Migration and Native Place: Qiaokan and the Imagined Community of Taishan County, Guangdong, 1893-1993." *Journal of Asian Studies* 59, 2 (2000): 307-31.

Huang, Evelyn, and Lawrence Jeffery. *Chinese Canadians: Voices from a Community.* Vancouver: Douglas and McIntyre, 1992.

Huffman, Ivy, and Julia Kwong. *The Dream of Gold Mountain.* Winnipeg: Hyperion Press, 1991.

Jensen, Lionel M. *Manufacturing Confucianism: Chinese Traditions and Universal Civilization.* Durham, NC: Duke University Press. 1997.

Kaplan, Anne, R. Marjorie, A. Hoover, and Willard B. Moore. *The Minnesota Ethnic Food Book.* St. Paul, MN: Minnesota Historical Society Press, 1986.

Kashima, T. *Buddhism in America: The Social Organization of an Ethnic Religious Institution.* Westport, CT: Greenwood Press, 1977.

Kim, K.C., and W.M. Hurh. "Beyond Assimilation and Pluralism: Syncretic Sociocultural Adaptation of Korean Immigrants in the US." *Ethnic and Racial Studies* 16 (1993): 696-713.

Knirk, Jason. *Women of the Dail: Gender, Republicanism and the Anglo-Irish Treaty.* Dublin: Irish Academic Press, 2006.

Kung, Hans, and Julia Ching. *Christianity and Chinese Religions.* New York: Doubleday, 1989.

Kuo Wei Tchen, John. *New York before Chinatown: Orientalism and the Shaping of American Culture, 1776-1882.* Baltimore and London: Johns Hopkins University Press, 1999.

Kuo, Ya-pei. "Redeploying Confucius: The Imperial States Dreams of the Nation, 1902-1911." In Mayfair Yang, ed., *Chinese Religiosities: Afflictions of Modernity and State Formation,* 65-84. Berkeley, CA: University of California Press, 2008.

Kutcher, Norman. "The Fifth Relationship: Dangerous Friendships in the Confucian Context." *The American Historical Review* 105, 5 (December 2000): 1615-29.

Lai, David Chuen-yan. "Chinese Immigrants into British Columbia and Their Distribution, 1858-1970." *Pacific Viewpoint* 14 (1973): 102-8.

–. *Chinatowns: Towns within Cities in Canada.* Vancouver: UBC Press, 1988.

–. "Home County and Clan Origins of Overseas Chinese in Canada in the Early 1880s." *BC Studies* 27 (1975): 3-29.

–. "Legends and Textual Research on the Origins of the Chinese Freemasons" (*Hongmen yuanliu zhi chuanshuo yu kaozheng* 洪門源流之傳說與考證). *Mingbao Newspaper* 明報 3 October 2001.

–. "Transformation of Chinatowns." Paper presented at conference entitled Chinatown and Beyond, Simon Fraser University, Burnaby, BC, 14 May 2009.

Lancashire, Douglas, trans., with introduction and notes. *Chinese Essays on Religion and Faith.* Hong Kong: Chinese Materials Centre, Asian Library Series 26, 1981.

Langlois, Janet. "Moon Cake in Chinatown, New York City: Continuity and Change." *New York Folklore Quarterly* 28 (1972): 83-117.

Lary, Diana. *China's Republic: New Approaches to Asian History.* New York: Cambridge University Press, 2007.

Lee, Rose Hum. *The Chinese in the United States of America.* Hong Kong: Hong Kong University Press, 1960.

Levenstein, Harvey A. "The American Response to Italian Food, 1880-1930." *Food and Foodways* 1, 13 (1985): 1-23.

–. *Revolution at the Table: The Transformation of the American Diet.* New York: Oxford University Press, 1988.

Li Chien-Nung. *The Political History of China, 1840-1928.* Trans. Ssu-Yu Teng and Jeremy Ingalls. Princeton, NJ: D. Van Nostrand, 1956.

Li Donghai [Lee, David T.H.]. *Jianada Huaqiao shi* [A History of Chinese in Canada]. Vancouver: Jianada ziyou chubanshe, 1967.

Li, Peter. *The Chinese in Canada.* 2nd ed. Toronto: Oxford University Press, 1998.

–. "Chinese Immigrants on the Canadian Prairie, 1910-47." *Canadian Review of Sociology and Anthropology* 19 (1982): 527-40.

–. "Reconciling with History: The Chinese-Canadian Head Tax Redress." *Journal of Chinese Overseas* 4, 1 (2008): 127-40.

–. "The Use of Oral History in Studying Elderly Chinese-Canadians." *Canadian Ethnic Studies* 17 (1985): 67-77.

Li, Peter S. "Social Capital and Economic Outcomes for Immigrants and Ethnic Minorities." *Revues de l'intégration et migration de l'internationale* 5, 2 (2004): 171-90.

Light, Timothy. "Orthosyncretism: An Account of Melding in Religion." In Anita Maria Leopold and Jeppe Sinding Jensen, eds., *Syncretism in Religion: A Reader,* 162-86. New York: Routledge, 2004.

Lin, Huping. *Surviving on the Gold Mountain.* New York: State University of New York Press, 1998.

Lloyd, Timothy C. "Folklore, Foodways, and the Supernatural." In Barbara Walker, ed., *Out of the Ordinary: Folklore and the Supernatural,* 59-71. Logan, UT: Utah State University Press. 1995.

Lockwood Yvonne R., and William G. Lockwood. "Pasties in Michigan's Upper Peninsula: Foodways, Interethnic Relations and Regionalism." In Stephen Stern and John Allan Cicala, eds., *Creative Ethnicity: Symbols and Strategies of Contemporary Ethnic Life,* 3-19. Logan, UT: Utah State University Press, 1991.

Louie, Kam. "Defining Modern Chinese Culture." In Kam Louie, ed., *The Cambridge Companion to Modern Chinese Culture,* 1-19. Cambridge: Cambridge University Press, 2008.

Lutz, Jessie Gregory. *Chinese Politics and Christian Missions: The Anti-Christian Movements of 1920-28.* Vol. 3: *The Church and the World.* Notre Dame, IN: Cross Cultural Publications, 1988.

Lyman, Stanford. *Chinese Americans.* New York: Random House, 1974.

MacDonald, John S., and Beatrice D. MacDonald. "Chain Migration Ethnic Neighborhood Formation and Social Networks." Milbank Memorial Fund Quarterly 42, 1 (1964): 82-97.

Maffly-Kipp, Laurie. *Religion and Society in Frontier California.* New Haven, CN: Yale University Press, 1994.

Mannheim, Karl. "The Problem of Generations." In Kecskemeti, ed., *Essays on the Sociology of Knowledge by Karl Mannheim,* 276-320. New York: Routledge and Kegan Paul, 1952.

Mannur, A. "Model Minorities Can Cook: Fusion Cuisine in Asian America." In S. Dave Nishime, and T.G. Oren, eds., *East Main Street: Asian American Popular Culture,* 72-91. New York: New York University Press, 2005.

Marshall, Alison R. "Moving the Spirit on Taiwan: New Age Lingji Performance." *Journal of Chinese Religions* 31 (2003): 81-99.

Marte, Lidia. "Foodmaps: Tracing Boundaries of 'Home' through Food Relations." *Food and Foodways* 15 (2007): 261-89.

Mazumdar, Sucheta. "What Happened to the Women? Chinese and Indian Male Migration to the United States in Global Perspective." In Shirley Hune and Gail M. Nomura, eds., *Asian/Pacific Islander American Women: A Historical Anthology.* New York: New York University Press.

McGuire, Meredith B. *Lived Religion: Faith and Practice in Everyday Life.* New York: Oxford University Press, 2009.

McKeown, Adam. "Conceptualizing Chinese Diasporas, 1842 to 1949." *Journal of Asian Studies* 58, 2 (1999): 306-37.

McLellan, Janet. *Many Petals of the Lotus: Five Asian Buddhist Communities in Toronto.* Toronto: University of Toronto Press, 1999.

McLeod, Alexander. *Pigtails and Gold Dust: A Panorama of Chinese Life in Early California.* Caldwell, ID: Caxton Printers, 1948.

Metropolis Conversation Series Report. *Transnationalism and the Meaning of Citizenship in the 21st Century.* 11 December 2007. Available at www.metropolis.net.

Miller, Hanna. "Identity Takeout: How American Jews Made Chinese Food Their Ethnic Cuisine." *Journal of Popular Culture* 39, 3 (2006): 430-67.

Miller, James, ed., *Chinese Religions in Contemporary Societies.* Frank Korom, series editor. Santa Barbara, CA: ABC-CLIO, 2006.

Miller, Stuart Creighton. *The Unwelcome Immigrant: The American Image of the Chinese, 1785-1882.* Berkeley and Los Angeles: University of California Press, 1969.

Millien, C., E. Woo, and Yeh. *Winnipeg Chinese.* Ottawa: Department of the Secretary of State, 1971.

Mintz, Sidney W., and Christine M. Du Bois. "The Anthropology of Food and Eating." *Annual Review of Anthropology* 31 (2002): 99-119;

Missionary Society of the Methodist Church. The Eighty-Fourth Annual Report of the Missionary Society of the Methodist Church. Toronto: Methodist Mission Rooms, 1908.

Moon, Richard, ed. *Law and Religious Pluralism in Canada.* Vancouver: UBC Press, 2008.

Morris, Lydia, and Sarah Irwin. "Employment Histories and the Concept of the Underclass." *Sociology* 26 (1992): 401-20.

Mullins, R. "The Organizational Dilemmas of Ethnic Churches: A Case Study of Buddhism in Canada." *Sociological Analysis* 49 (1988): 217-33.

Nedostup, Rebecca. "Civic Faith and Hybrid Ritual in Nationalist China." In Dennis Washburn and A. Kevin Reinhart, eds., *Converting Cultures: Religion, Ideology and Transformations of Modernity,* 27-56. Leiden and Boston: Brill, 2007.

–. *Superstitious Regimes: Religion and the Politics of Chinese Modernity* (Harvard East Asian Monographs 322). Cambridge, MA: Harvard University Press 2009.

Newton, Sarah E. "'The Jell-O Syndrome': Investigating Popular Culture/Foodways." *Western Folklore* 51, 3/4 (1992): 249-67.

Ohnuki-Tierney, Emiko. *Rice as Self: Japanese Identities through Time*. Princeton, NJ: Princeton University Press, 1993.

Orsi, Robert Anthony. *Between Heaven and Earth: The Religious Worlds People Make and the Scholars Who Study Them*. Princeton, NJ: Princeton University Press, 2005.

Osterhout, S.S. "Our Chinese Missions in British Columbia." *Missionary Bulletin* 13, 3 (1917): 499-500.

Penfold, Steve. *The Donut: A Canadian History*. Toronto: University of Toronto Press, 2008.

–. "'Eddie Shack Was No Tim Horton': Donuts and the Folklore of Mass Culture in Canada." In Warren Belasco and Philip Scranton, eds., *Food Nations: Selling Taste in Consumer Societies*, 48-66. New York, NY: Routledge, 2002.

Perry, Elizabeth J. "Chinese Conceptions of 'Rights': From Mencius to Mao – and Now." Association of Asian Studies Presidential Address, New York Conference on Asian Studies, 26 October 2007, Binghamton, New York, 6-37. With permission of the author.

Peterson, Glen. "House Divided: Transnational Families in the Early Years of the People's Republic of China." *Asian Studies Review* 31, 1 (2007): 25-40.

Pickles, Katie. *Female Imperialism and National Identity: Imperial Order Daughters of the Empire*. Vancouver: UBC Press, 2005.

Puett, Michael J. *To Become a God: Cosmology, Sacrifice, and Self-Divinization in Early China*. Cambridge, MA: Harvard-Yenching Institute Monograph Series, 2004.

Quo, F. Quei. *Chinese Immigrants in the Prairies*. Preliminary report submitted to the minister of the secretary of state. Special Collections Archives, Simon Fraser University, November 1977.

Rabinow, Paul. *Reflections on Fieldwork in Morocco*. Berkeley: University of California Press, 1997.

Ray, Krishnendu. *The Migrant's Table: Meals and Memories in Bengali-American Households*. Philadelphia: Temple University Press, 2004.

Reinders, Eric. *Borrowed Gods and Foreign Bodies: Christian Missionaries Imagine Chinese Religion*. Berkeley, CA: University of California Press, 2004.

Report of the Royal Commission on Chinese Immigration. Report and Evidence, Ottawa, Parliament, 1884-85. Sessional paper no. 54a, 1885.

Report of the Royal Commission on Chinese and Japanese Immigration. Ottawa: House of Commons Journals, 1879.

Rhoads, Edward J.M. *Manchus and Han: Ethnic Relations and Political Power in Late Qing and Early Republican China, 1861-1928*. Seattle: University of Washington Press, 2000.

Rowe, Allan. "'The Mysterious Oriental Mind': Ethnic Surveillance and the Chinese in Canada during the Great War." *Canadian Ethnic Studies* 36, 1 (2004): 48-70.

Roy, Patricia E. *The Oriental Question: Consolidating a White Man's Province*. Vancouver: UBC Press, 2003.

–. *The Triumph of Citizenship: The Japanese and Chinese in Canada, 1941-1967*. Vancouver: UBC Press, 2007.

–. *A White Man's Province: British Columbia Politicians and Chinese and Japanese Immigrants, 1858-1914*. Vancouver: UBC Press, 1989.

Sangren, Steven "History and the Rhetoric of Legitimacy: The Ma Tsu Cult of Tai-wan." *Comparative Studies in Society and History* 30 (1988): 674-97.

Seligman, Adam B., Robert Weller, Michael J, Puett, and Bennett Simon. *Ritual and Its Consequences: An Essay on the Limits of Sincerity.* New York: Oxford University Press, 2008.

Shah, Nayan. *Contagious Divides: Epidemic and Race in San Francisco's Chinatown.* Berkeley, CA: University of California Press, 2001.

Siu, Paul C.P. *The Chinese Laundryman: A Study of Social Isolation.* Ed. John Kuo Wei Tchen. New York: New York University Press, 1987.

–. "The Sojourner." *American Journal of Sociology* 58 (1952): 34-44.

Smart, Josephine. "Ethnic Entrepreneurship, Transmigration, and Social Integration: An Ethnographic Study of Chinese Restaurant Owners In Rural Western Canada." *Urban Anthropology* 32 (2003): 311-42.

Smith, Dorothy E. "Women, Class and Family." in Dorothy Smith and Varda Burstyn, eds., *Women, Class, Family and the State.* Toronto: Garamond, 1985.

Smith, Kidder. "Sima Tan and the Invention of Daoism, 'Legalism' et cetera." *Journal of Asian Studies* 62, 1 (2003): 129-56.

Spence, Jonathan D. *The Search for Modern China.* New York: Norton, 1990.

Srinivas, Tulasi. "Everyday Exotic: Transnational Space, Identity and Contemporary Foodways in Bangalore City." *Food, Culture and Society* 10, 1 (2007): 85-107.

Stanley, Timothy J. " 'Chinamen, Wherever We Go': Chinese Nationalism and Guangdong Merchants in British Columbia, 1871-1911." *Canadian Historical Review* 77 (1996): 475-503.

Stein, H.F., and R.F. Hill. *The Ethnic Imperative.* University Park: Pennsylvania State University Press, 1977.

Steinberg, Stephen. *The Ethnic Myth: Race, Ethnicity and Class in America Boston,* MA: Beacon Press, 1989.

Stoller, Paul. *The Taste of Ethnographic Things: The Senses of Anthropology.* Philadelphia: University of Pennsylvania Press, 1989.

Sun, Anna Xiao Dong. 2005. "The Fate of Confucianism as a Religion in Socialist China: Controversies and Paradoxes." In Fenggang Yang and Joseph B. Tamney, eds., *State, Market and Religions in Chinese Societies,* 229-53. Leiden: Brill.

Tam, Karen. *Golden Mountain Restaurant.* Montagne d'Or Montreal: MAI, 2006, 30.

Tan, Sor-Hoon. "Modernizing Confucianism and 'New Confucianism.'" In Kam Louie, ed., *The Cambridge Companion to Modern Chinese Culture,* 135-54. Cambridge: Cambridge University Press, 2008.

Taylor, Jay. *The Generalissimo: Chiang Kai-Shek and the Struggle for Modern China.* Cambridge, MA: Harvard University Press, 2009.

Thompson, *The Voice of the Past: Oral History.* Oxford: Oxford University Press, 1988.

Threadgold, Terry. "When Home Is Always a Foreign Place: Diaspora, Dialogue, Translations." *Communal/Plural: Journal of Transnational and Crosscultural Studies* 8 (2): 193-217.

Tsai, Kellee S. "A Circle of Friends, a Web of Trouble: Rotating Credit Associations in China." *Harvard China Review: Culture and Society* 1, 1 (1998): 82-83.

Tuchman, Gaye, and Harry Gene Levine. "New York Jews and Chinese Food: The Social Construction of an Ethnic Pattern." *Journal of Contemporary Ethnography* 22, 3 (1993): 382-407.

van der Does, Sonja Edelaar, Imke Gooskens, Margreet Lieftin, and Marijie van Mierlo. "Reading Images: A Study of a Dutch Neighborhood." *Visual Sociology* 7, 1 (1992): 4-68.

Van Esterik, Penny "Celebrating Ethnicity: Ethnic Flavor in an Urban Festival." *Ethnic Groups* 4, 4 (1982): 207-28.

Wang Gungwu. "A Note on the Origins of Hua-ch'iao." Seminar paper delivered in the Far Eastern History Department, Australian National University, 1976.

Wang Jiwu. "Organised Protestant Missions to Chinese Immigrants in Canada, 1885-1923." *Journal of Ecclesiastical History* 54, 4 (2003): 691-713.

Ward, W. Peter. "The Oriental Immigrant and Canada's Protestant Clergy, 1858-1925." *BC Studies* 22 (1974): 40-55.

–. *White Canada Forever: Popular Attitudes and Public Policy toward Orientals in British Columbia.* Montreal: McGill-Queen's University Press, 1978.

Warner, R. Stephen. "Enlisting Smelser's Theory of Ambivalence to Maintain Progress in Sociology of Religion's New Paradigm." In Jeffrey C. Alexander, Gary T. Marx, and Christine L. Williams, eds., *Self, Social Structure and Beliefs: Explorations in Sociology,* 103-21. Berkeley: University of California Press, 2004.

Warner, R. Stephen, and Judith G. Wittner. *Gatherings in Diaspora: Religious Communities and the New Immigration.* Philadelphia: Temple University Press, 1998.

Watson, Burton, trans. *The Complete Works of Chuang Tzu.* New York: Columbia University Press, 1968.

Weibaum, Alys Eve, Lynn M. Thomas, Priti Ramamurthy, Uta G. Poiger, Madeleine Yue Dong, and Tani Barlow. *The Modern Girl around the World: Consumption, Modernity, and Globalization.* Durham, NC: Duke University Press, 2008.

Wickberg, Edgar. "Chinese Associations in Canada, 1923-1947." In K. Victor Ujimoto and Gordon Hirabayashi, eds., *Visible Minorities and Multiculturalism: Asians in Canada,* 23-31. Toronto: Butterworths, 1980.

–. "Overseas Chinese: The State of the Field." *Chinese America: History and Perspectives* (2002): 1-9.

–. "Vancouver Chinatown: The First Hundred Years." A presentation given at Vancouver Chinatown: Past, Present, and Future, a workshop held at the Institute of Asian Research, University of British Columbia, Vancouver, 21 April 2001.

Wilbur, C. Martin. *Sun Yat-sen: Frustrated Patriot.* New York: Columbia University Press, 1976.

Wilder, Joseph E., with Fred C. Dawkins and Micheline C. Brodeur, eds. *Read All about It: Reminiscences of an Immigrant Newsboy.* Winnipeg: Peguis, 1978.

Willmott, W.E. "Some Aspects of Chinese Communities in British Columbia Towns." *BC Studies* 1 (Winter 1968-69): 27-36.

Wong, David Louie. *The Barbarians Are Coming.* New York: Penguin Putnam, 2000.

Yang, Mayfair Mei-hui, ed. *Chinese Religiosities: Afflictions of Modernity and State Formation.* Berkeley, CA: University of California Press, 2008.

–. *Gifts, Favors, and Banquets: The Art of Social Relationships in China.* Ithaca, NY: Cornell University Press, 1994.

Yee, Paul. *Chinatown: An Illustrated History of the Chinese Communities of Victoria, Vancouver, Calgary, Winnipeg, Toronto, Ottawa, Montreal and Halifax.* Toronto: James Lorimer, 2005.

Yu, Anthony C. *State and Religion in China: Historical and Textual Perspectives.* Chicago: Open Court, 2005.

Yu, Henry. *Thinking Orientals: Migration, Contact and Exoticism in Modern America.* New York: Oxford University Press, 2001.

Yung, Wei, trans. *The Cult of Dr. Sun: Sun Wen Hsueh Shuo.* Shanghai: Independent Weekly, 1931.

Index

Note: "(f)" after a page number indicates an figure; "(t)" after a page number indicates a table.

also Chinese Canadian foods; food as expression of identity; restaurants in western Manitoba
Freemasons. *See* Chinese Freemasons (*Hongmen*)
friendships: Chinese men linked by race and Sun Yat-sen's principles, 11; first relationships to form in Manitoba, 2-3; missionaries with bachelors, 148, 155; network of friends, 107, 109, 125, 126, 129; religious dimensions of everyday practices, 10-12. *See also* homosociality
Friesen, Gerald, 132
fundraising: campaigns for Nationalist cause, 28-29, 74, 150, 174-76, 188n62; during Second Sino-Japanese War, 44-45
funerary customs: *Chongyang* (autumn grave-sweeping festival), 11, 47, 160; *Qingming* (spring grave-sweeping festival), 11, 47, 48, 160. *See also* Decoration Day (*hangsaan/hangshan*)
Fung Quong, 68, 151

Gilbert Plains, Manitoba, 35
gods and goddesses: bachelors as god-like figures after death, 4, 47-48, 144-45, 169; Buddhist, 4, 19, 159, 169, 181n14, 202n27; Daoist, 4, 159, 169; misunderstandings about, 67; offerings to family gods, 61, 142-44; Sun Yat-sen as god-like figure in Manitoba, 4, 16, 44-45, 49-51, 55, 150-51, 169, 177
Goffman, Erving, 11-12
Gott Kee, 115
Goucher, Robert, 76
Guangong, or *Guandi* (Daoist god), 4, 19, 159, 169, 181n14
guanxi (personal connections), 156
Guanyin (Buddhist goddess), 4, 19, 159, 169, 182n14, 202n27
Guanyu. See Guangong, or *Guandi* (Daoist god)

haircutting, 73-74, 149, 173, 194n44
Han dynasty, 181n14
hangsaan/hangshan. See Decoration Day (*hangsaan/hangshan*)
Happy Dong, 86-87

Harrison, Henrietta, 72
Henderson's Directories, 30, 53, 62, 71
Hillman, Bill, 105
Ho Chung, 75
homosociality: Chinese homosocial networks, 1, 3, 59, 62, 71, 78, 151; through Chinese laundries, 62, 78-79; through Chinese restaurants, 88; creation of social cohesion and economic capital, 3; key dynamic of the way of the bachelor, 3; link to Chinese political and religous groups, 21, 177; religious dimensions, 4-5, 15; visits to KMT offices, 36-37, 54; way to survive in Canada, 18, 48, 51, 59, 88, 172
Hongmen. See Chinese Freemasons (*Hongmen*)
Huanghuagang, 30(f)
Hurley, W.H., 78

Ideal Restaurant, Brandon, 93
identity. *See* immigrant identity
immigrant identity: ambiguous and flexible identities due to public/private personas, 12-13, 22-23, 108, 121-22, 150, 184n3; authentic food available as well as Canadian dishes, 140-42; bachelors' acceptance due to acculturalization, 8; desire to appear Western and thus socially acceptable, 2, 10-11, 25, 26, 49, 72-74, 102, 108-9, 121, 149-50, 157, 158-59, 171; diasporic identity, 15-16, 136-37, 142, 145-46; "imagined community," 149; incorporation of Chinese, Christian, Confucian, and Nationalist ideas, 2; model of ideal Chinese immigrant identity, 2; Nationalist values, 2, 37, 55, 149. *See also* food as expression of identity; religious ambivalence
immigrants: chain migration by Chinese, 7, 92, 121; link between Ukrainian and Chinese immigrants, 131-32; restrictive legislation against Chinese of western countries, 4, 5-6, 18, 171
Imperial Order of the Daughters of the Empire, 24, 185n13
incense: offerings to ancestors, 27, 48, 135, 143, 144, 157-58; veneration of Chinese deities, 11

Printed and bound in Canada by Friesens

Set in The Sans and Palatino by Artegraphica Design Co. Ltd.

Copy editor: Joanne Richardson

Proofreader: Jean Wilson

Indexer: Pat Buchanan